PIERRE LAVAL

PIERRE LAVAL
Traitor or Patriot?

RENÉ de CHAMBRUN

TRANSLATED BY
ELLY STEIN
UNDER THE SUPERVISION
OF THE AUTHOR

CHARLES SCRIBNER'S SONS
NEW YORK

Special thanks are due Mr. Dennis L. Bark, Director of the Hoover Institution on War, Revolution and Peace, of Stanford University, California, whose cooperation in supplying documents is deeply appreciated. Acknowledgement with thanks also to Karen Poage for additional fact checking for the American edition.

Library of Congress Cataloging in Publication Data

Chambrun, René de, 1906–
  Pierre Laval : traitor or patriot?

  Translation of: Pierre Laval devant l'histoire.
  Includes bibliographical references and index.
  1. Laval, Pierre, 1883–1945.   2. France—Politics and government—1914–1940.   3. France—Politics and government—1940–1945.   4. Prime ministers—France—Biography.   I. Title.
DC373.L35C4813   1984   944.08′6′0924 [B]   84-14012
ISBN 0-684-18095-2

1 3 5 7 9 11 13 15 17 19   F/C   20 18 16 14 12 10 8 6 4 2

Printed in the United States of America.

CONTENTS

PREFACE TO THE
AMERICAN EDITION

In the minds of the men and women who lived through the Second World War or who have read about it since, the name of Pierre Laval is that of a traitor to his country. The associated names—Pétain, Vichy—evoke only condemnation for a puppet French quisling regime collaborating with the Nazis. The postwar trials in France are assumed to have sifted the facts and thus validated the common opinion. It is also remembered that although the life of Marshal Pétain was spared, Laval had to face a firing squad, his last words—"Vive la France!"—being interpreted as the last hypocritical gesture in a sinister role played to the end.

Nearly forty years have passed since those violent and confused events. Evidence about them has now accumulated to the point where a truly informed judgment is possible; and as regards Laval in particular, it seems that the time is ripe for reviewing the facts in the light of the record. Though the issues—quite properly—still arouse strong feelings, it seems clear that what Laval did and wanted to do is not what he is thought to have done. The court that sent him to a shameful death violated every rule of procedure and canon of justice; his side of the case has never been heard before the jury of public opinion.

This book is an attempt to present that side. The case to be made out is simple: Laval saw it as his duty to protect his country from the depredations of its Nazi enemies. He struggled to save the population from oppression and deportation, to ensure its livelihood by resisting requisitions of goods and equipment, and to maintain the republican tradition by opposing, at home, the elements gathered around Pétain, which wanted a rightist-royalist regime and genuine collaboration with the Germans.

The accepted view of the Vichy government is that it was at one on this main purpose. The documents show Laval steadily defeating that purpose. The accepted view is that Laval, at the request of the German authorities, aided the deportation of liberals and Jews. The facts are that he resisted in every way open to him. He saved many lives, including that of the former prime minister, Léon Blum. A famous and harrowing film, much later, cast Laval in the role of villain in the dark deeds of collaboration. Now the maker of that film has published a book in which he regrets his interpretation, saying it came about from photogenic rather than historical considerations (see page 205).

What must be understood at the outset is the situation of a people that has surrendered and whose country is occupied by an enemy still waging a desperate war on two fronts. The occupied land becomes a reservoir of supplies, human and material, and its spontaneous resistance must be repeatedly crushed. Meanwhile, the true government of that country is badly divided. Some of its former leaders have fled abroad (de Gaulle); others are in colonial North Africa (Darlan). Those who have stayed at home are of several opposite parties, each of the two main ones looking to the postwar period for the triumph of its special brand of revolution. In this situation, is there a place for the man who believes that the present health and wholeness of the nation should be the one overriding concern?

Such a place is at the center of danger; the enemies are foreign and domestic. Power is limited, and by the nature of the game to be played, motives and actions must alike be obscured. Allies and other friendly countries are bound to feel suspicion and to be misled, all being caught up in the vicissitudes of a global war in which neutrals, allies, enemies, partisans, and fifth columns continually change their spots and act with different ends in view— a grand confusion impossible to sort out at the time or for a good while after.

That position at the heart of the maelstrom Pierre Laval deliberately chose, in the belief that he was the only man who could save existing France. Others outside would in time liberate the country, but if they were to find anything but a despoiled and demoralized nation, that nation must be held together *now*.

The documents, recovered from many disparate sources, show that Laval not only intended this result but in large measure succeeded in bringing it about. He and some trusted associates scattered throughout France played a delaying game against German demands and sustained the republican, parliamentary ideal against its internal enemies.

Laval believed he could achieve his goal for a variety of reasons. He was, to begin with, moved by the passionate patriotism of a French peasant. He knew he was stubborn, as the men of Auvergne are reputed to be. He was conscious of a long and arduous political experience, dating back to 1914, when he was the favorite protégé of Jaurès and Briand. His record for integrity was unblemished. Before the war, whether in power or out, his foreign policy had been to warn against the dictatorships and by astute diplomacy to divide and diminish the threat from the Axis powers.

To act as buffer between the Nazis and the disarmed country, Laval knew he must compromise, not once but as often as he saw that toughness would ruin his cause. That is the reason why his actions can be misrepresented as compliance. Just so, the old Roman general Fabius could be accused of cowardice when he avoided engagement with the enemy, but in the end it was the Fabian tactics that won. To judge Laval and his purpose one must read the record in detail—both the description of typical maneuvers, as given in the body of this book, and the numerical measure of what he saved and protected, as given in the statistical summaries in the Appendix.

Two other sets of facts are relevant to the testing of Laval's integrity. One is the character of his statesmanship before the war. It is briefly reviewed here, and it poses the question Does a man with such a record suddenly turn about and pursue diametrically opposite ends?

The second set of facts is the story of his trial, also reported here. The proceedings were so obviously a farce played in a hurry, the work of a kangaroo court, that it raises suspicions beyond those of an ordinary miscarriage of justice. What did the judges and their instigators want to conceal? If Laval had been the criminal and traitor he was supposed to be and there was evidence of his crimes and treasons, its disclosure would have been an asset to the political elements that tried him. But no such evidence was disclosed. At the same time, the defense was never allowed to present its opposing evidence. Indeed, it was confiscated and hidden away, together with the prosecution dossier, for nearly a third of a century. Only lately has it been extracted from the archives and found to be such a corroboration of the testimony favorable to Laval that it made the writing of this book an inescapable duty.

Any situation as confused as French affairs were in 1940–45 leaves a picture even less intelligible in the minds of contemporaries. After another forty years of rumors and recriminations, it is hard to know the right place with which to begin a clarification. Each person's memory or preference would suggest a different starting point as the most logical. Some would be willing to go back to the diplomacy "between the wars" in which Laval took a leading part. Others would rather jump *in medias res* and see Laval at work after the catastrophe. And yet other beginnings—the trial, for instance—are possible, each logical from a given point of view.

Since I was myself involved in the events I have to recount, and being related, moreover, by marriage to the protagonist in this historic drama, I have decided that the simplest way to open the case is to begin with an episode that occurred at my house in Paris in December 1947. In keeping with this role of ocular witness, I shall reintroduce myself whenever it seems relevant along the way, for example, in my dealings with President Roosevelt and other American leaders or after the war with the British and French authorities.

But striking this personal note from time to time does not mean that I am writing a personal history or making a personal appeal. The case for Laval rests on facts attested to by many of the chief figures in the history of the time, some of the testimony being all the more convincing coming from the mouths of Laval's enemies, foreign and domestic. The reader will and should judge not by sympathy for the accused but, like a juryman, on the strength of the facts offered in evidence.

AUTHOR'S NOTE

It was December 12, 1947. Our regular dinner for three was about to end. Since getting out of prison, Mme. Laval had been living with us at the Place du Palais-Bourbon. A long ringing of the bell was heard from the floor below, and looking out of the first-floor window, I noticed a GI at the wheel of a large U.S. army car. I went downstairs and recognized my old friend Clark Denney, with whom I had started in practice in a New York law firm.

He had just made the trip from Nuremberg to Paris at one stretch and was planning to leave again the following morning.

"I was recruited," he said, "and assigned to the advocate general's office and named one of the assistants of Chief Prosecutor Robert Jackson. I helped prepare the indictments against the war criminals in the Luftwaffe—Goering, Milch, and Sperrle. Our consul, Fullerton, gave me your address, and I came to see you before my military discharge in a few months. I have something very important to tell you."

We settled down in the library, and as he took a bundle of papers from his briefcase, he explained to me the rough-and-ready way in which the documents had been organized since their discovery. Everything having to do with the Luftwaffe was translated into English; several copies were mimeographed and sent in bulk to the sorting department of the chief prosecutor. The documents dealing with the aircraft industry landed on Denney's desk. "I was surprised," he said, "when I read the telegrams and letters exchanged between the Ministry of the Air in Berlin, the Armistice Commission, the German embassy, the representatives of the French government, and your father-in-law, to realize the stubborn way in which Laval and his representatives opposed German demands."

And as if he were arguing a brief, he added: "As early as July 1940, the Germans tried to take over all the shares of France's nationalized aircraft companies—Laval played a game of hide-and-seek with them . . . The shares were nowhere to be found, not at the Bank of France, not at the Ministry of Finance. Then there were the formalities of the foreign exchange control. . . . Time was running on, and about 1942, Sauckel began to ask for more and more workers for the aircraft factories in Germany."

Denney went on to explain how Laval and Bichelonne succeeded in having Speer, the German minister of armaments, classify thousands of factories in France as "S-Betrieb," thus preventing the departure of tens of thousands of French workers for the Reich. Instead, they remained in France, where they were put to work making the most needed consumer goods.

Denney continued, "In 1943, the Germans feared the bombing by the

Allies of French factories making parts for the aircraft industry and demanded that Laval have the machinery transferred to East Germany. Laval objected strongly and won his point. The war came to an end, and the Germans had got neither the shares nor the workers nor the machines. I told Jackson I was a friend of yours, and he told me that many of the documents found at the Wilhelmstrasse showed how Laval had resisted Ribbentrop's demands."

As Denney went on I grew impatient and finally asked point-blank, "Couldn't we go to my office in your car? I could photograph all these papers in an hour."

"Can't be done. Those documents are now "top secret." They'll remain that way until the end of the lengthy trial of the high officials of the Wilhelmstrasse."

"So why show them to me if I can't make use of them?"

"I came to see you," Denney answered, "because I thought it my duty to tell you that they existed."

An idea occurred to me. "I know General Marshall pretty well; he was a great friend of my father's. He's in London right now, attending a summit conference with Molotov, Bevin, and Bidault. If I manage to see him before his return to Washington, the day after tomorrow or the next day, will you allow me to speak to him confidentially about our conversation?"

He thought it over and agreed to my proposal.°

Early the next day, I got in touch with a police inspector who was a good friend. In order to go to London, I needed a passport, and being the son-in-law of Laval, I was under indictment for "endangering the security of the state." The inspector told me that under the circumstances I would have to deposit 50,000 francs in order to have my passport signed by the police commissioner.

I did as required and arrived in London on December 15. I phoned the American embassy immediately. The ambassador, "Lou" Douglas, was also a friend. His secretary told me that he was with Marshall at 10 Downing Street. She advised me to call Colonel Hummelshine, his chief of staff. He told me that the conference, which was supposed to last several days, was coming to an end because of a serious split between the United States and the Soviets. The breakdown of negotiations would be announced in the evening papers. He was going to speak to the general about my errand and call me back before the end of the afternoon.

I did not stir from my room at Brown's Hotel. A little later, the Colonel called to invite me to "a dinner for three" at the embassy with the ambassador and the general. The latter would shortly fly home in the "Sacred Cow," which Truman had put at his disposal.

°I made notes then of the signatures and dates of several documents. The reader will find two of them in Exhibits A and B: telegrams signed Udet and Hemmen, dated September 9, 1940, and January 19, 1943, which I found later among a collection of several thousand documents.

I explained the reason for my trip. Marshall said, "Your request puts me in a delicate position with respect to our English Allies, and especially with the Soviets, because of the secret character of the documents. In principle, I should refuse, but I don't think I can say no to Josée Laval."

A few weeks later, Capt. G. Ullman, chief of the Information Control Division of the American Military Court, appeared in my office in civilian dress and asked if he could see Mme. de Chambrun. He had orders to speak only with her. But thinking it over briefly, he decided to see me. After asking me to give him my word that Mme. de Chambrun and I would be pledged to the same secrecy, he told me that he had received confidential instructions to turn over to her, in Paris, all the documents, translated from German into English, on all subjects in which the name Pierre Laval was mentioned. But all these communications were to remain secret.

During the following year, Ullman or his aide made thirteen trips to Paris, always letting me know in advance when they would arrive. Such was the way in which several thousand pages of documents were put in my hands, with this stamp and the certification of the translation on each page.

———————————————————————

DOCUMENT No. NG—5130

(Page 1 of the original)

Note: (Stamp:) To be treated as
Transmitted to special train   sealed matter only
as No. 1720

Berlin, 5 June 1943
Pers. Ch. Tel.

Telegram
(Secret code)

Paris, 5 June 1943   4 40 hours
Arrived: 5 June 1943   5.00 hours

No. 3651 of 4 June   Citissime !

*) at Pol. II—(Sealed matter)

A generous impulse on the part of an American friend had thus put me in possession of proof, originating with the enemy, of the unswerving patriotism of Pierre Laval. For twenty-seven years, from 1945 to 1972, I tried to gain access to the case for the prosecution of Laval, which Attorney General Mornet had refused to turn over to the defense. All of the material had been transferred to the French National Archives, where it was sealed and stamped "Prohibited Access" for fifty years, dating from October 15, 1945! Thirteen years later, President Pompidou and his minister of justice, Pierre Joxe, to whom I wish once more to express my gratitude, authorized an exception to the ban and allowed me access to the documents.

I spent thirty-four afternoons in August and September 1972 in a room of the Palais Soubise, examining eight large cartons, experiencing surprise after surprise, indignation on top of indignation.

The revelations of the Palais Soubise, coming on top of those resulting from General Marshall's kind action and supplemented by my personal recollections, make up the substance of the last part of this book, the story of the years of the German occupation and Pierre Laval's patriotic self-sacrifice.

Over the years, before starting to write this book, I tried to achieve a perspective on events, because I did not want my account to seem to be even in the slightest degree a pleading in appeal after Laval's trial. There can be no appeal, no talk of rehabilitation for an unjustly condemned man, for Pierre Laval was not tried. There was no trial. There was only, as the reader will see, a judicial crime.

PIERRE LAVAL

WHO WAS LAVAL?

It was during the Easter vacation of 1936 that I really got to know the Lavals at Châteldon in their native province of Auvergne.

Since I had married Josée, on August 20, 1935, I had spent only two or three short Sundays there. This had barely afforded me a glimpse of the man, whose practically uninterrupted responsibilities as head of the government and minister of foreign affairs during a particularly difficult time for France kept him from savoring the joys of family life. For him, our wedding day had been just another working day, interrupted only by the religious ceremony and a brief reception in the gardens of the French Foreign Office.

As I drew closer to my father-in-law, I began to witness the variations affecting the course of a political career. Through the inevitable ups and downs of difficult circumstances, there were signs of a fundamental continuity, and I was able to measure the scope of the grand design in foreign policy that this statesman had conceived and intended to carry out. He meant to take advantage of all possible opportunities for maintaining the peace that he loved passionately and that he could conceive only in terms of the defense of France's interests and the upholding of France's greatness.

Laval had had to work hard since childhood in order to find himself a place in Paris, where he was called to the bar in 1909. From the outset, he could not help fighting for peace and social justice. He joined the Socialist party and soon became a lawyer for trade unions and for the C.G.T. (Confédération Générale du Travail), where Léon Jouhaux had already achieved some prominence.

After union support had won him nomination by the Socialist Federation of the Seine, he was elected deputy on May 11, 1914, leading the slate for the district of Aubervilliers-Villemomble by 10,812 votes against 8,586 for the nationalist Marcel Habert.

The next day, May 12, L'Humanité, the Socialist party organ, announced the young deputy's victory in the following words: "Laval is the youngest of our party in Parliament, the defender of the principal workers' organizations. He goes and takes action everywhere, and his name will live as that of a participant in all the important workers' cases that have come to court in recent years. By virtue of his thorough knowledge of labor legislation and his skill as a speaker, Laval, who has already served the party so well, is now called upon to render it even greater services."

War broke out ten weeks after Laval's election. In the Chamber he battled against corruption and the high cost of living. Boldly, he challenged his older

1

colleague, Edouard Herriot, the minister of food supplies. Herriot politely answered his questions and added, "My dear colleague, if I could, I would load the barges myself." Laval replied: "Don't add silliness to impotence." It took eighteen years before Herriot forgave Laval for the laughter his impertinence had provoked.

On December 11, 1917, Clemenceau ordered Joseph Caillaux, a senator and former president of the Council of Ministers, imprisoned secretly and indicted before the Military Tribunal of Paris° for dealings with the enemy. Laval went to his aid.

At the time of his trial in the Senate, which had been constituted as the High Court, Caillaux had already been in prison for twenty-eight months. The trial itself was to last six months, from October 1919 to April 1920. The right wing of the Senate believed in his guilt. On March 24 and 25, Laval addressed the Right directly and demonstrated that in attempting to stop the killing of hundreds of thousands of Frenchmen, Joseph Caillaux did not betray his country. The victim of campaigns of hatred and slander, and found guilty by a vote of 150 to 91 of having communicated with the enemy, Caillaux then withdrew into semiseclusion and wrote *Mes Prisons,* an account of his persecution. In December 1920, he presented a copy of his book to Laval with:

> To my dear friend Laval, who defended me so nobly and so courageously, these pages of history—heavy with sadness—in token of my high regard for his talents and with deep friendship.

In the election of November 11, 1919, the first anniversary of the victory, the Socialist slate, headed by Laval, was swept out by the "National Bloc." The new Chamber (dubbed "Horizon Blue" from the color of the French soldiers' uniforms) followed a policy of extreme nationalism. Laval was nonetheless able to fight successfully to prevent the dissolution of the C.G.T., which had been decreed by the government after a ruling by a civil court.

On December 27, 1920, a party congress in Tours ended by splitting the Socialist party and bringing the Communist party into existence. Laval joined neither the Socialist nor the Communist group. He retired from politics and devoted himself to his legal career. Three years' work sufficed to earn him a position at the Palais de Justice and for the admired and respected Judge Henri Robert to state in the opening words of an article in the April 30, 1923, issue of the *Echos Parisiens:* "We know and love Laval. He has talent, he has heart, and he is loyal."

In the ensuing years, Laval became the owner of the provincial newspaper

---

°A certain Captain Bouchardon and a Mr. Mornet were put in charge of Caillaux's prosecution. Twenty-eight years later, General de Gaulle's provisional government was to call upon the same men to conduct the trials of Pétain and Laval. Though retired, they returned to public service: Mornet as attorney general and Bouchardon as president of the investigating commission.

Moniteur du Puy-de-Dôme; he thereby came to follow life in his native Auvergne more closely without having to give up residence in the suburb of Aubervilliers, which always remained dear to him. At the same time, a change occurred in his political thought. The extensive and practical experience of the previous four years gradually alienated him from those parties, adherence to which might preclude the exercise of one's freedom. While remaining true to his ideals, he decided "no longer to heed anything but the voice of conscience." When, in 1923, the socialists, who had broken for good with the Communists, asked him to make up a slate that he would head, he accepted as an independent. Thus, he was elected mayor of Aubervilliers by 29 votes to 1—his own.°

In 1924, the voters of the northern suburbs of Paris once more elected him to the Chamber of Deputies.

Laval's career as a statesman began on April 17, 1925, when he was just forty-two years old. Paul Painlevé, assembling his second cabinet amid the throes of an economic crisis, offered him the Ministry of Public Works and the administration of Alsace-Lorraine.

Laval recommended that Painlevé invite Caillaux into his government to help correct the financial situation. Painlevé agreed immediately and made Caillaux, who in 1920 had been sentenced to three years' imprisonment and five years' banishment from Paris, minister of finance. In that capacity, Caillaux devised and implemented the first French "personal" annual income tax.

For Laval, the years 1925 and 1926 were a time of intense political and ministerial training under the guidance of a great master, Aristide Briand. Born in 1862 (twenty-one years before Laval), Briand had also been a socialist and militant pacifist in his youth. This impassioned spellbinder was to be prime minister a record number of times under the Third Republic. On November 23, 1925, he formed his eighth government, following the fall of Painlevé, and offered his protégé Laval the post of secretary of state to the president of the council (i.e., the prime minister). Six months later, he gave him the opportunity to become the youngest minister of justice of the Third Republic; he saw in him a future successor to his own position. Laval was further gratified because Briand offered Caillaux a position as minister of state.

After Poincaré's return to power on July 12, 1926, Laval interrupted his work in central administration for two years in order to take up the political fight on home ground. Elected by the Department of the Seine in 1927, he left the Chamber for the Senate, "the house of reflection," where he would be able to watch events with more perspective than is possible amid the continual excitement of work at the Palais-Bourbon.

°In every municipal election up to the war of 1939–45, the Laval slate was elected in the first round. At the time of the last election under the Popular Front, his platform consisted of an ordinary photograph followed by the brief comment "In 1923, I put my hand in yours, and you have not withdrawn yours. Pierre Laval."

For him 1930 marked the beginning of great achievement: as minister of labor in the second cabinet of André Tardieu, he succeeded in accomplishing what was unanimously considered a tour de force—the preparation and presentation of the social insurance legislation.

SOCIAL SECURITY

Fifty years after its inception, people have forgotten that social insurance (renamed "social security" on October 4, 1945, so as to make it seem a fruit of the Liberation) is the work of Pierre Laval. Only M. Chaban-Delmas, who as prime minister celebrated the twenty-fifth anniversary of the decree in 1970, recognized that he was not dealing with a new piece of legislation. The law of April 30, 1930, establishing social insurance had changed its name, and the name of its creator was passed over in silence.

It is not so easy for me to forget the role Laval played. In the years just preceding the Second World War, he told me again and again that the social insurance law was the most important achievement of his political career. He once treated me to the full story of this law:

"What a job it was! From 1920 on, all governments—those of the center Right, the center, the center Left—tried to deal, always unsuccessfully, with this squaring of the circle. The worst failure came in April 1928, when a minister in the Briand government thought he was about to succeed. But just as he had carried the vote in Parliament, cries of protest broke out all over the country, and the law was stillborn.

"After two years of government instability (a cabinet under Chautemps, put together in mid-February 1930, lasted twelve days), President Doumergue asked Tardieu to form a government. Tardieu, who was on the verge of his second cabinet, called me immediately and said something like this:

"'Considering the difficult social situation in which France now stands, old man Doumergue is not doing me much of a favor. I will only agree to form a government on condition that you accept the Ministry of Labor and also make yourself responsible for working out a good law on social insurance. This must be done before May 1, to prevent unrest—perhaps even outbreaks—on that day, which is the traditional workers' holiday. We must be able to announce definitely that the administrative regulations will be drafted during the next two months so that, after passage, the law may go into effect on July First.'

"After a pause Tardieu went on: 'Well? Are you with me?'

"'Yes, I'm with you all the way.'

"I did not hesitate for a second, despite the enormousness of the task awaiting me. Improving the health and living conditions of the workingman has always been one of my main concerns. Its importance seemed to me all the greater since Germany was then ahead of France in the area of job security. I was convinced that a good social insurance law was the best guarantee against the spread of communism.

"As Tardieu was warmly shaking my hand, I added, 'I'm with you all the way, but under one condition: I want an absolutely free hand.'

"'Of course, but what exactly do you require?'

"'We have to do a thorough job of cleaning out the Ministry of Labor. We can't keep any of the present personnel: the top people, the advisers, the experts, and the like—all those who have been closely associated with the failures of these last ten years—must go. We must also create an office of undersecretary of state, to be put in the hands of Pierre Cathala. He is intelligent, hardworking, and would immediately help us to put together a team of handpicked members from the Council of State, willing, if need be, to work nights, Sundays, and holidays. But it must be understood that this team will have special powers. By this I mean that no one else will have the least right to look into what we are doing. We must keep those who have been swept out and who may resent it from attempting even the slightest obstruction.'

"'Agreed. You will have the special powers.'

"The next day, after the new government had been presented to Parliament, I went to work. First, I had to study in great detail the files that I inherited from my predecessors—to find mistakes, gaps, imperfections, which, when set right, would make for real progress; and then, too, so as not to be caught short by an objection or a question I could not answer.

"While I carried out this examination, I also decided on my own the principles of the only strategy that would enable me to succeed. It was out of the question to let a confrontation occur between union groups and management, for two reasons. While they were opposed to each other both ideologically and in their self-interest, they had a common opponent: the state; and they reproached it for wanting to meddle in an area beyond its jurisdiction. Big business certainly did not look favorably on this emerging power of the state, and the middle class was afraid of any law likely to increase taxes and the cost of living.

"So, I tried to arrange a series of conversations with the various parties separately and avoid or postpone confrontation. My object was to disentangle difficulties and forestall the predictable clashes among groups not inclined by nature to get along. I should add that I was holding a good card: Léon Jouhaux (the secretary-general of the C.G.T. and therefore very far to the left) understood and supported me.

"Furthermore, I had to win over everybody very quickly, beginning with the workers. I spent my first Sunday in Aubervilliers among employees and laborers. I brought along two experts in the use of actuarial tables. As I was familiar with my people, I spoke to them in a simple, direct, and concrete manner, which they easily understood. For instance, I would say to one of them:

"'You are thirty years old; you are earning so much. If you were asked to contribute five francs, and your boss and the state an equal amount, and when you retire you were to be paid so much, wouldn't you think it a good deal?'

"I then made the rounds of the employers and the unions, making sure to meet them at separate times and separate places. I also circulated in the hallways of the Chamber and the Senate, going around from one group to another and always meeting with my team in the evening to check things out and prepare for the following day.

"After three weeks of incessant work, the law began to take shape. An agreement among the various unions and employers' groups had been reached, and at least on paper, the financial feasibility of the project was assured; the total tax outlay would be covered by contributions from employers, workers, and the state.

"Came the day for the formal presentation to Parliament. Although I felt more at ease in the Senate than in the Chamber, I intended to face the deputies alone, and Tardieu graciously agreed to absent himself from those sessions. I had to fight a real war of attrition. I can't remember how often I had to intervene from the speaker's platform or from my seat, either to obtain the withdrawal of a series of amendments, or to oppose any number of attempts to send the law back to committee. I wanted to keep the debate from bogging down in minute details and carry out my promise to get the bill through within the required time. Finally, Parliament agreed to my proposals. Although the provisions of the law were to be elaborated later, the act itself had to be on the books without fail by May 1.

"The Chamber adopted the measure by a vote of 576 to 30; the Senate by 255 votes to 20. The vote took place at the Palais-Bourbon at four in the morning. I immediately rang and woke up Tardieu.

"'I congratulate you,' he said, 'I embrace you, and I'm going back to sleep.' The next day, he took me aside and whispered, 'The Chamber has just entered your name in the competition for president of the council (prime minister), with the grade of "high honors." I will always stand by you.'

The law was published in the *Officiel* on April 30. Five executive orders covering administrative regulations were promulgated in July, then combined into a statute of eight chapters and more than one hundred articles; over sixty decrees and as many executive orders were published between May 1 and September 1.

More than eight million eligible recipients had been registered, their declarations completed, their files set up. Offices that were to be managed by the insured themselves were established throughout the land. It was without doubt the most important law of the Third Republic.

THE FIRST FRENCH PRIME MINISTER TO VISIT THE UNITED STATES

Pierre Laval formed his first government on January 27, 1931. He himself took on the Ministry of the Interior, asked Briand to remain at Foreign Affairs, but watched its policies very closely, as if he had an inkling that he might soon have to carry on the work himself. On May 13, Paul Doumer was elected president of the Republic. As required by the constitution, the Laval cabinet resigned, only to be formed again the same evening.

Briand was approaching the end of a long political career; Laval was at the dawning of his own. On September 27, 1931, the two of them together were the first leaders of the French government to cross the Rhine since the war of 1914–18. Immediately, Laval was struck by the mixture of fear, hope, and menace that hung over Germany. The menace had a name: Hitler. He had already won a quarter of the seats in the Reichstag, and his growing success was generating justified fears. Hope, too, had a name: Brüning, who fought the accession of the Nazi leader with all his strength, backed by a population still suffering from the holocaust of 1914–18 and which did not want any more war.

Groups of German veterans and disabled soldiers greeted Laval and Briand enthusiastically in front of the Hotel Adlon in Berlin. For them, the two were not politicians but pilgrims of peace.

On their way back, when their special train stopped at the two border stations of Aix-la-Chapelle and Jeumont and the same crowds broke into applause, Laval understood the symbolic meaning of the trip to be quite simply the last chance—the last chance to establish an enduring peace between two countries that until then had spent most of their time preparing and waging war.

The whole cabinet waited for the travelers at the Gare du Nord, while under its roof could be heard the roar of thousands of veterans and disabled soldiers shouting their hopes of peace.

This double experience reinforced Laval's resolve to maintain the peace. He knew that he had the backing of the large majority of the French people. They would accept war only if it became necessary to defend their native soil or the independence of their nation against an aggressor.

In addition to trying to prevent another war, Laval addressed certain problems left over from World War I. At the end of the summer of 1931, he decided to go to the United States, to try once and for all to settle with President Hoover the irritating problem of war debts. Although the Dawes Plan of 1924 and the Young Plan of 1929 had greatly reduced the payments Germany had been required to make to the Allies under the Treaty of Versailles, Germany was neither able nor willing to continue to pay even these lesser sums by 1931. On June 20, 1931, President Hoover, recognizing the critical economic situation in Germany, called for a one-year moratorium on all Germany's war-debt and reparations payments. This was agreed to by France and Britain on July 6. At the same time, however, the United States continued to expect the repayment of debts owned her by other European nations. That it was France that should have received most in reparations from Germany and was thus bearing the greatest loss under the Hoover moratorium—2 billion francs—was not so much overlooked as ignored.

I was then living in New York, working for a law firm while preparing for admission to the French bar. The mood of the United States was peculiar. The country was still deep in the crisis that had begun with the stock market crash of October 24, 1929, but it was about to celebrate, with a great show, the 150th anniversary of the victory of Yorktown. Hoover had insisted that he himself lead the gigantic parade on the battleground where Americans had won their independence.

The French government seized the opportunity to celebrate French-American friendship by sending over two of its finest naval units, the *Duquesne* and the *Suffren*. On board were Marshal Pétain and some members of the great families whose ancestors had fought on the American side during the American Revolution.

This prestigious mission preceded Pierre Laval, who was to leave Le Havre for New York on the *Ile de France*. It was the first official visit of a French prime minister to the United States.

A parade down Broadway to city hall, under the usual shower of confetti (ticker tape), and a huge crowd of curiosity seekers awaited him.

Making my way through the throng, I found myself face to face with the motorcycle squad escorting the two official cars. In the first, I recognized Laval and Jimmy Walker, the mayor of New York; in the second, Al Smith, governor of the state. Next to him I saw a young girl, in a blue velvet beret, who was smiling and waving at the crowd.

New York wanted this to be an especially brilliant reception. While Laval was being made an honorary citizen (in the first bestowal of this privilege on a Frenchman since Lafayette's last triumphal visit of 1824), his daughter, in the blue velvet beret, was inaugurating the Empire State Building by pushing a button at the top of the building. This caused the torch of the Statue of Liberty to light up.

Once this spectacular display was over, it became necessary to broach the delicate question of war debts. In Washington, Laval had to face not only Hoover but the uncompromising isolationist Sen. William Borah. He argued that it was not equitable that France be required to repay her debts to the

United States when Hoover's moratorium delayed the repayment of Germany's debt to France.

Hoover and Borah were forced to agree. As long as Germany did not repay France, France need not repay the United States. Laval had won his point. *Time* magazine chose Laval Man of the Year.° The previous year it had been Gandhi. In 1932 he was followed by Roosevelt.

On January 14, 1932, Laval formed his third government. He asked Tardieu, a veteran of 1914, to succeed Maginot as minister of war, and for the first time in his career, he himself assumed the Ministry of Foreign Affairs.

Just then the approaching legislative elections were creating an atmosphere of political unrest, which was thought to favor the parties of the Left. The wind did shift: the Senate overthrew the Laval government, which was replaced by a transition cabinet entrusted with expediting current business while awaiting the results of the coming general election.

That took place in May. The Left won, and Edouard Herriot formed the new government. Though he was careful to name a homogeneous "radical" (moderate) cabinet, knowing that to bring in his socialist allies would cause him economic and financial difficulties, an atmosphere of unease pervaded the country; it was most apparent in Paris.

The radical governments that rapidly followed one another became more and more discredited. A veterans' organization, led by Col. François de la Rocque, conducted an "apolitical" operation "for the defense of great national values" then presumably under attack. Yet this group held the government of Daladier largely responsible for the explosive situation.

Suddenly, the accusations, discontent, and heat came together and exploded in the riot of February 6, 1934. In an effort to gain support on the Left, Prime Minister Daladier had dismissed the unpopular Paris chief of police, Jean Chiappe. Fascist and right-wing paramilitary groups launched a mass demonstration, including a march on the Palais-Bourbon where the deputies were meeting. The crowd tried to surge past the police barricades. Because of the threat to the elected representatives of the people, the government ordered the police to shoot at the demonstrators. Fifteen people were killed, and more than one thousand were injured. The next day, the government of Daladier was forced to resign.

Laval turned to Gaston Doumergue. As a former president of the Republic, a status that placed him above parties, he had not been involved in the confrontations of these last years. His good will and amiable character could be of help in returning the country to a state of calm. Laval therefore approached him at his retirement home in Tournefeuille, but Doumergue hesitated. He was old; he had been away from politics for a long time.

°In summing up the year 1931 in a two-page spread, *Time* magazine of January 4, 1932, noted that "France under Laval had the largest gold reserves and that the unemployed numbered only in the hundreds of thousands, while there were millions of them in the United States, England, and Germany."

Finally, Laval said sharply, "After all, you have an obligation to the country; you cannot refuse to answer such a call."

Doumergue replied: "I will be in Paris tomorrow."

The year 1934 began without any conspicuous difficulties: Laval accepted his much-desired Ministry of Colonies. He would often say: "My two favorite ministries? Colonies and Labor." He had, in fact, a passionate sense of empire unity.°

On October 9, 1934, King Alexander of Yugoslavia, and Louis Barthou, minister of foreign affairs, were assassinated in Marseilles by a Croation student. On the thirteenth, Laval had to leave the Ministry of Colonies to replace Barthou. In the interim, Doumergue's government had undergone the usual erosion of power. The resignation of the two "neosocialists," Marquet and Déat, hastened its disarray, so that at the beginning of November, Pierre-Etienne Flandin was naming a new cabinet in which Laval remained as foreign minister.

THE PARIS–ROME AXIS

In that capacity, Laval left for Rome on January 4, 1935, remained there until the seventh, and returned to Paris on the morning of the eighth.

Meanwhile, I had returned to Paris and had struck up a frienship with Josée Laval in the course of developing plans for the formation of a French Information Office in New York City. I was able to follow Laval's mission closely from the daily reports given me by Josée and then to relive it a little later, through confidential discussions with my uncle Charles, the French ambassador at Rome.

Since the formation of his first government in 1931, Laval had undertaken an in-depth study of all foreign-affairs papers. With his strong sense of the menace that German expansionism had let loose throughout Europe, he followed Hitler's successes and failures step-by-step. He had noticed that one of the major failures had been the action taken by Mussolini—and Mussolini alone—on the day after the Nazis' assassination of Engelbert Dollfuss, the

°He was the first prime minister to include an African in his government. On January 14, 1932, he offered the Senegalese Diagne the position of undersecretary of state for colonies. In November 1942, he named the first "Moselm Algerian," Chérif Mécheri, assistant prefect for Narbonne, then later prefect for the Haute-Vienne. After General de Gaulle's return to power in 1958, Mécheri was to receive a marshal's baton and was named chief of mission for African affairs at the presidential palace.

chancellor of Austria. The Duce, perceiving Hitler's design to annex Austria, had immediately sent three divisions to the Brenner Pass and received Doll-fuss's widow in Livorno. During this time, neither England nor France reacted.

Laval was aware that Mussolini was very anti-German. He had not for-gotten that in 1914 the Duce had founded the newspaper *Il Popolo d'Italia* in order to pressure the Italian government to enter the war on the Allied side, before he himself enlisted in the Bersaglieri, the Italian elite infantry corps.

Thus, by the time Laval succeeded Barthou as minister of foreign affairs, he had already decided to make the Franco-Italian alliance into the corner-stone of a policy that, by containing Hitler, would halt German expansion and avert another world war.

The assassination of the king of Yugoslavia had reawakened that country's hostility toward Italy and Hungary, both of which had granted asylum to Croatian conspirators, enemies of Yugoslav unity. At the General Assembly of the League of Nations, which met in Geneva on December 7, Laval pre-sented and carried the following resolution:

> No member of the League has the right to encourage or even to tolerate on its territory any political activity which might have a ter-rorist aim.

With this vote, Laval earned a double victory: he helped to placate Yugosla-vian anger toward Italy and to improve his relations with Hungary, and he had opened the door for his own negotiations with Italy.

On his return to Paris, the Senate, on December 18, 1934, unanimously approved the following motion: "We note with satisfaction Pierre Laval's declarations concerning the 'Eastern Pact,' as well as the current negotiations with the Italian government. The Senate wishes to congratulate him for the firmness and tact with which he defended and gained acceptance for the unchanging principles of French policy. He achieved this result in delicate and often critical circumstances, while in no way departing from the attitude of sympathy for Yugoslavia in its affliction." This was only the second time since the constitution of 1875 that the Senate had unanimously voted for a motion of this kind. The first had been adopted on November 7, 1918, to honor Georges Clemenceau and Marshal Foch for "having served their coun-try well."

In a cautiously worded opening, Laval had begun by minimizing the dif-ferences that existed between Italy and France. On the one hand, he said, Italy had major interests in Tunisia, a French protectorate, as well as eco-nomic designs on Abyssinia, which, in turn, was very close to Djibouti and to the French coast of Somalia; on the other hand, Italy was especially eager to defend the independence of Austria and to support Hungary's cause.

France, for her part, was linked by treaty with the "Little Balkan Entente,"° whose sympathies were not identical to those of the former Austro-Hungarian monarchy.

By Christmas the policy thus outlined was clear, and Laval, seeing no clouds on the diplomatic horizon, decided to act. On January 4, he arrived in Rome, where the agreements were to be concluded and the papers initialed.

His reception was triumphant. On January 5, Mussolini held a reception at the Venice Palace. The following day, there was a dinner at the Farnese Palace. Charles de Chambrun introduced the sixty guests to Laval and Mussolini, whose chest was graced by the red ribbon of the Légion d'honneur. Two days later, the French prime minister was received by King Victor Emmanuel III.

Laval had another good reason for playing the Mussolini card: the leader of Fascist Italy hated the leader of Nazi Germany. Their last meeting in Venice on June 15 had been not a meeting but a confrontation.

Laval also realized that Mussolini liked to flaunt his authority and missed no opportunity to prove that he was number one in his country. "When I presented my credentials to him," Charles de Chambrun reported to Laval, "he kept me a few minutes longer than planned, so that I would be a few minutes late for my first visit to Victor Emmanuel." Moreover, Laval understood that, like himself, Mussolini was a man of the people, and he therefore did not hesitate to breach the barriers of protocol and to address him man-to-man, directly, even familiarly. He stressed the similarities of their backgrounds. They were both born in the same year, "a good vintage," Laval said, smiling. They had both espoused revolutionary socialist ideals with equal dedication, sometimes approaching anarchist positions. Having grown accustomed to the obsequiousness of those around him, Mussolini responded with delight to Laval's sharp, quick, intuitive mind.

The spark was kindled into warmth between the pair, so that on two occasions they held their discussions alone. On January 6, when the Italian and the French missions encountered one last obstacle (the extent of territory in the extreme south of Libya to be given to Italy), Laval decided during a reception at the French embassy to have one last private conversation with the Duce. When the latter complained that Italy was forced to accept a reduced position in Libya, Laval came up with an unexpected rejoinder. "I am obviously not making you a gift of Paris, of Rome, or even of Aubervilliers, but you are the all-powerful leader of Italy, while I am only a French minister. If the success of these negotiations is important to you, it is for you to make a concession."

The Duce shook his hand, and opening the door of the room in which they had been closeted, announced to those present, "We shall sign tomorrow."

° The Little Entente was the alliance entered into by Yugoslavia, Czechoslovakia, and Romania for the safeguarding of the borders established in 1920.

With this agreement, Laval held the first link in the safety chain he wished to forge to strengthen the defenses of France against German expansion. For in signing with Mussolini, he never stopped thinking of Hitler. This explains his care to observe the rules of strick parity: the advantages and disadvantages for each side remained carefully in balance. In Libya, Italy was to receive 114,000 square kilometers of desert, and in Erythria, on the west coast of Somalia, 800 square kilometers. France retained economic control over the zone of the Djibouti–Addis Ababa railroad, but ceded to Italy a twenty percent share in the profits from the management of the line. As against this "partial waiver" by France, with which Laval had managed to impress Mussolini, Italy renounced its special regulations in Tunisia, which had long existed for the benefit of its nationals and their schools. In France, it was difficult for people to realize the extent of the sacrifice that this renunciation entailed. Laval made that clear: "Tunisia? It was the Alsace-Lorraine of Italy." Henceforth, Italy was now to recognize the French protectorate, without, however, ceasing to challenge it.

But for Laval the European scope of the Rome agreements was a source of great satisfaction. They entailed military cooperation in stated terms: in case of German aggression against Austria, France was to send one or two divisions to reinforce the Italian army; in return, in the event of a military reoccupation of the Rhineland by Germany, Italy was immediately to put a part of its newly modernized air force at France's disposal.

Apart from the benefits of this military cooperation, these agreements were to build a bridge between France and its central European allies, which otherwise could have been split off by a neutral or hostile Italy. France could then expect against Hitler the active military support of Poland, Czechoslovakia, and Romania.

The details of this cooperation were to be settled by the military staffs of the two governments in May 1935. The agreement further stipulated that should Germany decide unilaterally to rearm, the two governments were to consult immediately; a secret clause provided that they would assure themselves of a substantial margin of security under all circumstances: if Germany attempted to reoccupy the left bank of the Rhine and France went to war to prevent it, Italy would supply divisions to assemble in the Belfort region, while France would supply an army corps to assemble on the Yugoslav-Italian frontier.

Laval was well aware that he was the first French minister since 1871 to do so when he decided to pay an official call on the pope. But he did not hesitate. He had three favorable preconceptions about Pius XI. That man of decision had proved the extent of his openness to ideas of social justice in the encyclical "Quadragesimo Anno"; he condemned Hitler's racist and totalitarian principles; he was a lover of peace and on the side of all men of goodwill who were working for its realization on earth.

François Charles-Roux, the French ambassador at the Vatican, informed Laval of the strict rules of papal protocol. As soon as he was ushered in, the pope would ask him to be seated for a discussion that was to last exactly twenty minutes.

After a half hour, Pierre Laval, as required by decorum, moved as if to rise, but Pius XI asked him to sit down again. The discussion lasted almost an hour. Going very quickly beyond the formalities of their official positions, the two men spoke frankly. Pius XI confided his anxieties: "I can do nothing except to bless peace."

That evening, Laval said, "This pope reminded me of our country priests. If my dear mother could see me now!" At the end of the audience, the private chamberlain introduced Laval's daughter, to whom Pius XI offered a rosary. Then the group of her father's aides was brought in to meet the pope. Standing before his desk, the Holy Father reaffirmed in concluding remarks that France was the elder daughter of the church. "She will remain so, most Holy Father," said Pierre Laval.

All his objectives had not yet been achieved. He did not want to give the impression that during his stay in Rome he had tried to avoid certain groups. He therefore met with von Hassel, the German ambassador. Expecting a rather brusque reception, he was surprised to be told just one thing: "It will surely be necessary for my country to sign an agreement with yours one of these days, because no one can expect to face down the whole world alone."

He paid his last call on Sir Eric Drummond, the British ambassador, who also had only one thing to say: "I congratulate France and Italy!"

The "Stresa Front" was now a possibility.

A last surprise awaited Pierre Laval. Mussolini, in an unprecedented breach of protocol, came personally to escort him from the French embassy to the train. When the train was about to leave, he shook Laval's hand warmly, and in a last allusion to Franco-Italian friendship told him in French, "This friendship must not be allowed to be mummified in diplomatic formalities; it must be kept alive."

Six weeks later, the Chamber approved the Rome agreements by 555 to 9 votes, and the Senate ratified them unanimously.

LAVAL ENCIRCLES THE REICH

On February 2, Flandin and Laval went to London, where they concluded with Britain a treaty by which the two countries agreed to consult each other about the problems arising from German rearmament.

More particularly, they reviewed the situation in Central Europe as it had developed since the London Conference of April 1932. Italy's support permitted the conclusion of a tripartite agreement among the three allies of

World War I, the first to be reached since the Armistice of 1918. On February 3, a joint communiqué stated that London, Rome, and Paris "have agreed to consult one another on all questions raised by present and future circumstances."

Schuschnigg, the Austrian chancellor, judging the situation to be favorable, arrived in Paris on February 28, 1935, with his minister of foreign affairs, Berger-Waldenegg. He hoped to negotiate an agreement with France and England.

The leftist press raised a general outcry. They reminded readers that Schuschnigg had been Dollfuss's minister of justice when the beginnings of a riot in Vienna had resulted in the imposition of heavy sentences. The *Populaire* and *L'Humanité* printed the following slogan: "The people of Paris owe it to themselves to denounce the new chancellor as soon as he gets off the train."

Given this threat, the government felt compelled to take exceptional measures: the chancellor would arrive at the small station of Reuilly and would hear mass in the private chapel of the archdiocese. Laval did not hide the humiliation he felt on behalf of his country for having to treat in this manner the man who was carrying out Dollfuss's policies. To Chief of Police Roger Langeron, he said: "What a bitter irony! Does the Left believe that we can prevent the invasion of Austria if we are unable to prevent the invasion of a railroad station by demonstrators?"

This unfortunate incident did not, however, keep the negotiations from proceeding in an atmosphere of perfect calm and mutual understanding. Schuschnigg returned to Vienna completely reassured. A final communiqué based on public statements made by Berger-Waldenegg and Laval stressed that a "Danubian Pact" would very soon be signed, ensuring the protection of Austria against the designs of the Reich.

It was at that point that Hitler decided to stake his all. On March 9, he announced that Germany planned to equip itself with an operational air force, while military and paramilitary activities would continue throughout the Reich. The French government, in the person of Prime Minister Flandin, announced that the age group then drafted into the armed services would remain on duty for an extra six months. The Left, true to its antiwar principles, reacted violently.

Laval, continuing to steer the same diplomatic course, succeeded in having "the Three"—France, England, Italy—lodge a joint protest with the German government. Mussolini also called up a group of reservists.

On April 11, British Prime Minister Ramsay MacDonald, British Foreign Secretary Sir John Simon, together with Flandin, Laval, and Mussolini, met in Stresa and three days later adopted a resolution condemning Hitler's unilateral action. It affirmed "the close and friendly collaboration" of the three powers. England, Italy, and France were determined to "oppose by all appropriate means any unilateral renunciation of treaties such as would be likely to endanger peace in Europe."

Mussolini had requested the substitution in the text proposed by Flandin and Laval of the words "peace in Europe" for "world peace." This change, specifically intended to protect Austrian independence, left Mussolini a free hand in Abyssinia. In addition, the representatives of Italy and Great Britain reaffirmed their obligations under the Treaty of Locarno and declared themselves "determined to carry them out faithfully, should the need arise." After Laval's departure for Geneva, Mussolini and Flandin continued to work on the strengthening of their military agreements.

Laval, in the name of France, England, and Italy acting as "partners," proposed to the Council of the League of Nations a resolution solemnly condemning Germany for the violation of part V of the Treaty of Versailles. Two days later, on April 17, the resolution was adopted by the Assembly in a vote that was unanimous except for Denmark.

With Hitler officially censured, Pierre Laval proceeded full speed ahead. In April, he prepared for a trip to Moscow, where, with Stalin and Molotov, he hoped to forge the last link in the chain of alliances to ensure the security of France and Europe. In keeping with his prudent approach, he negotiated and signed, in Paris on May 28, with the Soviet ambassador, Potemkin, the protocol for a five-year agreement with the U.S.S.R. On May 12, Pierre Laval, accompanied by Josée, left for Moscow.

The first meeting between Stalin and Laval took place in the presence of an interpreter only. Without divulging any secret, Laval told me later that he had had a double aim: to prevent a Soviet-German accord; and to secure, if possible, Stalin's promise to have the French Communists end their opposition to the six-month extension of military service and the strengthening of the French military capacity.

The following day, Molotov invited Laval to lunch. Stalin, setting protocol aside, sat down like an ordinary guest at his minister's table. In the discussion that followed, Stalin promised to order the French Communists to support the military policies of the French government. In the evening, Laval read the final communiqué to the crowd of journalists around him, stressing each word of the final sentence: "Mr. Stalin understands and fully supports France's policy of national defense, intended to keep her strength at the level required by her security needs." Then he smiled, thinking of the pleasant surprise with which French moderates would react to this news and of the astonished Communists, who had just voted against two years of military service.

Because Marshal Pilsudski had died during Laval's stay in Moscow, Prime Minister Flandin proposed that Laval, together with Marshal Pétain, who was to arrive from Paris, stop over in Poland in order to represent France at the state funeral of the Polish chief of state. Goering was representing the Reich. As Colonel Beck invited the two delegations (the French and German) to lunch on May 6, it was quite natural that at the end of the luncheon at the House of France in Cracow, Laval and Goering should get together. Also present were Alexis Léger, secretary general, and Pierre Rochat, director of political affairs of the Quai d'Orsay. The meeting lasted more than four hours, during which Goering reproached Laval for having set up encircling alliances around the Reich. He also tried to justify German rearmament.

Laval replied, "Stop your rearmament. You have nothing to fear from France; no more in fact than from your other neighbors. Disarm, and France too will disarm."

On May 21, Hitler gave a speech in the Reichstag, whose peaceful tenor astonished the world. In five months of diplomatic activity, by remaining simultaneously flexible and firm, Laval had compelled the Führer to mark time.

HERRIOT SUPPORTS LAVAL

Though Laval could be proud of having halted Hitler's expansionism, he became daily more anxious when contemplating the American economic crisis. It had begun on a black day in Wall Street, and little by little it had turned into a worldwide crisis. It struck Germany, then France, where it manifested itself in the flight of capital and of gold, the fall of the franc, a decrease in tax revenues, increase in unemployment, and so on, just at the time when conditions began to improve in the United States.

Only if the government in France were granted special powers could the situation be rectified. Yet the radicals refused to vote these powers. The passionate pleading of Prime Minister Pierre-Etienne Flandin, though injured in a car accident on the eve of the May 30 debate, proved unavailing against the cold logic of numbers. The government fell.

The ensuing crisis was grave, owing as much to the situation itself as to the small number of persons to whom President of the Republic Albert Lebrun could turn to form a cabinet. François Pietri, a moderate and the first to be asked, gave up almost immediately; Jules Jeanneney, the president of the Senate, called on next, was told by his doctor that he was "no longer of an age to handle the strain of power"; Fernand Bouisson, the "technocrat president" of the Chamber, did in fact succeed in forming a cabinet, but it was overthrown on the very day of its presentation. There was only one recourse—Laval.

He had been expecting it, and when, seven years later, in April 1942, Marshal Pétain asked him to take up the reins in a country threatened with total occupation, it was of June 1935 Laval must have thought when he declared: "I have known difficult moments in my public life, when the fate of France was hanging in the balance; it is always at such times that I come to power."

In 1935, the problem he was called on to solve was a thorny one. The radicals' support was indispensable, and their support depended on Herriot, and Herriot alone. The leader of the Radical-Socialist party also knew that France was in danger. After a very long, private discussion with Laval, Herriot announced that he would become minister of state and take part in Laval's government with five of his fellow radicals.

When the day for presenting the cabinet to Parliament arrived, the prime minister had decided how to play his cards. He stressed the diplomatic initiatives he had successfully carried out and which he intended to continue in order to maintain the peace: "Our foreign policy based on security and peace, whose steadfastness everyone has acknowledged and whose wisdom you have eagerly ratified, could be compromised if you appeared to abandon us." The vote was 324 in favor, 160 against. Thus, the Assembly clearly gave the man who had contained Hitler a large vote of confidence.

But the crisis did not abate. The cost of government and the budgetary deficit rose steadily, while revenue continued to fall. French prices were higher than world prices, and this reduced exports, increased unemployment, and resulted in a dramatic drop in the gold reserves of the Banque de France—from 91 billion in 1930 to 71 billion in May 1935. On the single day of May 27, a record drop of 1 billion 223 million was registered.

Economists rushed to the aid of the sick franc. They made different diagnoses and argued from contradictory curves. Two experts, Paul Reynaud and Raymond Patenôtre, brilliantly urged that only a devaluation could launch an economic upturn and bring the crisis to an end. But Laval was unconvinced.

For him, the prerequisite to healthy financial management was a strictly balanced budget, which could only be achieved if outlays did not exceed income. After a balanced budget had been achieved, the government could plan a manipulation of the currency if that currency was strong. This was not possible as yet. To have devalued by 10 percent, for example, an already weakened franc, would have been to give the French ten francs in adulterated currency instead of nine francs in good currency.

The first order of business, therefore, was to reduce government spending. The government should set an example to the nation. In order to enact measures that were sensible and fair, Laval gathered a kind of brain trust around him, which included C. J. Gignoux of *La Journée Industrielle,* Jacques Rueff of the Ministry of Finance, and Raoul Dautry, head of the National Railroads.

Three long months of work—surveys, analyses, discussions, preparations—resulted in a group of coordinated measures, presented at the start of the October term.

1. Deflation was to be brought about by a 10 percent cut in salaries and pensions, as well as in appropriations for all public agencies and ser-

vices. This percentage was lower than the drop in the cost of living since the previous cut in public spending of 1930. This cut was also to affect services in the departments and communes, as well as arrears owed on annuities and war pensions, but it was not to affect welfare and unemployment benefits.

2. To counterbalance the sacrifice demanded of public employees, sacrifices were required of other groups of citizens: a tax on income above 80,000 francs, a tax on income from stocks and bearer bonds, and a tax on earnings derived from work and materials supplied to the state. What was important, salaries in the private sector were not affected.

3. These sacrifices were to be offset by a drop in the cost of public utilities (gas and electricity), by lower rents, and by a stabilization in the prices of certain everyday consumer goods, such as meat.

4. Finally, this deflation was to be temporary; it would end as soon as the situation improved—and it was expected to improve rapidly, because the economic recovery was to be sparked by allocations for large departmental and communal public works projects, a part of the money coming from the 10 percent being withheld.

Aware of the unpopularity of deflation, the prime minister made it his duty to explain it to the French people. In a radio address, he described the main points of the measures decided upon and summarized the spirit behind them. "The government is striving for fiscal independence and flexibility and for equality in sacrifice."

THE ANGLO–GERMAN
NAVAL AGREEMENT

As he worked ceaselessly to improve the economic and fiscal situation, a sensational event took place. On June 14, Lord Halifax, without informing the French, signed with Joachim von Ribbentrop a treaty that the two men had been secretly negotiating for several weeks. Under its terms, Germany was permitted to build a naval force, including submarines of a tonnage equal to 35 percent of that of the British fleet.

Mussolini and Laval refused on the spot to endorse this agreement, while

Hitler was reported to have said to von Ribbentrop: "It's the most beautiful day of my life!" He had good reason to say so: England was accepting the violation of the naval clauses of the Treaty of Versailles. Indeed, England was in effect violating them herself. Having demanded the almost total destruction of the German navy in 1919, she was now encouraging Hitler to rebuild it sixteen years later.

Only hindsight enabled British public opinion to measure the depth and breadth of its foolhardiness. Lord Tyrrell was to say ironically, "We made a slight error: we mistook the Germans for the English and the French for the Germans."

Churchill alone, when addressing the House of Commons on July 15, 1935, dared criticize the clauses of the Halifax-Ribbentrop agreement in strong terms. In his *Memoirs* he was to be still more definite and said what he could not say in 1935: "Laval saw clearly and far."

In France, Herriot, generally inclined to moderation, was beside himself. "I have often defended England, this time I condemn her absolutely."

Laval, as prime minister and foreign minister, was bound to be more reserved, but his taciturn face and worried look said much about the feelings that troubled him. From time to time, the same little sentence came like an obsession to his lips: "How could they have done it?" His sense of outrage was compounded by his memory of an episode in 1931, hitherto kept secret. My wife gave an account of it in the English edition of *Laval Parle:*

> During the night of the nineteenth of September, at about 1:00 A.M., my father was awakened by a telephone call from your chargé d'affaire, Sir Ronald Campbell. (Your ambassador, Lord Tyrrell, had been recalled to London for consultations some days earlier.)
>
> My father thought at first that there was some joke, because in those days, it was not part of British diplomatic custom to work at night. The weekends too were sacred.
>
> He quickly recognized the voice of Mr. Campbell, which sounded anxious and halting:
>
> "Mr. Prime Minister, I am calling you to request an urgent meeting."
>
> My father suggested the following morning at eight o'clock. Mr. Campbell, embarrassed, replied:
>
> "Mr. Prime Minister, I would like to see you immediately, the matter at hand is extremely serious and urgent."
>
> "Of course, come immediately," my father told him, as he began to dress. Mr. Campbell arrived a few moments later at the Ministry of the Interior, Place Beauveau.
>
> "I am instructed by my government to ask for your help and advice."

Then he described the situation of the Bank of England, resulting from enormous withdrawals of gold, and the inability of the British government to meet its obligations if France did not extend aid immediately.

My father replied: "Tomorrow morning I will call a cabinet meeting in order to discuss the question."

But Mr. Campbell countered: "Mr. Prime Minister, the question is much too serious and secret to permit twelve ministers to get wind of it. The slightest indiscretion by one of them would cause irreparable damage to Great Britain's credit. Furthermore, the matter is extremely urgent."

Mr. Campbell then handed my father the note he had written for the minister of finance, and about which he had just received instruction by telephone to communicate its contents to my father alone.

My father, moved by the predicament in which your country found itself, and by Mr. Campbell's mournful dignity, then said:

"You're asking for my advice. Here it is: let your government determine for itself the amount of credit it needs, and then get in touch immediately with Washington. Propose to the United States to subscribe one half of the needed credit, and tell them that France has already agreed to subscribe the other half. Come back and see me tomorrow, and if the United States has not agreed to take on one half, I will extend my offer alone for the entire amount."

Then he added: "In which case I will have to open wide the coffers of my country."

Two tears ran down Mr. Campbell's cheeks. He clasped my father's hand and said: "Mr. Prime Minister, I wish to thank you. My country will never forget."

The following morning he returned to tell my father that the United States had found it impossible to come to the aid of Great Britain. My father then reaffirmed his offer of the previous night, and that is how your country obtained a credit of three billion francs, which permitted Great Britain a few hours later to devaluate her currency under conditions that astonished the whole world.

Did my father have the right to act alone, when he made a decision that might have far-reaching consequences for the finances of his country?

Strange as it may seem, I, who admire him without reserve, do believe that he could have been accused of high treason for having decided to put all the financial resources of his country at Great Britain's disposal without consulting his cabinet, the Chamber, or the Senate. It is true that we were rich then, as France always was under the government he headed.

In 1935, after the low blow that Great Britain had just inflicted on France, Laval tried to find a plausible explanation for an apparently inexplicable action. At first he held one man responsible, or more precisely, the total lack of judgment of the man who was directing foreign policy in Great Britain, Anthony Eden. He said of Eden: "He is a perfect gentleman, very well brought up. But he lives on an island, and he wears blinkers."

Laval saw the effect of these blinkers in Eden's reaction to learning that France had decided to build the battle cruiser *Richelieu* (35,000 tons), to be followed by another cruiser of the same tonnage. After the launching of these two ships, Eden believed, the English fleet would no longer be supreme in the Mediterranean and Mussolini might seize two or three British colonies. It was imperative, therefore, to immobilize the French fleet in the Atlantic, and there was only one way of doing this: to give the Reich a naval force once again.

It was a case of simplistic and doubly false reasoning. Eden was wrong about Mussolini's intentions. The Duce was only looking for an outlet for Italian overpopulation. He could find this outlet only in the immense, under-populated territory of Abyssinia. France, England, and Portugal had divided the rest of the vast continent among themselves. In the second place, Eden was wrong about the enemy Great Britain would have to fight—not Mussolini's Italy, but Hitler's Germany.

Laval nonetheless felt no antagonism toward England. He said, "England has the perfect right to defend her vital interests." He regretted only that England lacked foresight to the point of unbalancing the structure he had erected patiently, brick by brick, to preserve the peace.

In spite of her ally's unfortunate gesture, France in 1935 was strong. Laval had no trouble demonstrating that fact before the Commission on Foreign Affairs of the Chamber, when he drew a broad overview in a speech over two hours long.

On the diplomatic front, the agreements of Rome, the Stresa Front, and the Franco-Soviet Pact both completed and reinforced the treaties signed with the Little Entente, and put France in an exceptionally strong position.

The improvement of France's military posture in 1935 followed the improvement of her diplomatic position. In materiel and equipment, the rate of production after the slowdown of 1933–34 markedly increased. The Somua tanks and the new model of antiaircraft guns were completely satisfactory.

As for general strategy, the Rome agreements had permitted the Army of the Alps to regain its entire freedom of movement, and the African troops to ensure a permanent link with the mother country, while also patrolling the Mediterranean without risk.

Cooperation between the French and the Italian military staffs had been established by Marshal Pietro Badoglio, head of the Italian armed forces, and General Maurice Gamelin, commander in chief of the French army. Their special care was shown in the details agreed on for the application of the treaty in case of an attack on Austria by the Reich. The Italian and the French armies were to intervene immediately. The Italian army was to move from south to north, with a French army corps acting as a buffer on its right to prevent any possible action by Yugoslavia. The French army was to cross the Rhine north of Alsace, near Belfort, with the support of an Italian army corps on its right. Apart from strategic plans, the two countries discussed the details of action on the ground, General Moyrand being present at the major maneuvers of the Italian army.

This year 1935 was also one of great moment for Josée Laval and me. Our marriage was celebrated on August 20. The religious ceremony took place at Sainte-Clotilde, the "parish" of the Quai d'Orsay where Josée was living with her parents. After the ceremony, there was a brief reception in the gardens of the Quai d'Orsay, to which friends, ambassadors, and members of the government were invited. I can still remember Herriot's smile when we said our good-byes on that happy day. No cloud had yet appeared to trouble the atmosphere of confidence and close collaboration between him and Laval.

Josée's little blue convertible awaited us for our trip to Cherbourg, and then to Canada and the United States. The car began to sputter along the coast of St.-Germain and finally stopped altogether. Being of a superstitious turn of mind, this breakdown did not seem to me to be a good omen; I was not mistaken.

LAVAL AND THE BRITISH ONCE MORE

Upon our return from the United States on September 15, we found Laval calm as usual, but overworked and preoccupied. He commuted between Paris, where he was preparing to govern by decree, and Geneva, where the diplomatic community was greatly agitated by the persistent rumor that Mussolini had decided to make a move in Ethiopa.

And indeed, on October 3, the Duce launched his "colonial" expedition against Haile Selassie, emperor of Ethiopia. On the fifth, Laval was in Geneva. The Council of the League of Nations decided to apply the economic sanctions against Italy provided for in Article 16 of the pact. From November 18 on, the shipment of arms, munitions, and most raw materials, with the exception of oil, would be suspended. France and England voted for the sanctions; only Switzerland, Austria, and Hungary abstained. It should be noted that the embargo was never extended to include oil.

Laval had just returned to Paris when the British ambassador, Sir George Clark, asked Alexis Léger, secretary general of the Quai d'Orsay, for an urgent appointment with the prime minister. A few minutes later, the Rolls-Royce, with its union jack aflutter, came to a halt before the ministry. Tall, thin, distinguished looking, Sir George Clark looked the archtypical British aristocrat, and not unexpectedly, he spoke excellent French. After a few words of greeting to Laval, he said, "My government has just asked me to inform you that the Home Fleet is to cross the Strait of Gibraltar in a few hours. I am empowered to tell you in confidence that right now, the fleet lacks certain supplies and is not combat ready. My country is asking for the support of your navy, in case Italy commits an act of aggression in response to the sanctions."

Laval immediately telephoned Charles de Chambrun at the French embassy in Rome. "Is that you, Chambrun? This is Laval. I have the British ambassador in my office, who tells me that the Home Fleet is about to cross the Strait of Gibraltar. I want you to ask for a meeting with Mussolini—tomorrow morning at the latest. You are to tell him that in the event of a conflict with Italy, England can count on the immediate support of our land, sea, and air forces, as I have just informed the British ambassador."

Sir George Clark, deeply moved, said, "Mr. Prime Minister, my country shall not forget."

He did not realize that he was repeating almost word for word what his predecessor, Ronald Campbell, had said on the night of September 18, 1931.

Nor did Clark realize that during dinner that same evening my father-in-law confided to us with a smile, "When I asked my chief of staff to place the call to Chambrun, he warned me: 'Mr. Prime Minister, the Italians have surely installed a listening device.' I don't doubt it; that's why I insisted on telephoning on an open line. I wanted Mussolini to get the news of my decision with full force, before Chambrun's visit, whose diplomatic language might soften it."

Ten years later, in his prison cell at Fresnes, Pierre Laval answered the chief prosecutor's charge of having "hated Great Britain" by recalling the decision he had imparted to Sir George Clark. Then he went on: "I have searched history for a precedent in which a French minister committed his country in that way to Great Britain, without being obligated by a military alliance. I did not find any."°

Following the launching of the Italian operation and the voting of sanctions, the international situation continued to deteriorate and seemed about to erupt. At this juncture, Stanley Baldwin and the conservatives won a decisive victory in the Parliamentary elections. The new minister for foreign

°Josée de Chambrun, ed., *Laval Parle* (Paris: Diffusion du Livre), 1948.

affairs, Sir Samuel Hoare, had a reputation for clear-sightedness. Laval invited him to Paris, and Hoare arrived on December 7. The two men conferred for a long time at the Quai d'Orsay and then at the British embassy. There, Laval met the Prince of Wales, the future Edward VIII, whom he was to see again the following day at Rambouillet.

At the end of these discussions, Sir Samuel Hoare and the Prince of Wales agreed that the solution proposed by Laval was the only one that might keep the peace and prevent Mussolini from aligning himself sooner or later with Hitler. The Prince of Wales had Laval's words repeated to him verbatim so that he might render them exactly to his father.

The positive result of the negotiations was the "Laval-Hoare Plan." Italy was to be granted a considerably increased portion of Somalia; Erythria was to be extended by the addition of the Tigris, which the Italian Expeditionary Force had just occupied; finally, a zone of "colonization" was to be offered to Italy on Ethiopian territory, under the sovereignty of the Negus. But under the same plan, Italy was to be denied the right to join together Somalia and Erythria, one of her most desired objectives. Abyssinia, in compensation for the agreed-upon sacrifices, would obtain an opening in Assab onto the Red Sea.

While Sir Samuel Hoare was still in Paris, Robert Vansittart, the secretary general of the Ministry of Foreign Affairs, returned to London. There he presented the plan in outline to Baldwin, who gave his approval.

The League of Nations would have no choice but to ratify it. For not only had France and England reached complete agreement in their negotiations, but one sentence—the key sentence of the draft—linked them directly: "The two countries are to use their influence in Geneva to have His Majesty the Emperor accept the plan and to secure approval from the League of Nations for the establishment in Southern Ethiopia of a zone for the economic expansion and the resettlement of population exclusively for the benefit of Italy."

Laval, moreover, pressured Mussolini behind the scenes with the help of Chambrun. No one doubted that the emperor would accept the Franco-British text if it was reinforced by an injunction from the League of Nations.

On the morning of December 13, the day after the League had received official notice of the plan, two obviously synchronized bombshells exploded in London and in Paris. The text of the agreement appeared in the *Daily Telegraph* in London and in the *Echo de Paris* in Paris. An official of the Quai d'Orsay had handed a copy of the secret document to François Quilici, the representative of the Havas Agency, who passed it on at once to Pertinax (André Géraud), head foreign correspondent of the *Echo de Paris*, who also worked for the *Daily Telegraph*.

Baldwin, newly come to power, was caught short. He did not have time to marshal his forces. Faced with a raging opposition, he had to ask Sir Samuel Hoare to resign. As Italy plunged deeper into war and Europe warmed to the excitement, Laval saw his work on behalf of peace rapidly reduced to naught. Ten years later, at Fresnes, he summarized the history of the Laval-Hoare Plan with clearheaded melancholy:

> All the attempts to solve by amicable means in Geneva the Ethiopian conflict had failed one after the other. Only a complete agreement between France and England could have achieved the desired result.
>
> Neither Italy nor Ethiopia would have been able to oppose a compromise imposed by our two countries. Sir Samuel Hoare understood this and with his strong realism and a wish to put an end to an adventure that might have serious consequences for the future of Europe, he agreed to discuss and elaborate a plan that I was sure Italy would accept, that he was sure the Negus would accept, and that we both were sure Geneva would accept.
>
> At that critical moment, there was a leak to the press, and much argument ensued. After questions in the House of Commons, Sir Samuel Hoare was forced to resign. He was, however, brought back into the cabinet, in a different position, several days later.
>
> I have always deeply regretted that the plan was not put into effect. I never thought that I should bear a particular grudge against England for the plan's rejection. In that country, as in ours, public opinion was in fact divided. It was generally more hostile in England, because in addition to the anti-Fascists, who alone opposed the plan here, there were some in England who believed that the route to India was also threatened. So the British were once more defending their interests which they believed to be threatened. Such are vicissitudes of international politics. I therefore had no reason to "hate" England. I only had cause to regret the lack of success that was, bit by bit, to throw Italy into the arms of Germany, to deprive France and Great Britain of the essential cooperation of the Balkans, and to bring so much misery to our land. I am very much surprised to find now, in an indictment as serious as this, such an accusation against me. It shows a grave misunderstanding of the facts of the recent history of our country.°

While clearing himself of the charge of having "hated England," he also repelled the charge of having been Mussolini's accomplice, who facilitated the conquest of Ethiopia.

As I write, I have before me all the warnings addressed to the Duce, in letters and telegrams between July 1935 and January 23, 1936, when Laval left the Quai d'Orsay. On that final date, he wrote a note to Mussolini that ends as follows:

> I have never given my assent to the war that you seem to have found it necessary to undertake. The debates in the French Chamber on December 27 and 28 have given me the opportunity to describe in

---

° Ibid., pp. 29–30.

detail the spirit in which I negotiated and concluded the Rome Agreements.

LAVAL THE VICTOR

Far from discouraging him, the failure of the Laval-Hoare Plan confirmed Laval's belief that he had been right. He was determined to have the Chamber approve the policy of peace that he had pursued since coming to the Quai d'Orsay.

The opposition was equally determined to get rid of him for good. It spent all of December sharpening its weapons and choosing its spokesmen: Léon Blum, Jean Zay, Gabriel Peri, Marcel Déat. Daladier preferred to remain behind the scenes and delegated Yvon Delbos, who yearned to be foreign minister, to speak for him. Lastly, the coalition obtained the support of one of the most brilliant debaters among the moderates, Paul Reynaud.

The debate opened at nine o'clock on the morning of Wednesday, December 27, continued without a break for two days and one night, ending in the evening of December 28. Laval underwent a gruelling test of physical endurance: he dared not leave the government bench for the entire day of the 27th and the entire night following.

From the afternoon of the twenty-seventh, the visitors' galleries were full. Léon Blum was the big attraction. In the incisive debate, he grew increasingly vehement in his attack on the Duce, whom he called "the tyrant of Italy" and the "assassin of his friend Giacomo Matteotti." He seemed strangely unaware of the existence of Hitler, the Reich, and the Nazi regime. For three hours, he aimed his fire at Laval and Mussolini exclusively.

After the night session, whose principal stars were Reynaud, Delbos, and Peri, Anatole de Monzie was one of the first to mount the rostrum on the morning of the twenty-eighth. He surprised the audience by calling Laval, whose friendship he had always claimed, the "Louis XI of the suburbs, plodding along and hoping to accomplish big deeds by means of little tricks." The Left laughed and applauded. From there on, they felt assured of victory.

Laval maintained a stony calm. None of the attackers succeeded in making him fly off the handle or lose his patience. During a longish break in one of the sessions, Laval met with Pietri, Cathala, and Mandel. Pietri said, "If we had bookmakers as they have in London, they would give the opposition odds of fifteen to one." Turning to Laval, he asked, "Is your brief ready?"

"When would I have had the time to prepare it? I've spent fifteen months fighting for peace, and now I've spent fifteen hours listening to tirades!" After a moment, he added, "What about you, how would you start off?"

"I would tell them, 'What you're really accusing me of is my politics.'"

At that point, the guard announced that the session was about to resume. Laval slowly made his way to the platform, holding a thick folder under his arm. The previous evening I had seen that same folder all tied up with tape, and I knew that it contained only official documents and no briefs with which to plead his cause.

President Fernand Bouisson solemnly announced, "Gentlemen, the prime minister."

The assembly, the public, the stenographers, the guards, all fell into an attentive silence as Laval opened his folder, and leaning toward the sea of faces, began.

"Gentlemen, in listening to so many brilliant speakers making so many heated attacks against my policies at the Quai d'Orsay, I questioned my conscience, and I asked myself what crime I might have committed against my country and against peace.

"What you have been doing is to accuse me of my politics."

Pietri had been right. But he had not realized that he had suggested the opening of one of the best speeches, or rather one of the best improvisations, of Pierre Laval's career.

As he continued to speak, silence fell little by little over the benches of the Left. They realized that they were listening not to a plea, but as Laval enumerated the secret memoranda exchanged between the military headquarters of the French and British armies, navies, and air forces, to a stark recital of unfolding events. After a pause, he continued. "These notes were exchanged at my request, in the course of carrying out my promise of September ninth." Laval needed no other justification: the fulfillment of a promise.

After a pregnant pause, he turned to the members of the extreme Left and hurled these words at them: "What did you take me for?"

Warm applause came from the Right, the center, and from a few benches on the Left. Josée, leaning toward me, whispered, "He has won."

He must have thought so, too. As he continued, his speech became more and more relaxed and serene. He concluded in an almost familiar, conversational tone: "I am done. The vote you are about to cast is important. Gentlemen, it is not the fate of the ministry that hangs in the balance. I have been at the Quai d'Orsay for fifteen months. I have been prime minister only since last June. I have not asked for anything. You have given me difficult tasks."

Again, there was applause on the Right, from the center, and from some benches on the left. He continued: "With the help of my colleagues, all of my colleagues . . ." Some exclamations were heard on the Left, so he took the opportunity to reaffirm: "Yes, all of my colleagues." The applause began again on the Right, in the center, and made inroads into more benches on the Left as he went on: "We have been able to defend the franc, and if the vote that the Chamber is about to cast permits it, the budget will be voted on in two days."

Again, there were outcries on the extreme Left. He waited for silence, and then added in a good-natured tone: "Oh, yes. Can it be that you're sorry about that?" With a motion of his hand, he stopped both the laughter that his answer provoked among the Communists and the continuing applause from elsewhere, and he concluded in a solemn voice:

"Mr. Léon Blum has presented here his electoral platform. Your own platform, for those of you who have supported the government, consists of the things you have accomplished, the courage you have shown, the spirit of self-denial and sacrifice you have displayed in the effort to defend the vital interests of this country.

"Gentlemen, the entire orientation of French foreign policy hangs in the balance. You are the representatives of the country and its responsible lawmakers. Choose!"

The applause redoubled, shouts of bravo filled the air, and hands reached out toward the prime minister as he returned to his seat. When calm was restored, Fernand Bouisson read the order of the day, presented by the majority, and for which the government had asked a vote of confidence:

"The Chamber, faithful to the noblest French traditions and approving the declarations of the government, entrusts the latter with the task of carrying on its work of conciliation, international understanding, and peace, within the limits of the pact of the League of Nations, and rejecting any amendments, proceeds to the order of the day."

The presiding officer announced the tally as follows:

Number of those voting	565
Majority	283
For adoption of the motion	304
Against	261

"The motion is carried."

While the majority rose in acclamation, the opposition left quietly through the concealed doors at the extreme left of the semicircular chamber.

LAVAL'S BALANCE SHEET

The vote of December 27, 1935, was an unequivocal reply to the third charge—or rather to the third falsification in the indictment of September 1945: "The French Parliament, whose confidence he had lost . . ."

But the opposition of the late 1930s did not give up. Although it had lost in open debate, it continued to work behind the scenes. It had already used slander and insult, as may be seen from such a document as this:

MINISTRY OF THE INTERIOR   The French Republic
Office of National Security   *Paris, November 4, 1935*

CONFIDENTIAL

The Minister of the Interior
Office of National Security
to the Prime Minister

In regard to insulting
remarks about
Mr. Laval:

I have the honor of informing you, for any useful purpose, that during a public meeting that took place in Metz on October 19, 1935, and was organized by the "Popular Front," a certain Mr. Midon, from the S.F.I.O. [Socialist] party of Nancy, made the following statement:

"Ten years ago, Mr. Laval had no money; today he gives his daughter millions as a dowry. Mr. Laval is therefore a thief and swindler. We cannot trust a man of that kind."

If I have chosen to keep this document from among hundreds of others of the same kind, it is because of the handwritten note that I found in the margin:
"Do not follow up. I scorn all insults. P.L."
But if slander and insults left him cold, he became angry when it was implied or insinuated that he had broken with the friends of his youth, who had also been his political comrade-in-arms. He reacted with great indignation when he read the opening words of the 1945 "indictment."

The indictment begins with an assumption with which I cannot agree: Having had my start in parties of the Left, I was supposed to have been "repudiated" by them. This statement implies that I was excluded from the Socialist party, to which I belonged. In fact, I left it of my own free will. Four years after my departure, the socialist candidates agreed to present themselves for the election of 1924, on a slate that I headed. At that time, I specifically stated that I would never again belong either to the Socialist or to any other political party.

As long as I belonged to the Socialist party, I always respected its discipline. In 1917, I refused to join Clemenceau's cabinet as undersecretary of state in the Ministry of the Interior. I refused because Clemenceau had asked me to offer the Socialist party a large measure of participation in his government and the party had turned the collaboration down as a matter of principle. In 1919, I had problems with my socialist colleagues, but I preferred to stand by them, because they had elected me in 1914. I did this even in the face of certain defeat, rather than accept the offer to head the slate of the National Bloc, which was, in fact, elected.

I have retained tender memories of my militant youth, not only because it was the time of my youth, but because in those days I found an enthusiasm, an open-mindedness, and a generosity of feeling that I did not find again later on, in other surroundings. I was imbued from then on with a *love of peace, of the workers, of the little people of the world, and of freedom.* I believe that I have proved my devotion to the working class by the enactment of the laws on family allowances and on social security in 1930, despite an atmosphere of almost general hostility. Thanks to these laws, I was able to settle peacefully the strike of textile workers in the north, which involved about 150,000 people.[°]

Despite the gravity of the crisis, Laval succeeded in keeping the peace. The special powers with which he hoped to spur an economic and financial upturn were approved by the Chamber. Even so, the government would have to last long enough for the beneficial effects of the economic measures to be accepted and appreciated by public opinion.

In June 1935, nine months before the legislative elections, Laval realized that a change in the majority would undo his work. He therefore obtained a promise from Herriot to support a six-months prorogation of the Chamber. On its side, the opposition was acutely aware of this threat of extension; it was all the more exasperating that the climate otherwise seemed favorable to the Left.

After the violent demonstrations of February 1934, which precipitated Daladier's resignation, there had been a paradoxical reaction from the countryside. It "repudiated Paris" and accused it of having wanted to overthrow the Republic. This can be seen from the depositions taken by the "commission of inquiry into the events of February 6, 1934" from many who had participated in the uprising. The commission was presided over by Marc Rucart, a radical socialist (moderate). All the witnesses protested their innocence and affirmed their strong loyalty to the regime and the institutions of the country.

This internal situation was tied to an external one that was to prove decisive: Stalin, realizing the menace of German expansion, wanted a strong France, as he had already told Laval at the signing of the Franco-Soviet Pact. To Stalin, however, a strong France implied a united Left. Stalin therefore wanted to see the large opposition parties—the radicals, the socialists, and the Communists—put an end to their differences (sharpened by the events of February 1934) and create a kind of holy alliance of the Left for the elections of April and May.

Stalin's wish was immediately realized. On July 14, 1935, radical socialists, socialists, and Communists, in a prefiguration of the Popular Front, marched

[°]Ibid., pp. 18–20.

from the Place de la Bastille to the Place de la Nation, chanting two slogans: "Laval must resign!" "Jail all the Fascists!"

Thus occurred the strange spectacle of Daladier marching at the head of the parade side by side with Léon Blum, Maurice Thorez, Peri, and Duclos, while Herriot and five other radicals in the cabinet were working furiously with Laval to set up the special powers. Daladier, held up to scorn after February 1934, was again on his way to power.

The opposition's first aim was to prevent the prorogation of the session of the Chamber, and for that they needed to overthrow the cabinet. But after the vote of confidence that the Chamber gave Laval on December 28, 1935, there was only one way of provoking a resignation: Herriot and the five radical ministers must leave the government. In June, however, Herriot had promised Laval to support him faithfully and to accept the extension of the Chamber.

Herriot was at a crossroads. His decision could determine France's destiny.

Daladier had made up his mind to play the game of the extreme Left. He led an offensive against the Laval government, the effect of which was to isolate Herriot and make him the hostage of the moderates. The early results of this offensive became quickly apparent. On December 18, Herriot felt obliged to resign as president of the Radical party. When the group met on January 16, 1936, Daladier was cheered; Herriot was only applauded. With his back to the wall, he spent five days pondering, hesitating.

On the evening of the twenty-first, as Laval prepared to leave for Geneva, his private telephone rang. Mme. Laval answered and told her husband, "It's Herriot. He is sure to tell you that he is resigning." A few moments later, the two men held a short, private meeting in one of the drawing rooms of the Quai d'Orsay. Herriot retracted his promise to accept the extension of the Chamber.

Laval, not wanting to miss his train, said little. He told his wife, "He's quitting. I should have had him put it in writing last summer. Tomorrow we will have the Popular Front, disorder, and perhaps even war."

On January 22 and 23, the only topic of conversation in Paris was Laval's resignation. He had just come back from Geneva. All the ministers met him at the Gare de Lyon—with one absent—Herriot. As soon as Laval appeared, applause resounded, but the same concern could be read on all the faces.

The prime minister made his way quickly through the crowd to his car, returned to the Quai d'Orsay, and on the spot, composed the letter of resignation of his government for submission to the president of the Republic in the morning.

When later in his prison cell he went over the matter of Herriot's "quitting," he showed no bitterness. He simply made an objective statement of his reasons for resigning:

I decided to leave office after returning from my trip to Geneva during which I had met with Mr. Eden. I informed him of my decision, and he seemed much surprised. He even had the courtesy to express his regret at seeing me resign. There are circumstances when the head of a government (especially when he is also minister of foreign affairs) has the duty to resign. It is the case when he lacks the cooperation necessary to assure the success of his policies.

I was not able to get Herriot's signature, which was necessary for the prorogation of special powers, already then called "full powers," and I knew that under these conditions, the policy intended to restore financial stability and to increase the country's production was doomed to failure.

Moreover, I knew that the so-called oil sanction against Italy was demanded by certain leftist elements in France and in England. I refused to consider it, because in my opinion the application of this measure would have dragged us into war, and I wished to avoid war. So I resigned.

I believed, moreover, that the same people who were opposing me would, once in power, and faced with responsibility, have the same apprehensions as I had. In fact, the oil sanction was never applied or ever proposed by my successors.

Moreover, several weeks after I left office, Germany was remilitarizing the Rhineland. This violation of the Treaty of Versailles should have been countered by sanctions, as provided for in the Treaty of Locarno. But this was not done. Aside from a speech and a few newspaper articles, there was nothing.°

A review of Laval's policies manifestly clears him of the charges that the prosecution leveled at him for his acts during this period, and it also shows that the prosecution lied. Nor is this all. That same review shows all that his country owed to his efforts. The numbers speak for themselves: when he became head of the government, France was suffering from galloping inflation, the budgetary deficit was more than 10 billion gold francs, and national production was in sharp decline. Seven months later, on December 31, France was the only country in the world to have a balanced budget (even a small surplus); the level of expenditures had been reduced; the cost of living had declined by more than 10 percent; interest, at 3 percent, was almost on a level with inflation. In the spring, the state debt showed a decrease for the first time since its adjustment under Poincaré in 1926. The index of wholesale prices was at its lowest: 332 (two years later, in 1938, it went back to 634). Production in the important sectors of industry (steel, automobiles, chemicals) reached record levels.

Finally, France had begun to rearm. Shipbuilding for the navy nearly tripled—from 15,950,000 tons in 1934 to 42,783,000 tons in 1935. It was to drop to 26,540,000 tons in 1938, less than a year before the war.

°Ibid., pp. 24–25.

THE POPULAR FRONT

Three months before the election of 1936, the Popular Front had already acted like winners. Laval, who did not expect to return to power soon again, organized his life by moving into his offices at 120 Champs-Élysées. In March, Pierre Taittinger, a deputy from Paris, had been the first to ask him to lead the opposition. But after the victory of the Popular Front, Laval preferred to stand aside; he answered those who asked, "I will not oppose their lies with truths that might hurt France abroad."

He turned to his new tasks. In Châteldon, he set up a mineral water business, La Sergentale, bought a radio-transmission station, Radio-Lyon, which had gone bankrupt, reorganized the newspaper *Le Moniteur du Puy-de-Dôme*, which he had bought in 1928. Later, when some Parisian papers had to escape to the free zone after the signing of the armistice, his own paper, *Le Moniteur*, enabled those papers to keep publishing.

These occupations did not prevent him from following politics closely. The state of grace of the first Popular Front government lasted only a few months. The public coffers soon emptied. While Germany was engaged in a huge rearmament, French production of military weapons, such as fighter planes, tanks, and antiaircraft guns, fell dangerously. The gold and currency reserves that had accumulated during the Laval government were melting so rapidly that on October 1 Blum and Auriol announced the largest devaluation of the franc since the start of the Third Republic—25 percent.

While Laval was following the course of European affairs very closely, certain foreign powers, in turn, watched Laval. One November night in 1936, Jacques Sadoul, a founder of the French Communist party, telephoned. "Someone very important, a friend of the 'Boss,' whom you went to see after your trip to Rome, is in Paris and wants to see you." Sadoul and Laval agreed to meet in Châteldon the next day. They had known each other before 1914 and had never stopped being on friendly terms.

Sadoul had an "in" in the U.S.S.R., where he was received by Stalin, the "Boss," and the next day he introduced the mysterious visitor: "Rudzutak, Stalin's man, and a member of the Politburo."

Rudzutak, in turn, introduced to Laval and to my mother-in-law the pretty young blonde who accompanied him: "My secretary." A moment later, he added, "She doesn't speak French."

After a little while, we sat down to lunch. Laval still somewhat puzzled, wanted to know more about the young woman. Did she really not know French? He told a rather daring story. The young woman blushed up to her ears. Laval laughed to himself. He had guessed that she was there to keep an eye on Rudzutak.

After lunch, Rudzutak got to the point, the reason that had brought him from Moscow to Châteldon. "Comrade Stalin is aware that Germany's military potential continues to grow, and he is worried when he sees that France, on the contrary, has slowed her efforts since you left office. He deplores the strikes and other social conflicts that are paralyzing your country. Since your trip to Russia was for him a notable event, he would like you to return to power and improve France's situation. He is ready to make things easier by telling the Communists to stop opposing you."

"That is a very flattering proposition—for me," replied Laval, "but I find it hard to imagine that Marty, Cachin, Thorez, and Duclos would be ready to salute my return to power."

"You need have no worries about that. I want you to know that whereas Stalin regards you highly, he has no confidence in Léon Blum. We are offering you the keys to the Popular Front; if you accept, we will support you."

"Please thank Comrade Stalin for his confidence in me, but tell him also that he would certainly admire me much less if I were to accept his proposition. I left the Socialist party because the international ideal that it supported did not seem to me compatible with France's interests, which have been my constant concern. If, one day, I return to power, it will be to serve those interests exclusively. I am sure Comrade Stalin will understand me."

THE CRY OF ALARM

During all of 1937 and 1938, Laval's concern continued to grow; it turned to anxiety as Hitler, given strength by the weakness of his enemies, broadened his conquests. Though blocked in his first attempt to annex Austria because Mussolini had decided to contain German expansion, the Nazi leader held all the cards when the war in Ethiopia led to sanctions being imposed against Italy. It was then that the Duce changed sides and threw himself into Hitler's arms. The Nazis immediately occupied Austria without firing a shot (March 11, 1938) and, next on the list, forced Czechoslovakia to give up the Sudetenland, mostly inhabited by Germans.

On the day following the "Anschluss" with Austria, my friend Ralph Heinzen, manager of the United Press, took me with him to see Laval, from whom he hoped to get a statement. But although my father-in-law knew and admired Heinzen, he would not break his silence. However, on condition that he not be quoted, he agreed to sketch a picture of the past fifteen years of French politics. He described how his country, which had known a brilliant past, was living in a difficult present and was facing a troubled future.

"Since the last war, out of four elections, France has voted three times for the Left: in 1924, in 1932, and in 1936. Each time, after less than two years, the government of the Left has put the country on the brink of fiscal and economic bankruptcy, with dreadful repercussions on our foreign policy. In 1926, it became necessary to draft Raymond Poincaré to rescue Herriot, the franc, and the economy. In 1934, I had to get Doumergue president in order to save the government of February 6, 1934. Today, two years after the third leftist election, we are on the road to catastrophe. We should get Clemenceau, but he's dead, and I'm afraid it's too late. The ogre opposite has a large appetite. Tomorrow, it will probably be Czechoslovakia's turn, and the next day Poland. Meanwhile, France will be diplomatically, morally, and materially too weak to go to war and win."

Faced with the spectacle of Central Europe being dismembered, France and England were becoming alarmed and finally getting to see that they were on the verge of armed conflict. Neville Chamberlain, the British prime minister, together with Daladier and Mussolini, who had offered his "good offices," tried to prevent war by going to Germany to negotiate with Hitler. For the French and the British, Munich was to prove a trap, if not an outright capitulation. The agreement they signed forced Czechoslovakia to cede the Sudetenland to the Reich, and Hitler, knowing he would now be free to do whatever he liked, annexed Bohemia and Moravia in March 1939, declaring himself their "protector." He created a Slovakia, whose "independence" was a fiction, and began to cast glances in the direction of the Danzig Corridor, which, though "guaranteed by the League of Nations," was, according to him, part of Germany's vital territory. Poland was directly threatened.

It was after this that Laval felt it his duty to ring the warning bell and wake up Daladier's government. Sadoul had warned him after Munich that faced with the capitulation of France and England, Stalin was planning a radical change of policy, including an agreement with Germany for a new division of Poland.

Laval asked that George Bonnet, the minister of foreign affairs, be questioned by the Senate Commission on Foreign Affairs. It met secretly on March 16, 1939, and the twenty-three senators who came to hear the minister's presentation were amazed to see Laval challenge the Daladier government. After listing all the errors that had permitted the spread of the "Nazi plague," he declared that the only way to bar the road to Hitler was by reestablishing "the chain." He insisted that there could be no "chain" without Italy:

Laval: The Reich wants central Europe; it's as clear as day. We're doing nothing to prevent it, and you quote newspaper articles at me! The tragedy that is playing itself out in our country is dreadful; France says nothing, because she is too complacent.

Bonnet: What would you do in my place?

Laval: I would resign. We are among Frenchmen here. What is going on is abominable. I am horrified by the present situation. Today, Germany, which lost the war, has more territory than she had before 1914. The Austro-Hungarian Empire has been destroyed. The Protestants, and I'm speaking freely here, did not want the continuing existence of this Catholic empire in the center of Europe. The forces of evil have joined together for the destruction of a group of countries that constituted a counterweight with respect to Germany, even after the victory of the Allies. The evil has been done, and today we see the plague spreading. Just a while ago, Mr. Bachelet put the problem very well: "If it's true that Hitler and Mussolini are in agreement, we will soon see what comes of it." Then we will have to defend ourselves, and as Mr. Bachelet said, we can count on the allies that we have. Nevertheless, I'm afraid that in listing them, he was too generous in our behalf, because the small countries of central Europe will be afraid. There is only one way to prevent Hitler from taking over Europe, and that is to make the "chain" stretch from London to Paris and on to Rome, Belgrade, Budapest, Warsaw, Bucharest, and Moscow. Otherwise, Germany will win. I used this same expression, even more strongly, when I spoke to Mr. MacDonald in Stresa.

Mr. Bachelet, can you and your friends realize that the interests of France as a whole must be put above those of our parties? If political passions have blinded us to the point where the Rome Agreements have been voided, today all French people must be united to block the road of Germany.

I am asking the government to find a solution. But there is one that it can't choose. That it is to permit Germany to continue to do what she is doing. I have had the privilege, during several months, of conducting the foreign policy of my country, and since that time I have seen all the advantages of the Treaty of Versailles fall away one by one. Today it is territories that are being added on to Germany one by one. I say this cannot be allowed to go on, or else in a few days, in a few months, French blood will flow, and hundreds of thousands of wooden crosses will be erected in our cemeteries. To keep this from happening, there is still time to make an effort, but no time to make more than one.

On March 23, before the business of Czechoslovakia, Mr. Paul-Boncour, who was minister of foreign affairs, seemed to understand—at least he said he did—that Italy would return to the Anglo-French orbit. I told him I was happy to hear him say so, but I added that it was urgent to do everything to bring Italy back. I used these words: "It is the only way I see to save our honor, defend our interests, and save the peace."

It was not done. We know what happened to our honor in Munich, we know what our honor was worth when we delivered homage of Munich to that unknown soldier, who, after having been killed in the trenches, sleeps beneath the Arc de Triomphe. You can see the condition that French interests are in today.

What was true on March 23 of last year is all the more true today. It was difficult then to have the policy of understanding with Italy that I advocated because of our internal politics and our divisions. Today, it is still difficult because of our internal problems. No matter: do you want to do something or don't you? Have you the will to try?

If so, go ahead and enter into discussions with Italy. Do you think that she is not interested in this problem, that she does not realize that once Germany is powerful, her turn will come, too?

In days of old, Charlemagne was a great man, a very great man, but he believed in God. Today Charlemagne does not believe in anything; he himself is God. That is without precedent in history. You will search in vain in our books, those in our high schools and our universities, for events resembling those of today. Do you not feel something impelling you to come to an agreement with all those who may be Hitler's victims tomorrow?

Again, won't you even try? If you do, you have a chance to save the peace; if not, you may well catapult our country into a tragic, fearful situation, the likes of which it has never seen.

I have shown the problem. Please forgive me for having been grandiloquent; I would have been even more so, had I expressed all I feel.

Oh, if Hitler could only guess—and he probably does guess—everything that is going on in Paris. Those exchanges with the minister of foreign affairs in the Chamber and in the Senate, where the latter explains to us in great detail how Germany has seized Czechoslovakia! Oh, how Hitler must laugh! If he knew how ashamed I am, how I become red in the face when I recalled to you the conversation of four hours' duration that I had in that little hotel room in Cracow with Goering. It was he, then, who reproached me for the measures we were taking, who reproached me for encircling Germany, who reproached me for always getting France to make plans against Germany. Today, Hitler's old enemies, the anti-Nazis, the anti-Fascists, all the irreconcilable enemies of tyranny, are the ones who are paving the way for Hitler's triumph.

I beseech you, wake up! All of us share the responsibility, because we are all representatives of our country. If I tell you that it is possible to get along with Mussolini, are you willing to give it a try? If you don't try, you are criminals; you are committing high treason against your country, the greatest that has ever been committed.

Bonnet: Does Mr. Pierre Laval then consider that negotiations with Italy would be possible at the present moment?

Laval: I consider that they are absolutely essential. Possible, you ask? That is between you and Mussolini. But I'm afraid that given the way you deal with him, you may find it very difficult for you.

If you want to reach an agreement with Mussolini, you must know what he wants before you enter into negotiations. You must be well informed, and he must be the one to ask; you should not be the one to offer an agreement, because he needs to show his people that he has won a victory. What he and the Italians reproach us with is Germany's presence on the Brenner Pass. It is therefore necessary, and I repeat it strongly, that we reach an agreement with Italy. The difficulty is to know whether we want to do it. And here I am really surprised by the questions that are raised. "Do you think," I am asked, "that Parliament will like it?" What difference is that to me? Don't you think Parliament has done France enough harm by now and that Hitler ought to be grateful for it? What counts is France's interests. They are what you are defending. Once you have the courage of your convictions, the deputies will run like rabbits as they realize that the people are with you. For the people, who are being deceived and lied to, will certainly be with you when they become convinced that you are defending the interests of the country. I cannot imagine a sadder meeting than this one, and yet, from your attitude, no one would suspect it.

In order to avoid looking at me with anger, Mr. Secretary, you are looking at that wall hanging behind you. How much better if instead of that hanging there were a map. They made fun of me when I asked for one. They also made fun of me when I put two world maps here. They were wrong. Mr. Secretary, if you had a map of Europe on which you could see Germany spread out bit by bit, you would see your duty clearly. You would understand that your agreements with Yugoslavia and Poland, your relations with Hungary, all of those are not worth much if you have no agreement with Rome. I am asking you again, Mr. Secretary, do you desire an agreement with Rome? Perhaps, as we leave, you'll tell me: "I would like to do it, but I'm not alone," and perhaps your boss will tell me, as he told me when I asked him to send a representative to Burgos, "I could lose the votes of twenty to thirty radicals." If that's how you think, I'll go back to what I said earlier. Resign, if that's how you think.

No British politician, no French politician, and above all no extreme leftist anti-Nazi had underscored Hitler's menace with the same perspicacity, tried to ward it off with the same firmness and constancy, or denounced the guilty apathy of the representatives with the same vehemence as Laval. None of them tried, as he proposed with stubborn clarity, to take the only course that could block Hitler's path and save the peace.

THE WAR

Daladier was shaken, yet for a good while he had been mulling over what Laval had told him. On the very day of my father-in-law's appearance before the Senate Commission on Foreign Affairs, Daladier asked Marshal Pétain to accept the post of French ambassador to Spain.

Franco was annoyed with the socialist government of Léon Blum for having wished for the *Frente Popular* to be victorious in Spain. Daladier calculated that only the attentions of a figure as prestigious as Pétain, the "victor of Verdun," could woo back Franco's sympathy toward France.

On September 1, 1939, five months after Laval's solemn entreaty of March 16, the Second World War began. Hitler invaded Poland. Laval dreaded the repercussions of the invasion, having in mind an account of the extreme weakness of the French air force, confidentially conveyed to him in July 1939 by General Denain, the minister of the air force in Laval's last government. France commanded a negligible number of fighter planes, not a single modern bomber, while the Reich had several thousand.

On September 3, before the opening of the Senate discussion of the proposed military appropriations, Laval made one last effort, as recorded in the *Journal Officiel:*

Laval: I wish to speak.

President of the Senate Jules Jeanneney: A communication from the government does not involve discussion. Therefore I cannot permit you to speak.

From many benches: Let him speak, speak!

Laval: Like all my colleagues, I have listened to the government's declaration with deep emotion. I have a short statement to make.

Henri Roy and several other senators: You may speak during the discussion of the appropriations.

Laval: In January 1935 . . . [mutterings here and there]

The president of the Senate: Please, my dear senator, do not insist.

Laval, who generally forgave easily, never forgave this refusal to listen to him at such a solemn moment. France slid into armed conflict in a condition of almost unbelievable myopia.

During the month of September, after hostilities had begun, the warring forces were busy with their respective reinforcement of the Siegfried and the Maginot lines. I was in charge of overseeing construction work on the casemates, set up at regular intervals, into which machine guns and 47-mm. antitank guns were to be placed. One could hear the Germans, working twenty-four hours a day, including Saturdays and Sundays.

Our side had at work one African battalion of convicts and some officers who had volunteered from the Third Army. Imagine our amazement when, on September 7, we received the following order: "Within the limits appropriate to the state of hostilities, the rule of the forty-hour workweek shall be observed, and work on Saturdays and Sundays shall be ordered only with permission from Third Army headquarters."

How could anyone hope to defeat a formidable enemy while continuing to apply peacetime labor laws? The opening of the war was, at least for France, so strange and unheard of that it came to be called the "phony war." For almost eight months the French and the Germans remained bogged down in preparations. At long intervals, the armies exchanged fire briefly or launched a raid. An atmosphere of false security, the climate of optimism that official circles wished to create, put the country to sleep. People went so far as to believe that the Germans were not attacking because they were afraid of France.

Laval, on the contrary, sensed that a disaster was threatening and its time coming ever closer. In March, he could restrain himself no longer. On the fourteenth, at a secret meeting of the Senate, he held the floor for more than two hours, drawing up the balance sheet of the long months of the "phony war," and voicing the strongest possible indictment of the Daladier government:

> Gentlemen, for four years I have often spoken before our committees (especially before the Commission on Foreign Affairs) about my fears and my hopes.

> Today I believe it to be my duty to come to this platform, not only to review with you certain events, not only to hold the government accountable, but to try to elucidate a certain number of ideas and principles that should be guiding us at this time.

> We are at war. We have been at war for six months. We are the ones who declared war, and we know why we declared it. We declared it to save Poland, yet Poland is destroyed. We declared it in the name of morality, in order to save small nations from aggression and brutality, yet chivalrous, sorrowful Finland has just succumbed, after fighting alone, without having received serious or sufficient help.

Today we see Germany taking the initiative. So far, all successes have been hers and the Soviet Union's.

What we are witnessing is the human spectacle of the weak, the neutral, the small nations being attracted to those that seem strong. What people, what small nation, will dare tomorrow to link its fate to the strength of our arms? Look where you will; none can be found.

In a few days, or in a few weeks, peace will most likely be offered to us, but we shall be unable to accept it, regardless of who initiates it, because under present conditions it can only be a peace of surrender, a peace with dishonor.

It is not enough to minimize the enemy's strength in the newspapers or on the radio. For we do have considerable means. But we must not pursue this course of dangerous indolence; it is real defeatism, in that it allows the country to hope that it need not make any great effort in order to bring Germany to her knees.

Gentlemen, have you ever seen a country revolt after as many victories as those recorded by Hitler? I do not know of any.

Mr. Daladier, it is generally said—please don't misunderstand me— that you are shrewd. I wish that you were shrewd not only with Parliament, but equally with the enemies of France.

We are living in a strange time. Perhaps we are not fully aware of it, while we live through it. But this is the most dreadful upheaval that has ever happened in Europe, and perhaps in the world, because man's diabolic inventions are increasing the means of destruction and of killing.

For us, what is at stake, is our life, our honor, it is France herself.

I want to leave this platform on a note of hope and with a word expressive of unity. We love our country; we don't want to see it die. We don't want it to be diminished or defeated. Well, whatever the errors of those who have led us in the past, or of those who are leading us now, let us unite! Let us set ourselves on the right course, which I outlined earlier! Let us make a start, but let us do it quickly; for I fear that the six months just passed have not been put to the right use.

My occupying this rostrum had no other object, it aimed at no other consequence (even if at times my manner proved irritating), than to call the attention of my colleagues and of the government to our failures, to what must be done. If I have succeeded, then I am happy to have spoken.

Daladier's government fell. In the hallways, in the usual commotion typical of a cabinet crisis, many politicians and officials kept mobbing Laval. Daladier, good loser that he was, approached him and asked, "You will shake hands, won't you?" Laval, thinking grimly of the days ahead and the gravity of the situation, answered sadly, "I can't. You already have blood on yours."

To make a new start and forge the union that Laval had urged so strongly at the end of his speech, France needed time. Hitler did not grant it. On May 10, he unleashed the Blitzkrieg. The Wehrmacht rushed through Holland and Belgium and broke through the northern border of France. During the battle, I interrogated the crews of German planes shot down by the British antiaircraft forces that were defending a sector of ten divisions pitted against the light and very efficient German bombers flying at low altitudes. My conclusion was clear. Although the German air force was strong enough to crush France, it was not strong enough to overcome England, which already possessed a large force of fighter planes, which grew stronger daily.

ON THE POTOMAC WITH ROOSEVELT

On the eve of France's defeat, I found myself in a unique position to witness and, I hoped, to influence America's role in the war. Because of my firm conviction that England could resist the German threat, I had been appointed in June 1940 special military attaché and sent to Washington to meet with Roosevelt.

On June 14, I arrived at the White House and was taken aboard the presidential yacht to spend the weekend there with Harry Hopkins and W. Averell Harriman. Just as we sat down to tea that first afternoon, Roosevelt learned by radio that the Germans had crossed the Seine near Paris and were advancing toward the Loire.

"The show is over," said the president, his arms dropping to the sides of his wheelchair. "I don't think Great Britain can hold on."

My campaign to strengthen American support of Great Britain began at that point. I said that if we had erred previously by underestimating the military power of the Reich, we should not make the opposite mistake of overestimating it. The English, I suggested, might misrepresent the Reich's power to Roosevelt in hopes of securing American aid. But the Luftwaffe had suffered more seriously than was supposed from the attacks of British fighter planes. As the British held the additional advantage of operating close to their own bases, any attempt by the Germans to land in Great Britain was likely to fail. If France kept her navy, I concluded, and if the United States could deliver supplies and bombers to Great Britain, it would eventually be possible to attack the heart of Germany—the industrial region of the Ruhr.

Roosevelt was silent for a long time. At last he said, "You are convinced. You have convinced me. It remains for us to convince this country."

The situation in America was particularly serious. Although American ports held fighter planes and weapons ordered by the French and the British, the German victories had triggered an outbreak of isolationist sentiment, with the result that the cabinet had decided on June 13 to keep this military equipment for the defense of the United States. To the Americans, as Roosevelt knew and as I had already seen, a British defeat seemed inevitable.

Roosevelt put me to work to counteract this corrosive pessimism. He made a list of twenty-three of the most influential politicians and directed me to meet with each of them.

The status of the French fleet troubled Roosevelt deeply. Still aboard the yacht, I drafted a telegram to Reynaud, the new head of the French government, to report the president's faith in Great Britain and to suggest that the Americans would follow Roosevelt into war only if England would stop demoralizing her allies by defeatist propaganda and if France could retain her empire and her fleet.

At the end of the weekend, we returned to the White House. Roosevelt's sense of urgency compelled me to telephone Reynaud. As I began my report to him, Reynaud interrupted me.

"But don't you know that I've resigned? Pétain is forming a government."

Full of surprise, I asked Reynaud to convey to Pétain Roosevelt's firm belief that the French must agree to an armistice but must not surrender her fleet.

Meanwhile, I prepared myself to battle American popular opinion, facing the Senate on the seventeenth and meeting with key figures thoughout my stay. False news influenced everyone. I heard that the bombing of London had begun, that an attack on Great Britain was imminent, and that the French fleet was about to be handed over to Hitler.

While I waited feverishly in Washington for an "authentic" piece of news, the situation in Bordeaux seemed deadlocked. Reynaud's government had resigned; Pétain's government seemed split. Some of its members, particularly Chautemps, Darlan, and Prouvost favored an armistice. Others, such as Campinchi and Delbos, thought it would be a dishonorable capitulation.

THE ARMISTICE

After the Panzer Divisions of the Wehrmacht had crossed the Seine and taken Paris, there were three huge breakthoughs. The spearheads of the tanks rolled swiftly west toward Brittany, south toward Bordeaux, and southeast toward Lyons and the Rhône Valley.

By June 12, the commander in chief, General Weygand, could no longer count on his orders being carried out; the entire French army was in chaos, split into isolated groups, retreating in disorder. Tens of thousands of soldiers were being captured every day, and on June 14, Weygand advised Pétain that the government had to choose between an unconditional surrender and an attempt to negotiate an armistice. The latter solution might not only preserve a substantial part of France's territory from total occupation, but save the fleet and the colonial empire in Africa.

The suggestion was made in later years that the army should have retreated to a bridgehead around Brest in Brittany under the protection of the British fleet. That was not possible: the Germans had complete control of the air, and streams of refugees—Belgians, Dutch, and French, men, women, and children—were blocking the roads.

On June 16, Paul Reynaud resigned as prime minister in Bordeaux. The president of the Republic, Albert Lebrun, immediately called upon his vice-president, Marshal Pétain, to form a government as rapidly as possible. This took place late on the sixteenth and in the early hours of June 17.

The government included General Weygand, Admiral Darlan, and Paul Baudouin, but not Laval. He was about to leave his home in Châteldon for Bordeaux and had not met Pétain since the marshal had gone to Spain as France's ambassador.

At noon on June 17, Pétain announced in a broken voice over the radio that he had asked the "enemy" to propose "an honorable end to the hostilities." Every attempt had to be made to negotiate with the conqueror so as to alleviate to some extent the load of suffering and hardships of the people.

At the end of the day on June 22, the armistice was signed at Compiègne between representatives of the two armies.

Like the overwhelming majority of the French at the time, Laval approved of the armistice as the lesser of two evils. I am certain that if he had participated in the negotiations with the Germans at Compiègne, he would, as he said when in prison,° have strenuously refused to surrender the German nationals, Jews, and Communists—mostly Dutch and Belgian refugees—who had fled to the South of France before the advancing Wehrmacht.

He also was of the opinion that on the day of signing, the French military delegation should have registered a general protest so that discussions and negotiations could later be undertaken to clarify and interpret the application of the document itself. These interpretations were bound to be called for in the sequel, and without the advantage of such a formal protest, the Germans could take advantage of French demands as a pretext for making counterdemands. Had the negotiators been refused the inclusion of a protest, then, Laval thought, they should at least have demanded a protocol outlining the conditions under which the armistice was to be applied.

°Ibid., p. 39.

The armistice saved French North Africa from the German wave, which was rolling southward. Two years later, in November 1942, the Allies and Generals de Gaulle and Giraud found French North Africa in the control and under the command of the French officers and soldiers who had been freed for this purpose by the government of Marshal Pétain and Pierre Laval in 1940 and 1941.

When de Gaulle chose to go to London to continue the fight, a few other political leaders might well have gone with him, but the overwhelming majority of deputies and senators at the time were convinced that it was their duty to remain with the 45 million French people. Pétain, Laval, and the members of the government thought it their duty not to abandon France to the cruel domination of a conqueror, as was happening in Belgium, Holland, Denmark, and Poland.

It was only the day after the signing of the armistice that Marshal Pétain asked Laval, along with Adrien Marquet, to join the government as minister of state. In the next few days, the government and practically all the members of the Chamber and of the Senate decided to meet at Vichy. It was to become the seat of the government, and there a National Assembly (joint session of the Chamber and of the Senate) was convened to change the constitution.

Pétain had realized that Laval loomed larger and larger as a statesman, a "resource" possessing the necessary prestige and experience to organize a National Assembly. He believed that Laval could obtain an overwhelming vote in favor of a change in the constitution, including the delegation of powers to Pétain and his government.

The marshal and the members of his entourage were political novices lacking any practical experience of governing. Given the general disarray into which the country had fallen, the meetings of the ministers were reduced to general conversations. Laval performed the first governmental task by sending out questionnaires, written in his own hand, to the managers of the largest businesses inquiring about their current manpower, equipment, and inventory situations. He also requested everybody there to return to work as quickly as possible.

Above and beyond the necessities of daily life, there remained the serious political problem of the regime itself. No previous one had ever survived a military disaster of such magnitude. The Third Republic, as the French people had known it for sixty-five years, would come to an end. But the change, the transition, would have to be carried out legally. The National Assembly, both the Chamber and the Senate, would have to vote special powers enabling Marshal Pétain to promulgate a new constitution.

The "Victor of Verdun" enjoyed enormous popularity. In those dark days, he represented for the majority of French people a symbol of the energy and hope that remained in them. Thanks to his proclamation, "I offer myself to France in order to alleviate her suffering," the nation sincerely believed that it had found its savior. Laval, for his part, was determined to achieve a smooth transition to the Pétain regime.

Pursuant to the old French constitution of 1875, the Chamber and the Senate were summoned to assemble in joint session at Vichy on July 9, 1940. Pétain presented a bill to amend the constitution. It is interesting to recall that the vote on the *principle* of revising the constitution was voted by the Chamber 395 to 3: Roche, Biondi, and Margaine. In the Senate, the only negative vote was that of my uncle, the Marquis Pierre de Chambrun, senator from Lozère.

During the debates that preceded the vote, President of the Senate Jeanneney declared, "I bear witness to our veneration for Marshal Pétain and our heartfelt gratitude for this new gift of his person to his country."

And Edouard Herriot, president of the Chamber, used similar terms.

The following morning, July 10, the National Assembly met in executive session so as to discuss freely what the government had proposed, prior to formal submission in the afternoon at an open session. An official shorthand report made at that meeting is in the National Archives. Here is the text of the government's proposal to the National Assembly:

> The National Assembly gives full powers to the government of the Republic, under the signature and authority of Marshal Pétain, president of the Council, to promulgate in one or more measures a new constitution for the French States. This constitution shall guarantee the rights of labor, of the family, and of the fatherland. It shall be ratified by the nation and put in force by the Assembly that it shall create.

The executive session was extremely long. A counterproposal presented by war veterans of 1914–18 led to an extensive debate and finally to a modification of the government's proposal. The war veterans had won their point, and the measure was redrafted and approved by 569 votes to 80, with 17 abstentions.

After this overwhelming vote, as Pétain began wielding the extraordinary powers that Laval had been instrumental in obtaining for him, Laval gradually began to realize the mistake he and all the concurring members of the National Assembly had made. They had not anticipated the "personal stamp" that the marshal and his entourage were going to put on his ways of governing. Significantly, he signed his first official decree and all those that followed: "*We*, Philippe Pétain."

Thus was the new "French state" with Pétain as its leader brought into being. Pétain was "formally" enthroned thanks to Laval's lobbying, casting the latter as "heir apparent" to the Vichy government. But what were the relations between Laval and Pétain to be, given that nearly everything—age, background, education, career, lifestyle—divided one from the other? How would Laval fit into a government largely made up of military men? Laval himself has told us about this difficulty:

> I was not asked to take part in the choice of ministers, and even less of course, in the choice of his aides. I noticed at once that the marshal had no regard for republican legality. I came to this conclusion from the pretentiousness and outdated style of his first decrees—"We, Philippe Pétain"—even more than from the large share of power he allotted to himself. The power was sure to be temporary, for like almost everybody else, I believed that the occupation would be of short duration.
>
> An enormous propaganda and publicity campaign was organized throughout the country to aggrandize the marshal. It was said that he incarnated France. He alone could save the country. His picture, his bust were everywhere. The newspapers, the radio, the movies, spoke only of him. His slightest gesture pushed all other news out of the headlines. There was a national song, "Marshal, we are here." There was a special decoration, the "Order of the Marshal," adorned with the Frankish battle-ax. Special organizations were created to spread the marshal's slogans throughout the country. In the occupied zone, there were the "Friends of the Marshal," and in the free zone, the "Legion." I doubt that such a great propaganda effort on behalf of any other man was ever undertaken in France.
>
> My relations with the marshal were correct, polite, but not close. After the vote of the National Assembly and the political situation that followed, the marshal kept his distance from me. Far from being his adviser, my advice, when I occasionally gave it, seems to have been systematically ignored. I therefore have the right to say that I cannot be held responsible for his measures; they were taken without my knowledge, against my will, and sometimes despite my opposition. The marshal was then head of state and lacked any consideration for ministerial practices, with which he was unfamiliar, and the ministers he had chosen did not know them either. He worked directly with them, and even the most important questions were only submitted to the Council of Ministers for a pro forma ratification. As a minister without portfolio, I did not take part in the drafting of texts. This was also the case with such decrees as these about the professional committees, the formulation of the labor charter, or the measures pertaining to the Jews and the secret societies. The marshal was jealous of his authority, and he would not have tolerated the slightest opposition. Such was the political situation following the vote of July 10, 1940.°

But the fact remains that Laval accepted the role of heir apparent. His "secret hope"—the indictment later charged—was one day to become dictator. Actually, his calculation was the opposite.

° Ibid., pp. 59–60.

As I was responsible to the National Assembly, I did not, at that time, refuse the title of "heir apparent," which would allow me, if the time came when the marshal was unable to continue in his position, to return to a normal and legal situation.

The intention that the accusation attributes to me could be explained only if I had been demented. I have too much political experience to believe that France, once she regained her freedom after the liberation, would tolerate a regime based on force and police power. In order to be a dictator, one must first seek popularity, and I have never bothered about that. The tasks I have taken on when other political leaders refused to serve at moments of crisis, gave me the opportunity to do my duty to my country but never brought me this required popularity. Even the most casual examination of the events in which I participated will prove that I never sought popularity or tried to become a dicatator.°

What is more, the very title of heir apparent immediately brought on the hostility that ambition arouses, in others, and I think that this was the true and deep-rooted reason for my removal from office and my arrest on December 13, 1940. The action against me on that date shows how limited my power was and how little it impressed the other ministers.

Laval, reared in republican institutions, was separated by a great gulf from Pétain, who considered himself virtually a monarch by divine right.

LAVAL AND COLLABORATION

The word "collaboration" has been used and abused to the point where it has come to symbolize for some people the opposition between the marshal and Laval. Many in France came to believe that Laval wanted "collaboration" with the Reich, and the marshal did not. In fact, their conflicting views related much more to internal policies. If Laval reconciled himself to collaboration, it was because he knew that the marshal favored a particular policy of inevitable collaboration with the Reich, indeed, the one policy that Pétain had most at heart.

To begin with, the word "collaboration," in its new sense, was not coined by Laval. It was written into the Armistice Convention, signed before Laval

° Ibid., p. 61.

joined the government. The term was accepted by the French representatives who affixed their signatures to the text:

> Art. III. In the occupied areas of France, the German Reich is to exercise all the rights of an occupying power. The French government promises to facilitate by all possible means the regulations relative to the exercise of this right, and to carry out these regulations with the participation of the French administration. The French government will immediately order all the French authorities and administrative services in the occupied zone to follow the regulations of the German military authorities and to *collaborate* with the latter in a correct manner.

In October 1940, Laval understood collaboration more or less in the same sense as Pétain. For both, to collaborate meant to give up the least possible in order to get the most. Laval, in his role of go-between, was forced to be in constant touch with the German authorities, to shift ground, to be wily, to plan ahead. All this, under the circumstances, drew more attention to him than to the marshal and made him appear to many Frenchmen as "the agent of collaboration"; to others, he was "the Germans' man."

Laval, "the Germans' man!" Laval, who had toiled with such success to contain Hitler that Goering had berated him.° Laval was the last man to deserve the title. As he pointed out in a memorandum confiscated at the time of his arrest, Laval, during the prewar years, whether in power or out, maintained a reserve in his relations with the Germans that sometimes bordered on aversion:

> On the personal level, there were no relations. I never belonged to any of those groups that intended to bring about a rapprochement and an understanding with Germany. I was only familiar with the name of the France-Germany Association. I had never seen Otto Abetz, who was widely known in Parisian circles before the war.

> When I was minister of foreign affairs, I of course received the German ambassador, like all other diplomatic representatives, but unlike some others, I never looked for any personal relations with the German representative.

> I had a particular aversion to von Hoesch. I found him too much inclined to meddle in our internal politics and too much interested in drawing certain French personalities, who showed great caution in this regard, to himself. When Chancellor Brüning, who came to Paris in 1931, asked me if I wished for anything, I asked him to send us another ambassador, even Neurath, if he liked, who was in London at the time.

°The minutes taken by Charles Rochat, who was present during the conversation between Laval and Goering on May 18, 1935, appear in Jacques Baraduc, *Les Archives Secrètes du Reich* (Paris: L'Elan, 1949), pp. 299–311.

I preferred a German, who presented himself openly, to a von Hoesch, who deceived his acquaintance with the false appearance of being a francophile.

I knew Koester in 1934–35, when I was at the Quai d'Orsay. He claimed to have been mistreated during the last war, and he did not like France. His feelings, which he hardly tried to hide, did not prevent him from being correct and courteous. He was a protégé of Marshal Hindenburg's and was not in favor with the Nazis. Later on, he was relieved of his duties and replaced by Count Welczeck, whose invitations I always declined without consideration for protocol. I always found a pretext for refusing without being insulting. That is what I did when Ribbentrop came to Paris to hold discussions with Georges Bonnet and there were receptions and dinners.°

With this background of experience, Laval in Vichy was extremely prudent, if not distrustful, about possible persons to talk to. He proceeded selectively, trying to find out whom to deal with, what he could hope for, and what he might have to fear from any particular person. He finally decided to meet with Abetz, the German ambassador in Paris. Gaston Henry-Haye, Vichy ambassador to the United States, who knew Abetz well, had spoken favorably of him to Laval and arranged a meeting of the two at the German embassy in Paris. Laval presented a list of demands:

1. Take all necessary steps to facilitate the return of millions of refugees (by eliminating formalities at the demarcation line, etc.).

2. Immediately stop the arbitrary evictions in the "forbidden zone" and permit the return of those already evicted.

3. Free all imprisoned farmers and peasants so that they can help with the harvest.

4. Reestablish telephone communications throughout the country.

5. Rebuild hundreds of destroyed bridges.

6. Stop the arbitrary dispatch to Germany of freight cars filled with goods needed in France to feed the population and supply factories with raw materials.

7. Reestablish rail service, with priority for those that supply the southern [unoccupied] zone.

8. Direct 3 million quintals† of wheat to the southern zone to alleviate the bread shortage.

9. Restore the authority of the prefects in all departments by reducing

°I copied this memorandum at the Palais Soubise in 1972.
†One quintal equals 100 kilograms.

to a minimum the acts of interference of the Kommendaturs, with the further understanding that the authority of the prefects of the twelve departments cut by the demarcation line would be the same in both zones.

10. Take the necessary measures not only to prohibit any German presence or interference in the colonies, but also to maintain the French military and civilian manpower at full strength.

11. Undertake not to apply that clause of the armistice that provided for the handing over to the German authorities those foreigners—almost all of them Jews—who had left the Reich to seek refuge in France. (Laval told Abetz: "I myself would never have put my name to that clause.")°

12. At the request of General and Mme. de Chambrun, not to touch the American Hosptial at Neuilly, which flies the American flag, or the American Library, where two English librarians are in charge of caring for the works of British and American authors.

Abetz's reaction? As Laval reported it to me, Abetz said, "Whatever depends on me is granted, and furthermore, I will make myself France's advocate with the military."

This answer appears less surprising when one remembers Abetz's recall to Germany in December 1942 for being a "francophile"and a "Lavalist."

Laval set Abetz apart from the other Germans. "Hitler," he told me, "was a fanatic, Ribbentrop hated me as much as he could, and Goering was a slave to his whims. As far as the local administrators were concerned, Hemmen often gave me trouble, and Sauckel was a brute. But I had good relations with Abetz, better than with the other Germans, and I always prided myself on the fact. Not on my own account, but on France's. The country gained a great deal from it on many occasions. "If Abetz had not been open to persuasion, I would not have kept up relations with him. I would have looked elsewhere."

No matter with whom he held such conversations, Laval approached the Germans with no thought of internal politics. He had only one and the same realistic, practical goal: "That France may live." He believed that this prime objective entailed a continuity and a flexibility in day-to-day decisions quite distinct from the usual political game. The importance of that attitude many French people, including members of the government, often misunderstood:

There were a great many problems, which, despite the occupation, remained essentially French problems, and which had to be taken care of every day. First of all, there was the problem of food distribution. Even if there was enough to eat in the countryside, the cities still had

°*Laval Parle*, p. 39.

to be taken care of. And I did not think that food supplies could be assured by destroying the storehouses where these supplies were kept. In order to feed the cities and to keep the factories working, it was necessary to maintain a minimum of transportation facilities in working order. And I also did not think that the best way to serve the country was to blow up the trains. I was not of the opinion that it was the right moment to destroy them.° It was important to try to help the prisoners by sending them food and clothing. It was important to keep our agriculture going, to provide it, as far as was still possible, with fertilizer, with seed, and with equipment. It was important that the children be able to continue to go to school and the students pursue their studies. It was important to watch over public health, which was seriously threatened by shortages, to keep hospitals open, and to ensure the manufacture of pharmaceutical products. It was important to ensure the functioning of the French administration and of all public services. In a word, it was important to do what every government worthy of its name must do, whether in time of peace or in time of war or when under the boot of the occupying power. That is why, for my part, I tried against all odds to do my best.

If those interested will look at the reports of the meetings of ministers that I attended, they will see what subjects I took up there and how I sometimes criticized certain ministers who seemed to have lost sight of the essential point of their task.†

The question of "collaboration" occupied a place above and beyond any "political" problem. Laval was forced into a certain kind of collaboration that was never cooperation. As he was to write when in prison at Fresnes:

Since there were needs that I could not deny and to whose creation I had not contributed, I was forced into what has been called collaboration; it was to save the essential minimum—that's all. If you examine my actions closely, you will see that, in fact, I did much more negotiating, discussing, arguing, and temporizing than "collaborating." Moreover, I did not collaborate in the same way with Abetz as with Sauckel. Once all the documents dealing with my relations with him have been collected, it will be apparent *how* we collaborated. I did not collaborate with Oberg in the same way as with Hemmen, the fellow from the Armistic Commission. I tried to extract French lives from Oberg. From Hemmen, who often gave trouble, I tried to salvage French property, food, and money. That is what my job was. That is how I carried it out. Let me have a genuine trial, and things will quickly become clear.‡

°These sentences allude to the movements that sought to rid France of the Germans by local sabotage.
†Notes by Pierre Laval copied from the archives at the Palais Soubise.
‡Ibid.

It is endlessly surprising to see Laval addressing the German conquerors with a self-confidence at times bordering on audacity, as in his negotiations with Abetz. But one of Laval's characteristic traits was his ability to approach any person, regardless of position or circumstance—be he a factory worker or the pope—in a direct and at times familiar manner. When I asked him if he had felt intimidated at his first meeting with Hitler, he answered: "Nobody has ever intimidated me when I was speaking in the name of France."

It must not be forgotten that he had fought desperately until the last moment to prevent France from declaring war on Germany, believing as he did that France could not win. The Germans were long familiar with his views, and this gave him a certain margin of freedom in his dealings with them that others could not have had.

THE LAST REPUBLICAN ELIMINATED

A large majority of the French people still remembered the war of 1914–18 and the devastation it had caused in the provinces of the north and east. Multitudes had been deported, their property and livestock stolen. As he made his way toward Paris in July 1940, Laval wondered what horrors the future held for a country defeated in a war it had itself declared.

During the first two months, the inhabitants of Paris and of other large cities had been surprised by the correct behavior of the German officers and soldiers. At the diplomatic level, Laval was heartened by Abetz's courteous, almost cooperative attitude, because the terms of the Armistice were so harsh that if they were applied to the letter, France could not survive. Hence, Laval's undertaking to try and loosen this iron grip. Harking back to his activities of that time, he wrote:

> If this is what is called collaborating, I would have been glad to collaborate for as long as I deemed it necessary in France's interest. I would not have hesitated to go quite far in that direction if I had thought it of use.

But the conversations he held with such men as Abetz, Hemmen, and Elmar Michel quickly brought him to the limits of possiblity. These officials lacked the power to take the steps Laval asked for. He himself had to take the next step:

> I told them that if they lacked authority, which I could well understand, it was absolutely essential that I discuss these matters with someone in a position to make decisions. And when they asked me what France might have to offer in return, I answered that this was a question that obviously could be discussed only during such a meeting. All these people must have written reports to Berlin. I am quite certain that they urged Hitler himself to come to Montoire.°

The meeting at Montoire needs to be demystified, and now it can be done. On October 20, 1940, a car took Laval and Abetz out of Paris to what Laval thought would be a conference with Ribbentrop. Only after traveling the whole day did Abetz inform Laval that he would be meeting with Hitler as well. They met in Hitler's private train in Montoire. On October 24, Hitler met with Pétain, Laval again being present.

Many have considered those meetings not only an insult to the national honor but also the initiation of a reversal of alliances that might have led to going to war against England. Laval responded to those suppositions.

> I am not a lunatic. A war? We had just got out of one and we knew what it had cost us. . . . Were we to have more French people killed? Were our cities to be bombed? Should the wounds of our people be reopened? You don't know me at all if you can imagine that I considered such a thing even for a moment.

> Neither the marshal nor I knew before it happened that there would be an event called "Montoire" or that it would acquire a certain importance later on. Still, everything I did tended to bring it about. In addition, the marshal himself had asked Goering, using Fonck, the "ace" of the war of 1914–18, as an intermediary, for a meeting with Hitler. I had no major policy plans. I was thinking mostly of the problems that caused suffering in our country: the demarcation line that cut the country in two in an absurd way; the joining of our Northern departments with Brussels by the German military administration; the case of Alsace-Lorraine; the very heavy burden of the occupation costs; and the fate of our prisoners.

> In the end, Montoire was nothing more than a conversation with no obligations on either side, and especially with no manner of military obligation on our part. I have never, at any time, subscribed to any military obligations, and I never would have. But a certain atmosphere

---

°Memoranda written for his attorneys Baraduc and Naud. The same idea is developed in *Laval Parle*, pp. 63 ff. Historians are urged to read the chapter on Montoire and the long deposition of Dr. Paul Schmidt, the German interpreter for the conversations held there. (Hoover Foundation Archives, no. 323.)

had been created; in fact, France was about to obtain substantial relief.°

On December 13, Laval was abruptly dismissed from power. It has been said repeatedly that this was the natural outcome of the policy of collaboration that Laval wanted to pursue and that Pétain only reluctantly accepted. The exact opposite is true: it was the marshal who had asked for a meeting with Hitler. Matters of policy were not discussed at Montoire. The one subject of conversation was the relaxing of the clauses of the armistice.

Of particular concern to Laval was the problem of the colonies. General Huntziger, the French minister of war, had declared, "The armistice conditions are harsh, but they are not dishonorable. France can keep her empire and her fleet." But Laval was only half satisfied. Among the approximately thirty requests he had submitted to Abetz at their first meeting had been one to exclude any German presence in French colonies. Their political and administrative structures were to remain absolutely unchanged, exactly as if France had not been defeated. On this issue, Laval obtained satisfaction.

Then, right after Montoire, internal politics undermined Laval's success at the expense of the Germans. Relations between the chief of state and the vice-president of the Council of Ministers continued to deteriorate. Laval removed himself bit by bit, not so much from the marshal as from Vichy, or, more precisely, from a part of the entourage of the chief of state. He did this for several reasons.

In spite of the existence of a so-called free zone, France, cut in two and subjected to the constraints of the armistice, was no longer the mistress of her own fate. Vichy had become a kind of Ruritanian, musical-comedy kingdom and could make practically no important decisions. Vichy only had states of mind.

Laval had perceived this very quickly. He knew that the only possibility for action open to him lay in direct discussion, with the hope that the German vise might be loosened and France "might live." He devoted his time and energy to this task.

He had also decided not to attend all of the ministerial meetings, which tended to degenerate into gossip. Early on, he began to skip one debate out of two, so that he might spend three or four days in Paris and then return to Châteldon after a short stopover in Vichy where he briefed the chief of state.

On top of this physical distancing, he gradually added intellectual and moral distance, owing mainly to the divergence between the republican ideal to which Laval remained faithful despite the change of regime and the creed that the marshal and his entourage intended to impose on the country. It was an antiparliamentary creed, pseudomonarchist, and it manifested itself in open hostility towards Jews and Freemasons,† taking the form of a shocking

°Notes drafted in Fresnes for Baraduc and Naud.
†See Schedule M.

guerrilla warfare. A section of the marshal's entourage, influenced by the reactionary Charles Maurras rather than by the marshal himself, encouraged these atrocities. Laval consistently protested.

Besides, Pétain, at the pinnacle of political honors, was extremely jealous of his own prerogatives and authority. As he had a great deal of free time, he undertook a series of visits throughout "his province" and discovered the joys of mingling with the crowd.

Laval thus felt himself more and more of an outsider in Vichy. Simultaneously, the marshal, to show that he had put an end to the parliamentary Republic, was successively eliminating the deputies and senators who were part of his government: Frossard, Chichery, Pietri, and Marquet were the last to be sacrificed in the summer of 1940. Laval could rely only on Jean Montigny, head of the information and press services, for any comprehensive view of what went on in Vichy while he was in Paris.

As the French proverb says, "Those who are absent are always in the wrong." The marshal's entourage did not miss an opportunity to present Laval's protracted stays in Paris as proof of his collusion with the Germans against Pétain. When Marcel Déat began to publish in L'Oeuvre a series of very harsh articles aimed against Vichy, Pétain's advisers told him that the inspiration for these articles came from Laval, a dangerous man who must at any cost be removed.

On December 12, at the Hôtel Matignon, Laval received Abetz, who told him that Hitler had decided to return the ashes of Napoleon's son, the "Aiglon," to France. The ceremony was to take place at Les Invalides on Saturday the fourteenth and Marshal Pétain was to be invited. The ambassador went on to say that as this gesture of Hitler's had high political significance, the Führer hoped that it would be understood and appreciated in France "as an act of sympathy of great historical importance." He added that the gesture underlined Hitler's desire to induce a spirit of reconciliation between the two countries. He pointed out that the marshal would thus have the first opportunity since the armistice to establish contact with the people of Paris and to preside at a national ceremony. He then handed to Laval Hitler's letter of invitation and asked Laval to transmit it to the marshal. Laval replied that it was already December 12, only two days before the proposed ceremony, that the marshal was old and the weather extremely cold, and that this might prevent his accepting an invitation so suddenly tendered.

Laval phoned Dumoulin de La Barthète, secretary of the cabinet, who replied that the marshal was not in a position to respond to such an invitation; its suddenness made it discourteous. He added that the marshal himself would fix the date that he deemed fitting for his visit to Paris and that as he had not been previously informed of the return of the "Aiglon's" ashes, he would not attend the ceremony. Laval at once notified Abetz, who came back to see him at the Hôtel Matignon. Laval said that he regretted the lateness of the invitation but that he had conveyed it upon receipt. According to

Abetz, it was Hitler's way to make rapid decisions. He begged Laval to remember only the friendly intention that had inspired it, and he added that a refusal such as Laval was transmitting—having slightly softened its wording—might result in grave consequences. He became very insistent, begging Laval to persuade the marshal to reconsider so as not to complicate Franco-German relations.

This second talk with Abetz, and the scarcely veiled threat about grave consequences, prompted Laval to leave at once for Vichy. Distrusting Dumoulin de La Barthète, he thought it his duty to explain the situation fully to Pétain in person so that whatever decision Pétain wished to make would be his alone.

Laval reached Vichy about a quarter to one, and he met the marshal returning from his walk. They made an appointment for three o'clock. The conversation lasted nearly an hour. Laval repeated Abetz's exact words and was surprised by the difference between the marshal's own attitude and that conveyed by Dumoulin de La Barthète when transmitting Pétain's refusal the day before. The marshal definitely agreed to come to Paris and expressed his intention to stay at the Hôtel Matignon. He even decided to give a small official lunch. The conversation throughout was of the utmost cordiality.

Laval returned to his office, where he received the Spanish ambassador, de Lequerica, at four o'clock. At five, he presided over a brief cabinet meeting. All the ministers were present, with the exception of Alibert, who was, with Dumoulin de La Barthète, putting the last touches to the plot that was to unfold less than two hours later.

At the end of the cabinet meeting, Laval stopped by Dumoulin's office to read and, if necessary, modify the text of the marshal's answer to Hitler. Laval made the change in the last sentence from *"mes sentiments les meilleurs"* to *"mes sentiments de haute considération."*

While Laval was in Dumoulin's office, General Laure, chief of Pétain's military staff, entered and announced that a Council of Ministers was to take place at eight o'clock. Laval did not know of such a meeting being called. Dumoulin feigned the same ignorance, and Laval surmised that the marshal wished to inform the ministers of his departure for Paris.

Laval had hardly entered the council room when the marshal came in, accompanied by Baudouin. He was extremely pale and nervous and said, "I wish every minister to sign and hand in his resignation."

All signed, and Laval thought that the marshal, who at the time was in disagreement with Belin, then minister of labor, wished to designate his successor. The marshal retired for a few minutes, returned, and announced: "The resignations of M. Laval and of M. Ripert are the only ones accepted." At this, Laval, thoroughly indignant in the face of such ingratitude, asked Pétain to explain the reason for so sudden a decision. Pétain replied that he could not tell when Laval returned from Paris what bad news he would bring back, that Laval had put obstacles in the way of his installation at Versailles and inspired the articles written by Déat in Paris against him and his ministers. Laval answered that he had always given a full account of his trips to

Paris, that it was not, alas, in his power to prevent the Germans from taking decisions disagreeable to them all, and that, on the contrary, he spent his whole time intervening to prevent such actions. He had done everything in his power to facilitate Pétain's installation at Versailles, which the Germans had been putting off; and as for Déat's articles, he had absolutely nothing whatever to do with them. Then, raising his voice, which he seldom did, he spoke these last words before leaving the room: "I hope, marshal, that your alternating and contradictory decisions will not cause our country too much harm."

By eight-thirty, Laval was back in his office, telling members of his staff that he was going to phone Madame Laval and his daughter and arrange to take the midnight train to Paris. A car would follow the next morning with his papers and baggage. While he was talking, all the outgoing phones from the "Hôtel du Parc" were being cut off. The marshal and his entourage were vanishing from the premises, while one of the top officials of the police was knocking at Laval's door to inform him that pursuant to an "order" given by the marshal to the minister of the interior (Peyrouton), Pierre Laval was to proceed to his home where he would be under house arrest with Madame Laval and Madame de Chambrun.

The next day, December 14, in the picturesque old château of Châteldon, the Lavals could not use their phone—cut off as it was in Vichy—but they were able to follow events on the radio. They heard Marshal Pétain's statement that he had parted from his vice-president, Pierre Laval, for "reasons of internal policy." A later broadcast described the ceremony at Les Invalides of the return of the ashes of Napoleon's son, the "Aiglon," which were placed next to Napoleon's tomb. Admiral Darlan represented the marshal, who returned to Vichy about the same time as Abetz. There the marshal told Abetz that there had been a vast misunderstanding and that he intended to offer Laval the Ministry of the Interior. Abetz confessed that he could not understand why, if the marshal had had any grievance against Laval, he had assigned him the post of Minister of Foreign Affairs, put him in direct contact with the German embassy, and entrusted him with the talks at Montoire with Hitler.

On the morning of December 16, the same police officer who had knocked on Laval's door in the evening of December 13 called at Châteldon at 9:00 to inform "Mr. le Président" that all "orders" had been canceled. A couple of hours later, Dumoulin de La Barthète, terribly embarrassed, arrived from Vichy and asked Laval if he would come and talk with the marshal. Laval entered Dumoulin's car, as the marshal had remained in Vichy, and during the ride, asked Dumoulin what the reasons were for "such an odious and grotesque adventure." Dumoulin tried to evade Laval's question and ended by saying, "It's that idiot Alibert who managed to make the marshal believe that you wanted to lure him into a trap in Paris with the intention of having him arrested."

The conversation between Laval and Pétain took place at the Pavillon Sévigné. Laval was harsh and bitter. "I must thank you for the treatment you inflicted upon my wife and daughter." The only answer the marshal could give was that all had been done against his will.

Laval refused to come back into the government. After talking to Abetz (who had remained in Vichy), he returned to Paris.

A few weeks later, Laval and Pétain met again in the little town of La Ferté Hauterive. Pétain had motored up from Vichy; Laval, down from Paris. Laval, again, refused to enter the government, but to Pétain's question "Do you still hold a grudge against me for a decision that was not really mine?" Laval answered, "It will be hard to forget." In fact, it was to take sixteen months filled with sorrowful events.

Laval was replaced as minister of foreign affairs by Flandin, who resigned a few weeks later. The Germans paid no attention to the new government. Since the dissolution of the Assemblies, domestic public opinion mattered little. But the measures taken concerning the Freemasons and the Jews, at the instigation of a part of the marshal's entourage, provoked in many quarters unfavorable and even hostile reactions.

In these conditions, Vichy felt the need of a larger base of support and created the National Council, a hybrid assembly whose members, appointed by the government, were chosen from among the most eminent people in all sectors of the country. Not surprisingly, this gathering had little power and soon fell apart and disappeared amid general indifference.

As far as Franco-German relations were concerned, Flandin preached patience, explaining that things would become clearer by the beginning of 1941. But the Reich continued to remain aloof, and the marshal, realizing that the dismissal of Laval had been a serious error, turned against those who had urged him to it. Raphael Alibert, minister of justice, was forced to resign at the end of January. Flandin left on February 9, and on the fourteenth it was Peyrouton's turn to leave. The road was henceforth clear for the man who, after waiting in the shadows for his turn, now came forward openly. This was the man who had been designated "heir apparent" by the Constitutional Act IV. This man was the minister of the navy; he was Admiral Darlan. He was to remain in office for fifteen months, and Germany obtained from him concessions in the naval and military sphere that, one may be sure, the "pacifist" Laval would never have made.

MEANWHILE IN WASHINGTON

In the days following the armistice, I continued to carry out the assignment given me by Roosevelt. General Marshall, the army chief of staff, put a plane at my disposal, and I went from one city to another, arguing that

England would hold out if she could get planes and antiaircraft guns. I observed the reaction of the American public to the new French regime and its leaders. One question was raised everywhere: was Pétain a Fascist?

William C. Bullitt, who had returned from Europe and was passing through New York, confirmed this atmosphere of unease. For the ambassador, Vichy was a subject of concern. Didn't Pétain dream of becoming dictator? And why was Laval increasing his contacts with the occupation authorities? I tried to set these people straight. One doesn't suddenly plan to become a dictator at the age of eighty-five. As for Laval, he felt like the official receiver in a bankruptcy for which he was not responsible. When he negotiated, or rather, argued with the German authorities, he was not talking politics. His sole concern was to enable the free zone of France to survive; it was overcrowded with refugees and must first of all be supplied with food.

Everyone worried whether these supplies would not be diverted into the hands of the occupying power. The United States argued the question of a possible food blockade of France. Although Secretary of State Cordell Hull favored the supplying of the free zone, Secretary of the Treasury Morganthau opposed it. His aversion to totalitarian regimes made him feel friendly to democratic France, but the latent fascism in the Vichy atmosphere made him support the possible blockade.

After over a week of discussions with opinion leaders, trying to ease their fears, I saw Roosevelt again. He was no longer as receptive as he had been on the *Potomac*. Pétain, Laval, the armistic, the collaboration—those words recurred in his conversation; those were the subjects that preoccupied him. I spent two hours reiterating that it was absurd to accuse Pétain of fascism and that Laval was pursuing one aim only: doing whatever would help his country, crushed and under occupation, to survive and from day to day trying to lessen its suffering.

To my plea that the United States send food to France, Roosevelt replied that the Nazis would confiscate any supplies he might send. I replied that I doubted very much that the Germans would commit the grave error of crossing the demarcation line and take away condensed milk or other foodstuffs that might be sent. The Germans were trying to pass themselves off as generous victors. France, I argued, would not soon forget that the United States had reached out a helping hand when she was plunged in misery. Furthermore, I had thought of a scheme that would minimize the risk—small successive shipments, every three or four weeks, instead of a few big ones. As long as the Germans let them through, the shipments could continue, and the Americans would gain enormous political and moral goodwill. At the first case of seizure by the Germans, the shipments would stop, and French public opinion would know what to think about the Germans.

Roosevelt accepted my suggestion. He asked me to make a proposal to Pétain: if he agreed to a meeting of American journalists in Vichy and to a pro-American declaration approving of the U.S. rearmament and reasserting French democratic ideals; and further, if he stopped the attacks on England by Baudouin and the Vichy radio, Roosevelt would arrange for the free zone to receive regular shipments of food—in particular, condensed milk—until the end of hostilities.

As I prepared to leave for France, I received a letter from the British ambassador:

Washington, August 9, 1940

My Dear Captain de Chambrun:

I am happy to provide you with a diplomatic visa for your return to your country, together with a letter of introduction to the governor of Bermuda.

I am glad to inform you that it has been my privilege in recent weeks to inform His Majesty's government of the splendid work you have done in Washington and throughout the United States in support of the cause for which the British Empire is fighting. You have been able, almost alone, to change official public opinion in favor of my country. Your astonishingly energetic activity during the dark days of June was an inspiration to us all. You were able, at the right moment, to find the arguments and the words that convinced the highest authorities of the United States and the Foreign Affairs Committee of the American Senate.

For all of this, I want to assure you that Great Britain will never forget everything that you have done for her during her days of misfortune and distress.

I wish you a good trip and beg you to believe in my faithfully devoted sentiments.

Lothian

On August 18, I arrived in Châteldon, and on the nineteenth, Laval and I set off for the Hôtel du Parc. My father-in-law went straight to his office; I approached Pétain. The marshal wanted to hear about everything. I began by telling him that Roosevelt insisted on my mission remaining strictly confidential. Pétain, who cultivated secrecy, was happy to comply. I reported Roosevelt's proposal; Pétain summoned Baudouin, who was told firmly and simply, to stop his attacks on Great Britain and to publish no communiqué or other statement that might cast a slur on that country.

Pétain was delighted at the idea of speaking to American journalists. "Do you know that it will be my first press conference? Set it up for five o'clock so that I'll have the time to draft a statement and prepare myself for their questions."

I phoned Ralph Heinzen, the senior American reporter, and asked him to alert his colleagues, then returned to help Pétain prepare. At 5:00 P.M., the representatives of the United Press and the Associated Press arrived, together with the correspondents of the *New York Herald Tribune*, the *New York Times*, the Baltimore *Sun*, and the Chicago *Daily News*.

The marshal read his statement:

It is a real pleasure for me to greet the representatives of the American press and to welcome them. I am happy to take advantage of this occasion to express France's sincere friendship for the two Americas. France will remain firmly attached to the ideal that she shares with the great American democracy, an ideal based on the respect for individual rights, devotion to the family and the fatherland, love of justice and of humanity. France will try harder than ever to extend cultural and economic exchanges between the Old and the New World, in order to create an atmosphere of understanding and friendship among peoples.°

A stream of questions and answers followed. At the close of the conference, it was unanimously agreed not to mention it in the occupied zone.

On August 26, the marshal finished drafting the letter Roosevelt had asked me to obtain and signed it the next day, when I should be leaving again. Here is the text:

Mr. President,

France is at present going through the most tragic time of her long history. Three-fifths of her territory is occupied. Few are the households not anxiously awaiting the return of one of 3 million prisoners held by Germany. Millions of refugees from the most fertile regions of France, who were able to bring with them only their exhaustion and misery, are awaiting the hour of deliverance, when they will be able to return to the land they were forced to abandon. Today they are sharing their pain and their need with Belgian, Austrian, Czech, Spanish, and Polish refugees who have settled in our territory.

In an unprecedented event in our annals, war has ravaged half of our land within a few weeks and destroyed our bridges, our roads, our railroad stations, and a large part of our factories.

Our land, the cradle of a civilization that has astounded the world, is today in mourning and in distress.

In the wake of the voices that until very recently fed the French people with words of illusion and optimism comes now the sad voice of one who can speak to each person only of his wretchedness and deprivations, though not despairing of the future.

My government's principal concern, its daily care, is to help the whole French people to bear the burden of its suffering. I know our

° *New York Herald Tribune*, 21 August 1940.

task will be hard, yet we shall count ourselves successful, albeit in a small way, only when we are able to offer every man, woman, and child, rich or poor, a system a little less harsh than hitherto.

I know that your generous country, which is linked to mine by an age-old friendship, wishes now to take part in the effort to aid and relieve the French people.

Problems concerning the purchase of food and control over its final destination, of relief, of allocation of transport facilities, and of the coordination of individual tasks are bound to occur in France and in the United States. I believe that an unbiased person could materially assist in this relief work, in concert with our embassy in Washington and the American and French Red Cross organizations.

I have therefore asked Mr. René de Chambrun, a citizen of both our countries,° to devote his time to this task, supposing that you yourself and the American relief organizations agree that this help would prove useful.

I beg you, Mr. President, to accept the assurance of my highest esteem and firm friendship.

Ph. Pétain.

Josée and I arrived in New York on the afternoon of August 31. Without delay, I called Miss Le Hand, the president's secretary.

"When shall I be able to see the president?"

"Harry Hopkins heard that you'd arrived; he is on a plane to New York and will have dinner with you this evening."

"Rather a good sign," I told Josée.

"No, it's rather a bad sign."

She was right. Harry Hopkins seemed very much embarrassed. After we had eaten our first course in silence, he said nervously, "The president has had to give up the plan of shipping condensed milk. Churchill telephoned him insisting that we maintain the blockade."

I reminded him that with my help Roosevelt had concluded an agreement with Pétain. I also recalled what I had done for Great Britain, and even more to the point, what the United States was doing for her, all of which put Roosevelt in a position of strength with respect to Churchill. It should permit him to regard the supplying of the free zone as the modest and legitimate counterpart of the help the United States was giving Great Britain. But Hopkins could not be persuaded.

I had no recourse but to ask private relief agencies to supply part of what the official ones were refusing. My book *I Saw France Fall, Will She Rise*

°As a direct descendant of Lafayette, who was honored by Congress in this manner for his participation in the War of Independence.

Again?° had sold 80,000 copies. I decided to use my royalties to pay for tens of thousands of packages for French prisoners of war. I put myself in the hands of the Quakers in Philadelphia and of two selfless women—Anne Morgan, who had been awarded the Legion of Honor and the Croix de Guerre: 1914–18 for managing a military hospital in the war zone, and Mrs. Seton Porter, who had founded the organization Packages for French Soldiers. Its name was simply changed to Packages for French Prisoners of War.

RETURN TO PARIS

By the end of November, Josée, who was anxious to see her parents, took the plane for Portugal, while I continued my work as traveling salesman, trying to sell a product called England to a still skeptical United States. I kept in constant touch with Mrs. Eugene Meyer, the wife of the chairman of the Federal Reserve Board and of the *Washington Post.* She was trying in particular to protect the German Jewish intellectuals who had fled the advance of the Wehrmacht and were now in the southern zone. It was at this time that Josée was in touch with her father to arrange for these Jews to leave France and cross Spain and Portugal, ultimately to reach the United States. Here I was able to get them preferential visas through Mrs. Shipley, the director of the visa section. René Mayer was one of the first Frenchmen to arrive, via Canada.

The "13th of December,"† when it was headlined in the newspapers, came as no surprise to me, but I awaited a cable from Josée with growing impatience. It finally came: "STAY AMERICA STOP NO REASON TO WORRY EXCEPT FOR COUNTRY STOP ALL LOVE."

"Except for country." Those words followed me about in the holiday atmosphere of New York, where I spent the saddest Christmas of my life. France was constantly in my heart and mind. I felt almost a stranger in the United States, which had eyes only for England, still on its feet though reeling under the relentless bombardment of the Luftwaffe.

Had I not carried out the assignment I had willingly accepted? Josée had advised me: Stay in the U.S.; but I had only one thought—how soon could I leave? Plane service had ceased, and there were only two old tubs, the *Escambion* and the *Excalibur,* which made a ten- or eleven-day crossing from New York to Lisbon under terribly overloaded conditions. By resorting

°New York: William Morrow, 1940.
†Laval had been dismissed from Pétain's government on December 13, 1940.

to the black market, I managed to get a bunk in a cabin for four for a crossing in mid-February.

As soon as they knew of my decision, many acquaintances, such as the Strassburgers, Mrs. Seton Porter, John Jay, and others, stuffed my pockets with letters, messages, paper and gold dollars, which I was to hand to their faithful servants still living on the properties these Americans owned in France. I spent my last hours in New York with Simone and André Maurois. We left each other with heavy hearts, comforted only by the knowledge that we shared the same feelings.

Submarine warfare was at its height, so the route taken by neutral ships curved more and more southward. I arrived in Lisbon after a thirteen-day crossing, just in time to catch the night train to Madrid. The sleeping cars were full. I finally found a corner seat in second class, but could not sleep. When I arrived at the French embassy in Madrid, I sent three wires to the three places where Josée might be: Châteldon, the Place du Palais-Bourbon, and the Villa Saïd, and I gave the address where I would be the next day, the Grand Hôtel Tivolier in Toulouse.

There was, of course, no question of trying to cross the border at Hendaye, in the occupied zone. François Pietri lent me an embassy car to get to the French border crossing of Canfranc. As I was stuffed with gold and dollar bills like a big-time smuggler, I didn't feel particularly safe. Fortunately, the diplomatic passport given to me by Ambassador Henry-Haye in Washington forestalled any incident, and when I arrived at the Tivolier, I had the pleasure of having the concierge announce to me with a big smile, "Here is the key to the room where Mme. de Chambrun is waiting for you."

The next day we left for Paris to join our parents and parents-in-law. As we approached the demarcation line, a strange idea crossed my mind: the Germans I had met so far, the pilots shot down by British antiaircraft guns, had been "our" prisoners. Wasn't I now to be a prisoner of the Germans?

When I arrived at the National City Bank building, where my office was, the gate was open: the United States was not yet at war. I went into my office. Everything was in its place, but I saw only two photographs, facing each other: those of Laval and Pétain. The marshal had written in his careful handwriting, "To little Bunny, as a souvenir of the trip to the United States in 1931, when he showed so much considerateness and affection for his old friend. Paris, May 3, 1933. Ph. Pétain."

Josée refused to be mollified by this inscription, and I heard her voice: "I don't want to see your marshal next to my father!"

So I exiled the marshal to a far corner of the room. For forty years now, the two men have been watching each other in silence.

When we had had lunch, the subject of December 13 came up again, and my father mentioned the part played by the marshal. I watched Laval. He was thoughtful and quiet. I had the fleeting impression that he might in the end forgive, whereas I saw in Josée's eyes the fire of a resentment that might well never go out.

DARLAN AT THE HELM

While I was resuming my career in France, Darlan began his reign. As he embarked on his political career, he was considered a great sailor, combining daring with a skill for maneuvering. Being an officer, he understood how to give orders, but also had a tendency to come down hard on what he considered acts of disobedience, even by civilians. He believed internal politics to be a simple matter of administrative management that could be turned over to trustworthy people.

Foreign policy was his main concern, and the improvement of French-German relations, which had reached a deadlock. To unfreeze them he counted on a certain amount of personal credit: since Mers-el-Kebir,° for which he wanted no retaliation, except symbolically, he had earned England's hatred, regularly informing the Reich of the British fleet's position in the Mediterranean, indicating the safest routes for the convoys of the Axis to take. He had the help of men like Jacques Benoist-Méchin. He was Darlan's secretary general as well as the author of *History of the German Army*, and thus was friendly with the leaders of the Reich. With Darlan also was Paul Marion, an ex-Communist converted to totalitarianism, who, in *Their Struggle*, showed how Mussolini and Hitler had come to power. These semi-official contacts with the Germans created a certain détente. The new ministers, for example, were allowed to move about freely throughout the country. But there was as yet no question of any major renegotiations between the two countries. During March, Darlan hoped for an invitation from Hitler, which did not come. In April, the Wehrmacht stormed through Yugoslavia and Greece. Finally, on May 10, the admiral left for Germany amid great secrecy. But Hitler, receiving him in Berchtesgaden, merely wanted to test him by a new demand. Rachid Ali, the head of the government of Iraq, had just turned against the British and asked for Germany's help to continue the war. Hitler needed the use of Syrian airports, then part of the French mandate, so that the Luftwaffe could land there and deliver arms.

Darlan agreed. General Dentz, French high commissioner in the Middle East, was flabbergasted by the admiral's orders but carried them out nevertheless. Darlan hoped that the meeting in Berchtesgaden would lead to general negotiations. And sure enough, Hitler asked that the bases in North

---

°A port on the Algerian coast where, in July 1940, an English fleet summoned a French squadron to join them in the war or disarm. On Admiral Gensoul's refusal, the British attacked, killing 1300 sailors and destroying or damaging several of the French ships.

Africa be put at the Reich's disposal, in return for which the line of demarcation would be abolished, prisoners would be freed, and war compensation would be reduced. But no agreement was reached, and Darlan returned to Vichy empty-handed.

From Darlan's accession to power, Laval became more and more anxious and watchful. He reacted with anger to Darlan's first public message: "The victor could have erased us from the world map." Syria was the last straw: He saw with fury Darlan not only yielding to German demands, but indirectly involving France in a war with Britain, a situation which Laval had steadily striven to prevent.

Though eager to make his views and feelings known, Laval was aware of the difficulties that a man who was only an ordinary citizen, shunted aside from the affairs of state, was likely to face. He finally thought of an adroit device to make his position known. Ralph Heinzen was the chief of the United Press Services in Europe. I traveled to Vichy to get him; Laval would give him an interview. First, Laval recalled the tradition of friendship that permitted him to count on a sympathetic hearing from the American people. Then he stated categorically that the peace he wished for in no way implied submission to German hegemony. He stressed how greatly the policy of collaboration, as he understood it, differed from Darlan's policy of surrender—though he did not name Darlan directly. He recalled what he had said to Hitler at Montoire, in particular the famous statement: "If you want to crush us, so be it; one day we will rise up again—it is the law of history."[*]

June and July passed uneventfully, but at the beginning of August, the marshal, influenced by his regular antirepublican entourage, made several decisions that shocked Laval—the suspension of all political parties in the free zone, the cessation of parliamentary allowances, heavy penalties against Freemasons who had made false statements, and the creation of a Council of Political Justice, which sentenced Daladier, Blum, Reynaud, Mandel, and Gamelin to be detained forcibly while the Court of Riom debated the charge of culpability for failing to prepare France's defenses before the war; finally, all holders of high office would henceforth be required to swear an oath of allegiance to the marshal.

A BULLET NEAR THE HEART

The date was August 27, 1941. Josée had left for Châteldon to be with her mother. In the silence of the Place du Palais-Bourbon, the telephone rang.

[*]See for example, le Figaro, 26 May 1941.

Automatically, I looked at the clock It was 7:00 P.M. A deeply distressed voice was at the other end of the line. "This is Pagès.° The prime minister has been shot.† It's serious; he is being operated on. Come quickly to the Versailles Hospital."

At ten o'clock in the evening, I saw my father-in-law. He had regained consciousness and immediately asked to speak to his wife. The doctor, Pierre Barragué, hesitated, but Laval insisted that the surgeon bring the telephone mouthpiece to his lips, and he whispered into it: "The car has left for Châteldon. See you tomorrow. Kiss Josée." Then he turned to Barragué. "Make sure that nothing is done to the one who shot me."

Barragué nodded, and taking my arm, led me to the door. In the hallway I met Pagès, who told me what had happened. He had been working with the prime minister on the Aubervilliers files. At 5:30, Laval realized that the first contingent of volunteers going to fight *"Bolshevism"* was on the point of leaving. He and Pagès left the town hall and arrived at the scene just as the band struck up the "Marseillaise," to which the crowd listened quietly. As they finished, one of the volunteers left his place and shot Laval, the colonel of the regiment, and Marcel Déat. Pagès rushed to Laval, who was losing blood rapidly. With the help of two soldiers, Pagès moved him to his car, got him inside, and sat down next to him. Just as they arrived at the hospital, Laval lost consciousness.

One 6.35-mm. bullet had struck the shoulder and another penetrated the lower right side of the chest. It stopped about one-half centimeter from the heart, virtually touching the far side of the left ventricle. Dr. Barragué chose to perform a minimal operation because Laval was a heavy smoker. The crowd was besieging the operating room, and the doctors had to lock themselves in.

For the next several days, all visitors were excluded, but an exception was made for Barthélemy, the minister of justice, who had come from Vichy at Pétain's request. Was it a shadowy indication of remorse?

"I only hope that Collette's life may be spared" said Laval of his would be assassin. In the days that followed, the attempted assassination was much discussed. Eyewitness reports seemed to confirm that Deloncle, one of the leaders of the "ultracollaborationist" movements, had urged Collette to join the "anti-Bolshevik legion," and Deloncle had twice urged that Laval should attend the ceremony.

Two weeks more of medical care enabled my father-in-law to leave with Mme. Laval for a rest in Châteldon. Later, he returned to Paris, where he spent the fall and winter.

On December 7 came the attack on Pearl Harbor. The United States

---

° Pagès was for many years Laval's assistant at the Aubervilliers town hall.

† Although Laval was out of office, French custom requires that he be addressed and referred to by his former title.

entered the war. The Chambrun family felt duty bound to arrange as quickly as possible for the safety of American interests in Paris.

Already, during the summer of 1940, Laval had received assurances from Abetz that the American Hospital in Neuilly, one of the most modern in Europe, would be placed under the protection of the French Red Cross. That is how this American institution, of which my father, General de Chambrun, was the volunteer manager, had escaped the greediness of the Wehrmacht.

But with America's entry into the war, all American establishments were put under German sequestration as "enemy property," and the American Library among them presented a special problem. My mother, an American by birth, was its president. The townhouse on Rue de Téhéran contained 120,000 books of English and American literature, of which a large portion had been put on the index (blacklisted) by the German Propagandastaffel agency. These books had to be saved from burning or "deportation" to Germany. We decided to remove the names of the Jewish and foreign subscribers from the Library's list and organize a personal delivery of the books to their homes.

As for the rest, we had to wait and see, telling ourselves that Dr. Aschenbach, the councillor of the German embassy, who was married to an American, might perhaps help us out.

RETURN TO POWER

The Russian winter slowed the German advance, and the occupation grew harsher. The French people were becoming less cooperative. German soldiers would be killed at night. In reprisal, the Germans would take hostages, execute suspects, and step up the arresting of Jews.

Near the end of March 1942, Laval met Col. Helmut Knochen, the chief of the Sicherheitspolizei in occupied France, and told him bluntly, "I am surprised and distressed to see the occupation bear down so heavily on the French people. Your wrongdoings are becoming more and more serious. I am telling you all this before I leave Paris for a prolonged stay in the Auvergne."

A few hours later, Knochen telephoned.

"Mr. Prime Minister, Marshal Goering will be in Paris tomorrow, Thursday, March 29. He wishes to see you around noon and wants the meeting kept secret."

The next day, Goering told Laval that the Germans were about to unleash a second offensive against the Soviets, on a front more than two thousand kilometers long, which would force a decision before winter came. Soon after, he said, the Germans would attack England in her African empire in such a way that the United States would not have time to intervene. Goering insisted that Laval maintain a strict secrecy about the entire interview. He went on with a stern warning: While Germany concentrated its forces on the Eastern front, no resistance or unrest would be tolerated to the rear of the Wehrmacht. He reminded Laval of the way the Nazis had solved "the Polish Question," and spoke darkly of Hitler's displeasure at the intrigues and shilly-shallying of the French government.

Not intimidated, Laval retorted that ever since he had left the government, German policy in France had been nothing but an accumulation of mistakes.

Goering countered by saying that even if Pétain were to ask Laval to return to power, it would be either too late or too soon. Laval, he said, had been an honest foe, strong in defense of his country's interest, whom the Germans would doubtless meet again after peace was made.

It seemed most unlikely that Pétain would ask Laval to come back, but through a series of odd circumstances, I became liaison between the two and lived to see Laval's reentry into the government. After my return from the United States, I had decided not to go to Vichy again. But on March 31, François Monahan, a childhood friend, came to ask me a favor on which he set great value. His father-in-law, Captain de Marenches, had been an aide to my father, then Colonel de Chambrun. The two together from 1917 on, directed the liaison between Pétain and Pershing, the commanders in chief of the French and the American armies. After victory in 1918, Chambrun and Marenches collaborated on a book, *The History of the American Army in the European Conflict*, with the approval of the two generals.

As the American law office where François Monahan worked had closed down after the United States entered the second war, he had asked to be admitted to the Paris bar. He was told at the Palais de Justice that if he could put a copy of his father-in-law's book with the marshal's dedication in his file, the various obstacles to his application would vanish.

Monahan knew me well enough to be aware of my reluctance to ask for an interview with the marshal after the affair of December 13. So he suggested only that I see Pétain's secretary, Dr. Ménetrel, and persuade him to get the book inscribed.

Two days later, I made my way up the stairs of the Hôtel du Parc so as to avoid a possible meeting in the elevator. Ménetrel agreed to help. I was leaving when the door opened and I heard the marshal's cheerful voice, "You, here? Where have you been?" And before I was able to open my mouth, he pulled me into his office.

"Sit down in this chair—a little closer, so I can hear better." Our knees were almost touching as he asked, "How is Josée? How are your parents?" adding quietly after a pause, "Is your father-in-law still angry with me?"

"Marshal," I said, "I have never lied to you, and I'm not going to start now. Yes, Pierre Laval is angry with you, not for what you did to him or to his wife and daughter, but for the harm that your move of December 13 has done to the country. He was sure that nine days later, on the twenty-second, he was going to obtain the release of a contingent of 150,000 prisoners, the reduction of the occupation costs from 400 million to 180 million and the rejoining of the northern and Pas-de-Calais departments with Paris, not to mention a major relaxation of rules governing the demarcation line. Abetz had shown him the memorandum of these changes initialed by Ribbentrop. It would have been very difficult, Laval thinks, for the Germans to go back on their promises. Now he is deeply worried. After the very harsh terms of the conversation he's just had with Goering, he fears the worst."

When I told the marshal of Goering's threats, he cast a wandering glance around his office and whispered rather than spoke, as if the walls had ears. "I am sorry for what I was made to do. Your father-in-law was a good negotiator. He should have come up to see me more often and submitted written reports on what he was doing. I was wrong to listen to the bad advice of Alibert and La Barthète. Since Laval's gone, I've had to face the Boches alone, without infantry." After a while, he went on, "Laval knew how to talk to the Boches, how to gain time. Darlan is a good sailor, but on land he can't manage."

One thing still bothered me—the imputation that Laval had had a hand in the antigovernment campaign led by Déat in *L'Oeuvre*. "Marshal, did you really believe that Laval urged Déat to write those articles?"

"They tried to make me believe it. Your father-in-law's enemies circulated many lies. They went so far as to say that I gave the order for his arrest. That's not true. It was Peyrouton's idea. I never sent policemen to Châteldon."

I posed another question. "Did you believe that Laval would maneuver the country into a colonial war in Africa without your knowledge?"

"No, I didn't. That idea came from Darlan and Huntziger. After the business of Dakar, they wanted to take Chad back from the dissidents."

The word "dissidents" will sound odd, but the marshal never spoke to me of "Germans" or "Gaullists." He always used "Boches" and "dissidents."

I was about to leave when he held me back by the arm. "Do you think that in spite of everything that's happened, your father-in-law would consent to come back and help me?"

"Perhaps, but I know that Mme. Laval and Josée will do everything to prevent him."

At this point, the marshal called Ménetrel, and a few moments later I left with the book, the eagerly awaited book, warmly dedicated, with an equally warm letter from the head of state.

I returned to Paris that same evening and on the next day had a phone call from Ménetrel. "The marshal wishes to see Prime Minister Laval as soon as possible. The meeting could take place in the forest of Randan, at the crossing of two riding paths, safe from curious onlookers. I will pick you up at Châteldon so we can make sure of the place."

We marked the intersection of the two riding paths, not far from a wooden hut that could shelter us from the rain if necessary. We set the meeting for 4:30 the next day.

My father-in-law and I arrived at 4:25. A little later, we saw the marshal's car. As he was getting out, I leaned toward my father-in-law and told him what Josée had asked me to say: "Don't give in. Remember December thirteenth."

Actually, it was to be neither yes nor no: faced with the gravity of the situation and the marshal's insistence, Laval agreed to meet Darlan in Châteldon.

During the entire trip back, he did not say a word. He was deeply upset. I did not need to ask in order to understand his inner struggle. Three years later, when I read the lines he had written in his cell in Fresnes, I saw that I had not been mistaken:

> At no time in my life was my conscience so troubled. Sometimes it is difficult to find the true path to which duty leads. I sympathized with the objections raised by my family. It was impossible to keep public opinion informed, and I knew that later I might be held responsible for the demands and hardships imposed by the Germans. But even in matters where personal interests may suffer, I stand ready to accept all risks and dangers if it is to perform a duty for my country. I would have felt it extremely wrong to shirk my responsibility, if by my presence, my actions, and my words I were able to alleviate even a little the miseries of France and of the French people.[*]

THE FIFTH LAVAL GOVERNMENT

On April 17, 1942, Laval formed his fifth government. He himself took Foreign Affairs and the Ministries of the Interior and Information. Darlan was named commander-in-chief of the army, navy, and air force. Lucien Romier became minister of state, Cathala went to the Ministry of Finance, Abel Bonnard to National Education, Raymond Grasset to Health, Max Bonnafous to Supplies, Jacques Leroy-Ladurie to Agriculture, Hubert Lagardelle

[*] *Laval Parle*, p. 96.

to Labor, Robert Gibrat to Communications, and Jean Bichelonne to Industrial Production.

There remained the task of finding a minister of justice. Laval called Léon Bérard, the French ambassador to the Vatican. "I'm forming a government."

"Pierre, you know how much I like you."

"I understand. *Au Revoir.*" He hung up, sure that Bérard guessed he was about to be asked to be minister of justice, and knowing from Bérard's words that he would refuse. Later, Laval said to him: "You're like a fireman: you like your job well enough, but you don't like fires." Joseph Barthélemy became minister of justice. A capable lawyer and a member of the law faculty in Paris, Barthélemy had strongly opposed France's entry into the war.

On April 20, Laval addressed the French people, both those of metropolitan France and those of the empire. He did not mask the truth:

> Several days ago, during a very moving conversation with the marshal, I told him of my anxiety concerning the external situation of our country. Today, speaking as the head of the government, I must tell you that the situation is serious.

> Frenchmen and Frenchwomen of our empire, all of you who are listening to me this evening, in Africa, in Asia, in the islands of the Pacific, in those countries of America where the colonizing talents of our people first proved themselves, Frenchmen and Frenchwomen whether by origin, by adoption, or by choice, I sense your feelings as you share our anxiety concerning the fate of the empire. To you, who inhabit our faraway territories, and who remain attached to France, I say to you: We will not abandon you. You will remain French.

> I thought of the words I would speak to you when I was in my native village, there on the soil of Auvergne, there where I was born, the place to which I feel so closely attached. At this very moment, spring has come to that village. Will spring not also come in time to our country? For my part, I dedicate myself to the assigned task, and will not give up before the well-being of France has once again been assured.

He was put to the test immediately. He received two ultimatums, one after the other. The first came from the United States and demanded that Adm. George Robert's squadron, stationed in the Antilles and on which the gold reserves of the French Central Bank were kept, head for an American port to deposit the gold there.

The second came from the Reich and demanded, under threat of reprisals, that the fleet be scuttled without delay, and that the gold reserves be sunk.

Laval's double counterthrust was as swift as the attack. On April 27, he reassured the United States. "Your fears are unfounded and make you seem to forget the age-old friendship that unites our two countries." With the Reich, however, he remained on the plane of strict legal discourse. His official memorandum of April 28 read: "Your request constitutes a flagrant and unacceptable violation of the Armistice Convention."°

"The prime minister has just surpassed himself," Charles Rochat, the secretary general of the Quai d'Orsay told me. "His double thrust is a diplomatic masterstroke."

AN UNEXPECTED VISITOR

Laval was not yet done with the business of ultimatums when the news about General Giraud came out. An incident that was ordinary enough was about to become an affair of state, because it had made Hitler furious. Suddenly, it seemed there was no longer any chance that Laval could negotiate for advantages. Rather, France would have to pay the price for a general's escape. On May 12, five-star General Giraud escaped from the prison for high officers at Koenigstein by sliding down a knotted rope. Generals Charles Mast and Alphonse Juin had been freed from the same prison in the previous year to restore leadership to the French empire in North Africa. Giraud managed to cross Germany from east to west toward the Swiss border, reached Vichy, and presented himself, smiling, before the marshal.

In Koenigstein, the prison guards were understandably distressed. Fearing Himmler's reaction, they lied and argued that Giraud was a prisoner bound only by his pledge of honor. Himmler, in turn, fearing Hitler's anger, accepted the excuse. Hitler feared in his turn that Giraud, supposedly a tactician for offensive tank warfare, was returning home as part of some plot. The Führer ordered him seized and brought back to Koenigstein, and suspended all releases and furloughs from captivity, including those given for health reasons.

The marshal asked Giraud to stay for lunch, and turning to my father-in-law, said, "Mr. Laval, try to arrange this matter with the occupying powers."

The first step was to get in touch with the right parties. Abetz agreed to a meeting in Moulins, where Abetz himself, with a general representing General Keitel, the commander in chief of the Wehrmacht, and Laval accompanied by Giraud, would confer. Because Moulins lay on the wrong side of the demarcation line, Laval insisted that if the parties failed to reach agreement, Giraud would be free to return to Vichy.

In Moulins, the general representing Keitel was more than merely cour-

° Both documents are in the Ministry of Foreign Affairs.

teous; he offered several concessions if Giraud would return to Germany of his own free will. Giraud would be "the guest of honor" of the Reich, residing at the Hotel Adlon in Berlin; an aide-de-camp would be put at his disposal; his family would be permitted to join him; and, if he desired, he could inspect the camps where French prisoners were kept.

The general thought it over for a good while, but finally declined the offer and returned to Vichy with Laval. He had decided to sign the declaration of loyalty, as he had indeed promised the marshal. He expected Pétain to appoint him to the position Georges Scapini held in the Delegation on Prisoners, with the rank and the privileges of an ambassador.

My father-in-law felt greatly embarrassed to have to call Scapini, the respected head of this important delegation in Berlin, which also had representatives in Paris and in Vichy. Scapini's responsibilities already carried with them the rank and privileges of an ambassador. Laval was not surprised to hear him answer: "To be exchanged for a general? There can be no question of it."

The only action Giraud could take was to write his declaration of loyalty to the marshal. This he did on May 4, in the form of a letter from Lyon, to show that he had not been subjected to any pressure.

Lyon, May 4

Marshal,

Following our recent discussions, and in order to dissipate any possible doubts concerning my attitude, I want to express to you my feelings of complete loyalty.

You, as well as the prime minister, have explained to me the policy you intend to follow with respect to Germany.

I agree with you completely. I give you my word as an officer that I will do nothing that might in any way interfere with our relations with the German government, or hamper the mission that you have entrusted Admiral Darlan and Prime Minister Laval to carry out under your high authority.

My past record is the guaranty of my loyalty. I beg you, marshal, to accept the assurance of my complete devotion.

A. Giraud

After he delivered the letter, he drove away in the direction of Lyon. A few days later, he reached the Mediterranean coast, where he spent several months before boarding a submarine that was to surface near the Algerian coast only at the time of the American landing there. Laval had been kept informed of his movements. The idea of preventing his possible escape never entered his mind.

LAVAL VERSUS SAUCKEL: THE TWO-YEAR STRUGGLE BEGINS

The American ultimatum, the German ultimatum, the Giraud affair—Laval was still dealing with these three crises, when a fourth occurred: Fritz Sauckel, the "Gauleiter" of Thüringen, asked to see the prime minister.

Hitler had assigned this former longshoreman from Hamburg, a prisoner in France from 1914 to 1919 and a militant Nazi from the first, to recruit manpower throughout the occupied territories. Ever since 1940, the Reich had appealed to French volunteers, to whom it offered tempting salaries and conditions. As the war continued and the need for manpower increased, all salaries had been raised, and by May 1942 between 100,000 and 150,000 volunteers had left to work in Germany.

Sauckel nonetheless told Laval that the number of volunteer workers from France was insufficient. If this number did not reach 250,000 before the end of July, he would requisition workers and recall to Germany those prisoners of war who had been repatriated (600,000 sent home "on furlough" during the year 1941).

Laval, shocked by this harsh request, solemnly protested against demands that flagrantly violated the armistice provisions. He added that such a policy would end any possibility of reconciliation between the two countries.

Sauckel remained unmoved. Laval was especially angry because this about-face by the Reich was sprung on him bluntly, without warning, by a man of whom he had just heard for the first time. Laval argued so fiercely that he felt ill, and the discussion halted for a few moments. The indisposition passed, and Laval realized that fighting head-on in this way would lead nowhere. Sauckel was not only "a brute," as Laval put it later, but—even more serious—he had Hitler's trust.

Laval then thought of linking the recruitment of volunteers to the return of prisoners: for each worker leaving for Germany, one prisoner would be returned to France. The proposition made Sauckel smile. He reminded Laval that since General Giraud's escape, the release of any French prisoners had been prohibited by Hitler.

Laval made one last effort. If Germany went so far as to refuse even the principle of freeing prisoners, he said, the French government would find it impossible to assist in the volunteer workers' departure.

At that point, Sauckel realized that the inertia of the French government would force him to use duress, which might cause serious trouble. He agreed to telephone Hitler. The next morning, he brought the Führer's reply: 50,000 peasant prisoners would be freed in return for the departure of 150,000 skilled workers for Germany. Sauckel added that although the exchange might seem heavily unbalanced, a numerically even exchange would be a minus transaction for the Reich, for in one way or another all French prisoners in Germany performed some useful task.

Laval tried in vain to strike a better deal. He was more and more worried about the future. Sauckel would surely return, and in August, once the volunteers who had left for Germany were checked in, he would very likely turn up with new demands.

Laval very quickly came to the conclusion that he had only one weapon, namely, his personal reputation, and that he could only maintain his reputation if he could convince his opponents that he was doing his best. "Convincing the Germans" would mean giving the Germans compensation for refusing or delaying the execution of their demands. And compensation would mean uttering "certain words" pleasing to German ears, but which would surely irritate feelings in France.

So it was that on June 22 he declared, "Germany is fighting communism. Great battles are taking place in the east, from Petsamo to the Caucasus. I wish for a German victory, for without it, Bolshevism will take over everywhere in Europe."

A few hours after Laval had delivered this message, Maurice Schumann, de Gaulle's spokesman in London, crossed out both the beginning and the ending. The Propagandastaffel in Berlin performed the same amputation, so that the statement became "I wish for a German victory."[*]

Although he could not have foreseen the editing by the propagandists, Laval well knew that he would collide head-on with public opinion. But as he said more than once, he preferred personal unpopularity to the grave dangers that threatened his country.

The Germans, of course, were not meant to understand his ploy, but Laval tipped his hand to three hundred schoolteachers who came to hear him in Vichy on September 3, 1942:

> I went quite far in my remarks, as far as it is possible to go. I want you to understand me: I am willing to run any risks to myself so long as it permits France to have a chance.[†]

The unanimous applause of the audience demonstrated that they had understood him very well; this was his way of offering himself up to mitigate his country's woes.

---

[*] See also Exhibit D.

[†] The entire text of the speech is at the Hoover Foundation, under no. 221, together with stenographic copies of eighteen other speeches by Laval, taken down without his knowledge. See, for example, the entire text of his speech to the mayors of Cantal, on November 9, 1943, in Exhibit E.

The speech of June 22 had succeeded in partly disarming the Gauleiter on his first visit. Laval had two months' respite before he had to face this obtuse and stubborn person again. Alert, clearheaded, and always looking to the future, Laval tried to do two things: on the one hand, to effect a few democratic reforms—the first; and on the other hand, to sustain France under the burden of military occupation as well as defend the country against an insidious infiltration by German civilians—they were operating with the support of the Wehrmacht in many sectors important to national security.

Laval began by breathing a bit of "republican air" into the administration. As minister of the interior, he appointed Georges Hilaire and René Bousquet secretaries-general—the first in charge of administration, the second of the police. The administration was to be completely transformed. All the prefects previously dismissed because they were suspected of not agreeing with the ideology of a part of the marshal's entourage were recalled, while the men installed by Pétain and by Darlan were either sidelined or transferred, but not confirmed. Laval did not require allegiance to his own person, as the marshal was wont to do. Henceforth, the choice of prefects was to depend on competence, courage, and patriotism only. The long list of dismissals, transfers, reinstatements, and new appointments, a sampling of which is given in Schedule K, proves this in detail.

Though he cared about the republican tendencies of his prefects, as well as about the other requisite qualities, Laval did not in any way try to ascertain the extent of their anti-German feelings or their degree of sympathy with the Resistance.

André Sadon, the regional prefect of Toulouse, has told of the conversation he had with Félix Bussière, prefect of Marseille, who later died in deportation. "One day, a visitor, trying to flatter the government, said something uncivil about the Resistance. Laval stopped him at once, saying that in these troubled times it was difficult to know where one's duty lay. Everybody doubtless tried to do his best, and if a government resisted, it was good that in addition to its passive resistance there existed also an active one. In any case he would not listen to any criticism of the Resistance."°

Laval always covered for and fiercely defended the "resisting" prefects who were courageously serving France's interests. He resorted to all possible means to save them from deportation and death. At the same time, he eliminated from administrative and prefectorial service all those who, under pretext of collaboration, put themselves at the service of the occupying power and received favors from them. It was the pro-Nazis and not the resisters Laval found fault with.

There was the particularly delicate problem of the police. The army of occupation set up, at least in part, its own police force on French soil. Behind it, of course, lurked the Gestapo. Laval, however, insisted on a national police

°Declaration of A. P. Sadon, the Hoover Foundation, under no. 155.

whose duties were to be clearly defined, its authority recognized—in short, an independent police force, answerable only to him. To obtain this status, the Germans had to be approached, for they preferred to let matters stand. By the end of July, General Oberg, head of the SS, had agreed to discuss the matter with Bousquet, and on August 8, Oberg concluded an agreement satisfactory to Laval. It kept the German police from interfering in the sphere reserved for the French police.

In such attempts to defend the administration and the police, Laval had to struggle against both the greed of the occupying power and the antiparliamentarian anti-republican attitudes of the chief of state's entourage.

THE JEWS AND THE FREEMASONS

In the vexed matter of the Freemasons, Laval's chief opponents were French. As early as July 20, 1940, just after the post-Republic government had been sworn in, the hatred of the Freemasons on the part of men close to the marshal assumed the aspect of a witch hunt. Freemasons were tracked down and pursued. They were regarded as "damned," and so must be excluded from all public functions. This anti-Masonic bigotry seemed to Laval thoroughly unjust. Before Montoire, when he had to leave Vichy so frequently for negotiations with Abetz in Paris, he deplored the anti-Masonic acts of the marshal's team, but he had neither the time nor the means to oppose them effectively.

During the sixteen months when he was out of power, he saw the Freemasons driven out of national life. Although a law of November 10, 1941, created a procedure for exceptions, it was so carried out as to allow only the fewest exceptions.

Once returned to power, Laval began to change all that. A law of June 21, 1942, put all matters having to do with secret societies under his direct control; a law of August 19, 1942, gave the "Special Commisssion" the power to reinstate Freemasons in the positions they had held until deprived of them by anti-Masonic decrees. Freemasons began to be "reprieved." But Laval could not abrogate the share of power that Admiral Platon, a fanatic anti-Mason, wielded as secretary of state. Platon, on his side, bided his time.

Similarly, Laval's struggles to protect the Jews had to be carried on not only against the Germans and the ultracollaborationists, but also against the anti-Semitic faction within Pétain's staff. Later Baudouin, never a Lavalist, affirmed that "Laval was the most opposed [of those in the government] to the anti-Jewish measures."[*]

[*] *Neuf Mois au Gouvernement* (La Table Ronde, 1948), p. 341.

When Laval returned to power in April 1942, there were interned in the unoccupied zone 30,000 civilians; 12,000 communists had been interned by the Daladier government in 1939–40 after the dissolution of the party and the signing of the German-Soviet Pact. The Pétain-Darlan government interned 18,000 persons, among whom were many Jews and Freemasons. When Laval came back to power in April 1942, he liberated 20,000 of those interned. The prefects' statements at the Hoover Institution and, in particular, the report by Colonel Bernon, who headed the commission that supervised these mass liberations, testify to the change. Again, on resuming office in April 1942, Laval also abolished the so-called anti-Jewish police, which had been set up after he left the government on December 13. Finally, he instituted the Maurice Reclus Commission for the reinstatement of the Freemasons.

Two months later, in July 1942, Himmler ordered the mass deportation of all foreign and French Jews in the occupied zone. Looking back on the events, Laval wrote:

In July 1942, I received a call from Colonel Knochen. The object of his visit was to notify me that the German government had decided to deport every Jewish person in the occupied zone. No distinction was made between Jews of French nationality and others. The prefect of police had already been notifed by the German authorities of their decision.

I protested vigorously and immediately saw the German ambassador, who said that he was helpless. The news had already been given to the Paris press. The ubiquitous Darquier de Pellepoix had already issued a statement. I interceded with General Oberg, who made his position painfully clear to me: "The Jewish problem has no frontiers for us," he said. He repeated to me once again that it was the intention of the German government to set up a Jewish state in the east, carved out of Polish territory.

On my return to Vichy, I spoke with Mr. Rochat,° who at once notified on my behalf the foreign ambassadors and ministers and urged them to intervene, without delay, with the German authorities to save their nationals of the Jewish faith then resident in France. I recall that the Spanish and Turkish ambassadors took immediate action, as did the Romanian and Hungarian ministers. I happen to know that the Spanish ambassador intervened successfully.

I informed Marshal Pétain and the Papal Nuncio of these deplorable events, and I concerted with Bousquet to place every difficulty in the way of carrying out the move. The Germans continued to threaten us with the deportation of the French Jews. I summoned all the prefects

°See depositions by Rochat and Dinu Hiott at the Hoover Institution, under nos. 22 and 100.

and explained what was going on. Moreover, in the teeth of German opposition, I managed to obtain exceptions from this measure for all foreign Jews married to French nationals and all Jews who had rendered distinguished services to France.

Hundreds of pages of the German secret files (telegrams, reports, documents of the Nuremberg trials) demonstrate that the Germans themselves knew of Laval's subversive attitude. On August 15, 1943, for example, S. S. Rothke and Geissler, heads of the Gestapo in the southern zone, sent the following telegram to Knochen, the head of the SS in Paris:

> Laval refuses to put at our disposal for these arrests the French police of the occupied zone. If we want to carry them out with our own means, he is not in a position to prevent us from doing so. To sum up, the French government refuses to follow us in the Jewish question. I foresee that at the next cabinet meeting the Bousquet project will be opposed and stopped. We also have the impression that Pétain wants to prevent the application of the law that many Jews have been asking him to protest. A few minutes before receiving Geissler and myself, Laval had received the Jew Lambert, president of the Union Générale des Israélites of the southern zone.°

In September Geissler further informed Knochen:

> President Laval often receives calls from Jews or persons who intervene on their behalf. Certain members of his entourage are friends of the Jews. One must distrust him altogether, for he will not support our anti-Jewish action even though many segments of the French population regard it sympathetically.†

Knochen himself encountered resistance from Laval.

From personal conversations it was clear that by his repeated interventions Laval always delayed the solution of the Jewish question demanded by the government of the Reich.

When Dannecker, the special delegate for Jewish questions, called him, Laval realized that he was a fanatic and refused almost immediately to continue talking with that young fanatic.

It was impossible to find arguments that would persuade the central office in Berlin to recall Dannecker as its representative, for he had worked to their great satisfaction in Austria and Czechoslovakia. He succeeded in obtaining his recall in October 1943 on disciplinary grounds. That brought about a delay of many months in settling the Jewish question in France. During that

---

°Jacques Baraduc, *Les Archives Secrètes du Reich*, (Les Éditions de L'Élan, 1949) p. 189.
†Ibid., p. 192.

time, the political situation changed completely, and in 1943 and afterward, Laval was able to oppose with all his might the deportation of Jews of French nationality.

As soon as Laval realized that the wording of the instructions from Rome received by the Italian authorities in France differed from the text of the German orders coming from Berlin, he used this fact as the pretext he had been looking for to turn the Jewish question into a political one. He treated it as a problem in foreign affairs affecting the relations of the Axis. With his great experience in foreign policy, playing sometimes on Franco-German relations and at other times on Franco-Italian relations, he took advantage of every chance and used the Jewish question to weaken Axis relations by exploiting the opposing conceptions of the Germans and Italians on this subject. He saw that the Italian and German authorities in France could not reach an understanding and that negotiations between Rome and Berlin would become necessary, a fact that meant at least that he had gained more time.°

Laval instructed the French prefects (regional and departmental) to do all in their power to protect the Jews, as well as the Freemasons and other victims of German persecution. The testimony of Jean Chaigneau, prefect of the Alpes-Maritimes, is typical of the dozens of depositions on file at the Hoover Institution:

> With regard to the measures taken against the Jews and the Freemasons, we always found him at our side or ahead of us, protecting us in the actions we took to make sure that the new measures should be as ineffective as possible.†

Similarly, Alfred-Roger Hontebeyrie, prefect of the Herault, declared,

> At the same time at Vichy—this was toward the end of 1943—Pierre Laval instructed me to do everything and take every possible step to save any Jews that still remained in the Montpellier region. Thanks to his support when the German army took police measures in the maritime departments, I was able to transfer the Jews into the Aveyron and Lozère. President Laval's intervention prevented the *Sicherheitsdienst* from becoming involved in the operation. . . .‡

Apart from his protests and refusals to cooperate, Laval took action to save Jewish lives. During the time when he was officially receiving representatives

---

°Deposition of Knochen, head of the SS in France, at the prison of the Cherche-Midi., March 24, 1948. The Hoover Institution. A4, vol II, p. 1778.
†Document no. 31 at the Hoover Institution.
‡Document no. 154 at the Hoover Institution.

of those countries that were either German satellites or occupied by the Germans, doing so with the hope of inciting them to intervene on behalf of their Jewish nationals, he also suggested to Pinkney Tuck, the American chargé d'affaires, that the United States send ships to Marseille to save as many foreign Jewish children as possible.

Tuck left my father-in-law assured that the State Department would agree. Tuck returned the next day, distressed to report that his country could not assume this responsibility, as Germany might consider such an intervention a hostile act. This was several months before the American landings in North Africa.

Again in this time of anxiety, Laval used the printing plant in Clermont-Ferrand that issued *Le Moniteur* to aid Jews and resisters. Forged certificates of baptism, identity cards, and ration cards were made at the plant, the only one in France that steadily refused to print anything for the occupying power. During Pétain's postwar trial, reference was made to the 150 Jewish children who were saved at the Centre de Jeunesse de Moissac. When it became known that the Germans were about to round them up, they were hidden in various schools and homes, and the prefect furnished each child with false ration and identity cards. All these had been printed at Laval's printing plant.°

A tragic balance sheet was published by the Anglo-American Commission on the Palestinian question. The commission drew up an approximate census of the number of Jews (nationals and foreigners) residing in the following seven countries in 1939, before the German occupation, and in 1946, after the defeat of the Reich:

	1939	1946	Losses
Belgium	90,000	33,000	57,000
Czechoslovakia	315,000	60,000	255,000
Greece	75,000	10,000	65,000
Holland	150,000	30,000	120,000
Poland	3,351,000	80,000	3,271,000
Yugoslavia	75,000	11,000	64,000
Austria	60,000	15,000	45,000
	4,116,000	239,000	3,877,000

For these seven countries, the surviving Jewish population was exactly 5.80 percent.

France numbered 330,000 Jews in 1939, of whom about half were foreigners. In 1946, there were about 180,000 Jews, of whom 160,000 were French. The foreign Jews suffered appalling losses, but Pierre Laval and his aides, and notably the admirable corps of Prefects and their staffs, helped to

°See evidence before the court of appeals at Riom, 1956 in re Laval; *Le Moniteur du Puy-de-Dôme* v. the state.

save 95 percent of the French Jews, as well as kept a great many foreign Jews from being deported. To close this painful enumeration, it should be noted that every Jewish war prisoner from France, being protected by the Scapini embassy, came back unmolested at the end of the war. The Great Rabbi Weill stated this under oath in June 1947.°

The Great Rabbi Hirschler of Strasbourg was able to measure the sacrifice Laval was making by remaining at his post in November 1942, at the time of the North African landings and the occupation of the southern zone. On November 14, he called to see Laval, recently back from Munich and in Paris mainly to oppose German pressure for more workers. The great rabbi was received by Secretary-General Jacques Guérard. He had heard that Pétain and Laval were about to flee to North Africa. "All the Jews are my children," he said. "What will happen to them if President Laval abandons them?" Told in confidence by the secretary that Laval would not abandon his post, the great rabbi left him a message: "I am well aware of your difficulties; do not lose your courage. The French Jews will never forget what you have done for them."†

In retrospect, the prominent Jewish writer Léon Poliakoff concluded: "Vichy was, in fact, the major factor that contributed to the relatively merciful fate of the French Jews." Quoting this statement, Alfred Fabre-Luce of *Le Figaro* added, "The Jews much preferred the free zone of the south to the northern, occupied zone, even after the southern zone was invaded [in 1942]."‡

Meanwhile, there had occurred a strange interlude in domestic politics. The marshal asked my father-in-law to stop in, because of a bothersome visit about to take place—that of the count of Paris, traveling incognito under the name of Major Bertrand. He had written to Pétain that he had something very important to tell him, so a member of the marshal's staff, Colonel de Gorostarzu, had picked him up in Spanish Morocco. Pétain, believing that the count, pretender to kingship in France, was thinking about being the marshal's successor, asked Laval to take the delicate task of discouraging him.

Laval met the pretender at a private dinner and later reported the exchange to us.

"Do you prefer that I address you as 'Your Majesty' or as 'Major'?" began Laval.

The count answered with a smile: "Say Your Majesty from time to time." He got to the heart of the matter fairly quickly, recalled his rights and duties as pretender, and concluded by saying that he could not wait much longer— he had already been waiting twelve years.

°Document no. 53 at the Hoover Institution.
†Document no. 258 at the Hoover Institution.
‡*Le Figaro*, 30 June 1981.

"May I be permitted, Your Majesty, to ask how old you are?"

"I am thirty-three."

"At the age of thirty-three, I was still an apprentice minister, and I had to wait before becoming president of the Council [of Ministers]. Do you think, Your Majesty, that the present time, when France is in such deep distress, is the right moment to serve the cause you represent?"

The count recited the benefits he could confer on France by reason of his friendships, in particular with the sultan of Morocco and other important foreigners.

Laval could sense the count's surprise and especially his disappointment, but was suddenly inspired. "Your Majesty, do you absolutely insist on becoming king despite the tragic times in which we are living?"

"Why not?"

"All right, then! I can see only one solution."

"What is that?"

"I offer you the Ministry of Supplies. If you succeed in feeding the French people for the next several months, nothing can prevent you from becoming king of France."

LAVAL AND LABOR

At the end of July 1942, Laval was again awaiting Sauckel. The Gauleiter had got a menacing order from Hitler. The Soviet campaign, and especially the battle of Stalingrad, had caused so many German casualties that Hitler demanded an immediate increase in the number of workers sent to Germany, to make up for the mass reinforcements going to the Eastern front. Hitler decreed that "all men and women between the ages of twenty and sixty-five in the occupied territories are requisitioned by the Reich for forced labor." Newspapers in the occupied zone published the Diktat at the order of the Propagandastaffel, which also demanded that it be published in the free zone.

Laval formally protested against the publication of the order in the press of the occupied zone and objected that the order was in violation of the armistice provisions. He forbade publication in the free zone and told Abetz that if the order were carried out in France, he would resign.

Hitler agreed to modify the order: in all of occupied Europe, French women only would be exempted from work deportation to the Reich.

This first victory did not blind Laval. He did not forget Goering's words of May 1941 that France could not hope for a special fate when all the other countries were being bled white by the occupier.

But to maintain contact so that Germany would continue to believe he was doing his best—the kind words of June 22 no longer sufficing—he issued a ruling on September 13, 1942, that declared "all persons of the male sex between the ages of eighteen and fifty, and all persons of the female sex under the age of thirty-five can be compelled to carry out any kind of work that the government may consider necessary in the higher interests of the nation." It stipulated that "idlers will be tracked down."

Now it was no longer a German order but a French law. It was no longer a sentence of forced labor, but a statement that the government might permit itself to act not on Germany's behalf but in the higher interests of France. Only the clause about "tracking down idlers" was capable of stimulating the flow of volunteers toward Germany. But the negotiations between the two parties, the preparation of the texts, the delays in putting them in proper form, created obstructions. Sauckel expected 250,000 workers. The number of those leaving remained "insignificant," as Hemmen reported to Ribbentrop.

The Gauleiter knew perfectly well that he had received satisfaction in name only. But while he was getting impatient and angry, months passed— months that were so much gained for France. Without changing his strategy, Laval had modified his tactics of flexible defense. As he said to his friends, "Sauckel wants men? Well, I'm giving him legislation."

August, September, and October 1942 went by, Laval dealing with the usual domestic questions. Admiral Platon, the undeterred "anti-Mason," asked for the repeal of the two liberal laws that Laval had had adopted on June 21 and August 19, 1942, and proposed a text to reinforce the statute already in effect. Laval postponed its consideration to February 4, 1943.

Aside from such problems, he derived some satisfaction from success in the several sectors of which he was in direct charge. A detailed list can be found in the thirteen schedules of the Appendix to this book, but a few of these bright spots from the period June–November 1942 deserve to be emphasized.

The Comités d'entraide created in 1942 in the Maison du Prisonnier grew so rapidly that they numbered thousands of volunteers. By 1944, they had collected and distributed 3 billion francs, while avoiding the temptation to involve themselves in politics, something that Laval had warned them against.

After the Germans' refusal to reduce the occupation costs to 180 million (a blow that was a direct result of December 13), Laval succeeded in restoring good public finances by raising taxes, deferring payments, stopping increases in public spending, and suppressing illegal speculation. These measures ensured the strength of the franc and protected the value of French currency abroad.

Laval gave the Committee of the Cinematographic Industry the means to produce films superior to those of the German "Continental," and to form a professional organization for the first time.

Laval gave Colonel Pascot, the high commissioner for Youth and Sport, a free hand, which enabled him to disguise the number of his active workers. Despite German prohibitions, Pascot succeeded in buying fields and equipment. "Go ahead," Laval told him. "At least they'll remain on French soil and Sauckel will not get these men!"

Finally, he authorized the reform of the Agricultural Loan Agency, which henceforth functioned as a bank. Exactly at the moment when this reform was about to take place, on November 7, 1942, came the landing in North Africa.

THE ALLIES IN AFRICA

No sooner had the Americans landed in Algiers than Krug von Nidda, the German consul in Vichy, solemnly handed the prime minister a personal message from Hitler. It offered France an immediate alliance *"durch dick und dünn"* (through thick and thin). Laval spoke with von Nidda for an hour, but he had instantly decided to refuse the offer. Pétain sided with Laval, who prepared to leave at once for Munich to see Hitler. He asked Jacques Guérard to open the safe, took out certain documents, opened all the drawers of his desk, sorted his papers carefully, and then locked them up again, as if he were preparing for the possibility of a very long absence.

That night Laval and I left for Châteldon. "I am meeting Abetz tomorrow morning in Dijon," said he. "The trip to Munich won't be pleasant and my reception there even less so. Last year they shot one hundred hostages in retaliation for a noncommissioned German officer found dead in a metro station. How is Hitler going to make us pay for the defection of the African army, almost all of whose general staff and field officers I freed in 1940?"

We ate our dinner quickly, and then the long vigil began. He planned to leave just before dawn. He put his wallet on the table and handed me his watch. Josée immediately understood the gesture.

"I beg you," she implored, "resign!"

He shook his head, but she went on. "You know perfectly well that your presence can no longer accomplish anything."

He stopped her. "You don't understand! The Germans will become tougher; their toughness and their demands will increase with their military defeats."

He paused, then, emphasizing every word, said, "Resigning means deserting. I must remain here to protect the prisoners on furlough, the refugees, the people of Alsace-Lorraine, the Jews, the Communists, the Freemasons.

If I were to quit, France would be transformed into a vast underground. How many thousands of French people would pay for my cowardice with their lives?"

After a second pause, he added, "Look at what is happening in Poland, in the Balkans, everywhere."

The next day, Abetz urged Laval to reconsider, warning that Hitler might react violently. Laval would not listen.

It was 4:30 A.M. when they reached the outskirts of Munich; the meeting had been set for 8:00 P.M. The night before, Hitler had waited for Laval until midnight. At five o'clock, Laval and Abetz, exhausted, arrived at the Vier Jahreszeiten Hotel, where they rested for a couple of hours.

At midmorning, the Italian delegation, headed by Galeazzo Ciano, Italy's foreign minister and Mussolini's son-in-law, arrived in Munich and was received by Hitler. The leaders of the Axis held a military staff meeting. Hitler, who had heard meanwhile that Darlan had joined the Allies, kept Laval waiting for two hours.

At last, Laval, in civilian clothes, was brought before what seemed a tribunal of judges in military uniform, a tribunal presided over by Hitler, who opened the session by railing against Darlan's defection.

Then he turned to Laval and announced that France would keep only those parts of its empire that it had successfully defended. Reiterating threats in a hoarse voice, he was nearly overcome by fury. While Hitler caught his breath, Ciano interjected, "Italy will occupy Tunisia, Nice, and Corsica."

Laval, who had not moved a muscle during Hitler's diatribe, now turned toward Ciano and, in a voice that brooked no reply, said, "You keep quiet. Germany beat us, not you. You never even fought." Ciano did, in fact, keep quiet. The amazement in the room was such that Laval was able to present his country's defense in a few sentences.

Dr. Paul Schmidt, Hitler's interpreter, understood both Laval's opening move and Hitler's reaction when he wrote in his Memoirs: "Laval gave Hitler reason to distrust him, owing to the delaying tactics through which he tried to gain time for France."[*]

Ciano similarly observed: "Laval, like a good Frenchman, tries to gain time for his country."[†]

At 4:00 A.M. the next morning Abetz telephoned Laval to inform him that the Wehrmacht would cross the demarcation line at eleven o'clock that day "for reasons of military necessity." Laval protested immediately and requested that Abetz communicate his indignation to Hitler without delay. He told Abetz that he would put his protest in writing that very moment.

[*] *Statist auf diplomatischer Bühne* (Bonne: Athenäum-Verlag, 1949), p. 564. Dr. Paul Schmidt, who was the official translator of the German heads of state from 1928 to 1944 and after the war became president of the Translators' Institute in Munich, also deposited at the Hoover Foundation (no. 323) a twelve-page report dated February 14, 1961 on the conversations of Laval that he had translated.

[†] See Galeazzo Ciano, *Journal Politique* (Paris: Baconniere, 1948), vol. 2, p.211.

Abetz was accustomed to Hitler's shows of strength, but he was not familiar with Laval's. He was so impressed that he completely revised the letter in which Hitler informed Pétain of the occupation of the free zone. The letter was presented to the head of state at 11:10 A.M. by Marshal von Rundstedt, commander in chief of the German forces in the west, accompanied by Consul von Nidda.

Considering what had taken place in the Führerbau, the tone of the letter was indeed surprising:

> The action of the German troops is not aimed against you, head of state and venerable commander of the valiant French soldiers of the world war, or even against the French government, or those French people who want to keep their country from again becoming a theater of war: this entry of troops is not aimed at the French administration.

Laval's outburst also brought two almost unhoped-for sources of satisfaction. The Alsatians living in the southern zone and their institutions (which had been shut down) would be protected. The 90,000 escaped prisoners and the 650,000 prisoners on furlough would not be challenged. Laval could not help wondering if France had been spared the worst because of his "I wish" victory speech of June 22.

Laval and Abetz left for Vichy by plane. A few days later, Abetz was harshly recalled by Ribbentrop for having informed, advised, and helped Laval.

On his return, Laval briefed Pétain on the essentials of his trip and gave approval to decisions made in his absence.

For Hitler's benefit, the marshal had officially renewed the order to defend Africa. At the same time, Admiral Auphan, head of the naval forces, secretly informed officers of the true intentions: the marshal, who did not want a civil war any more than a foreign war on African soil, had released all military commanders from their oaths of allegiance to him. But the "official" order to defend Africa might be enough to avoid reprisals against metropolitan France.

Laval also agreed to let the more compromised officers of the intelligence services disappear, and he permitted secret documents to be destroyed if no absolutely safe hiding place could be found for them.

Major Bonhomme, now a lieutenant colonel, told me that the marshal, if he wished, could always take the plane kept ready for him and two hours later find himself among the cheering crowds of Algiers, all his old popularity restored. But this idea, said Bonhomme, had not crossed his mind.

Despite their unbridgeable differences, Pétain and Laval were as one in their determination to stand by France in its perilous hours.

A few weeks later, Anatole de Monzie approached Laval to try to obtain the release of two friends arrested by the SS, then asked him why he hadn't left for Algiers, taking Pétain with him. "One should either have a grand policy," he said, "or resign." Laval's answer is a clue to his thinking: if he had executed a "grand" policy, if he had left for Algiers, he couldn't telephone Achenbach to ask him to intervene for Monzie's friends. Achenbach would do the impossible to save them. To any grand policy Laval preferred a useful one in defense of France's interests. He had joined Pétain's government only for that reason, and for that reason he remained.

AT HITLER'S HEADQUARTERS

A few days later, one of the most tragic events of those painful years occurred—the scuttling of the French fleet in Toulon. Laval described it later from his prison cell.

At 4:30 A.M., November 27, Krug von Nidda telephones me in Châteldon. For the past half hour, our fleet has been encircled by a German squadron, which is about to seize the ships. I protest indignantly against this act of aggression and rush off to Vichy to confer with the marshal and the ministers. Admiral Leluc tries to communicate with Admiral Marquis, the maritime prefect of Toulon. We finally learn that explosions aboard the ships had begun about four o'clock that morning and had continued without interruption. Admiral de Laborde, the navy chief of staff, was at his command post on the *Strasbourg* and refused to leave; he was going to go down with his ship, but he agreed to leave on Pétain's orders. The marshal was his only superior, and he took his instructions from him alone.*

Laval could do nothing.

The order to scuttle had been given to all the squadrons by the admiral [Darlan], after the armistice. It may have been renewed; it had most certainly never been revoked. Each captain had the absolute order never to let his ship fall into the hands of a foreign power. Before the armistice, the government had entered into an agreement with England that the French would never surrender their fleet to the Germans. The other agreement, at Rethondes, which permitted us to keep the fleet, required that it never be put at the service of Germany's enemies. This double bond is what prompted the government and

Laval Parle, pp. 146 ff.

Admiral Darlan to give the scuttling order for the entire fleet, lest it should fall into the hands of a foreign power.°

Laval saw the disastrous consequences of the new catastrophe. In spite of the removal of the demarcation line, many obstacles hampered the traffic of people and goods from one zone to another. The Wehrmacht engaged in an extensive black market, which exacerbated shortages caused by barriers between the free and occupied zones. Max Bonnafous, minister of supplies, told Laval that the Wehrmacht transported entire truckloads of scarce foods across France. At the same time, despite the difficulty of crossing from one zone to the other, it had become so easy to move between France and Belgium that the two countries seemed to blur into a Franco-Belgian territory, their borders and autonomy erased.

But the worst was to come. The escalation of the war required that German workers leave for the Eastern front to replace their fallen comrades, which in turn meant the deportation of civilians from occupied countries to replace the German workers. Sauckel's shadow loomed. Abetz, recalled to Germany in disgrace, was replaced by his second-in-command, Counselor (Minister) Schleier, a party hardliner. With Abetz gone, Laval had no recourse but to appeal to Schleier. The new ambassador advised him speak directly to Hitler. On September 23, 1943, at a meeting of prefects at the Hôtel de Ville, Laval had said, "They blame me for going to see Hitler as if he were the devil. I want you to know that I would see the devil himself in order to save French lives!"

On December 3, he asked for an audience through official channels. On the evening of December 15, he was told that the interview would take place at Hitler's headquarters in Eastern Prussia on December 19.

Accompanied by Jean Bichelonne, the minister of industrial production, Laval made the grueling trip to the forest of Görlitz, where Abetz greeted him. The sight of the former ambassador comforted Laval, but he soon learned that Abetz's presence there in no way signified his return to Paris. Ciano then arrived with Marshal Cavallero.

It seemed a replay of the Munich "tribunal," until Goering himself appeared. Hitler resumed his Munich tirade against the French. He declared that the French generals, whom he had freed, had committed treason, that Darlan had committed treason, and that enormous deposits of arms had been found in the southern zone. He enumerated the various charges, Laval responding to each one by one, sometimes with a touch of humor. "If you have found arms in the southern zone, we, too, found a great many after 1918; cannons were sticking out of rivers."

At that point, Goering rose, pointed a finger at Laval, and demanded information about the "scandalous" black market operated by the French.

°Ibid., p. 146.

Laval opened his briefcase, took out Bonnafous's report of the German black market, and slowly recited the entire record of the Wehrmacht's illegal operations, which were causing starvation in France. He noticed in passing that the interpreter, Dr. Paul Schmidt, was translating everything perfectly. He was not surprised. He and Schmidt were old acquaintances. The doctor, who had the rank of minister at the Wilhelmstrasse, had already served as Brüning's official interpreter at the time of Laval's meetings with the German chancellor.

Goering, realizing that he had blundered, tried to accuse France of other wrongdoings. But Hitler signaled Laval to continue. Laval presented the remaining fourteen claims. Ciano was not saying a word. But in his *Journal*, he recorded Laval's success:

> The Germans, with the exception of Hitler, are charmed by Laval. They are eager to talk with him, to be near him. It's as if a great, dethroned lord had landed in the midst of newly rich boors. Ribbentrop, too, tries hard, but he ends up by committing a blunder. He reminds Laval that his "eminent compatriot" Napoleon once was in this same forest. Of course, [Ciano concludes humorously,] the circumstances had been somewhat different.[*]

Bichelonne, too, impressed the Germans with his penetrating intelligence, the breadth of his knowledge, and his talent for organization. Albert Speer was to remember particularly Bichelonne's dictum that "for efficiency, it was better that the French should work for the Germans on French soil rather than on German soil." From this remark, Speer conceived the idea of classifying French factories and relieving most of them from sending workers to Germany ("S-Betrieb"-protected enterprise).

Adjourning the meeting, Hitler announced that qualified experts would examine the demands of the French government. One month later, Schleier reported Hitler's decisions. Stern measures would be taken at once against any member of the Wehrmacht implicated in any black market traffic in France. General Keitel, commander in chief of the Wehrmacht, requested that the regional prefects inform the Kommendaturs of any such offenses known to the French police. Schleier added that he shared Laval's sense of outrage at these activities; it was not decent, he felt, that German soldiers living in France be treated better than their comrades fighting on the Soviet front.

Beginning March 1, moreover, traffic would be allowed to move freely throughout France. Mail service and trade would be reestablished with the departments of the north and the Pays-de-Calais. The checkpoints on the French-Belgian border would be put in the hands of the French authorities.

[*]Ciano, *Journal Politique*, p. 225.

THE LAST MEETING WITH HITLER

Although these successes to some extent mitigated France's hardships, 1943 began badly. On January 11, at a meeting of the German departmental chiefs, Sauckel attacked Laval and his government: "The Laval government consists only of specialists in the art of temporizing. If workers had arrived in Germany in time, new divisions could have been assembled, and the encirclement of Stalingrad would not have occurred."* On January 13, Sauckel demanded 250,000 workers by March 31, of whom 150,000 were to be skilled. For every three workers leaving for Germany, one prisoner would return to France.

On February 10, Bichelonne (who, since September 1, 1942, was handling the transfer of workers to Germany) reported the count. By that date, 76,000 had left, of whom 56,000 were skilled, and an additional 45,000, also skilled, would leave before March 31. That left a requirement of 129,000 men.

Bichelonne used the tactics recommended by Laval. He did not confront Sauckel with any positive refusal, but he made up administrative instructions that would slow down departures and make them more difficult in the future. To begin with, he ordered that a general census be taken of all French males born between January 1, 1912, and December 31, 1921.

Then he sponsored a bill (Act of February 16, 1943), relating to the department of Compulsory Work. Work was made compulsory for all young men born between January 1, 1920, and December 31, 1922, but farmers could not be forcibly displaced. The law also halted the recruitment of unskilled industrial and commercial workers and provided increased recruitment of men born in 1920, 1921, and 1922 and of men fitting certain other categories so as to replace subsequent losses of manpower. Exemptions were made for young men who worked as farmers, railroad workers, miners, firemen, and policemen. Students were given deferments until September 1943.

Departures for Germany had passed the 200,000 mark (March 31) when, on April 9, Sauckel formulated new demands: 120,000 men in May, 100,000 in June. But he was not aware that various developments in the Reich would enable Laval and Bichelonne to thread their way through these mounting difficulties. Rostov had just been recaptured by the Soviets, and the Wehrmacht was retreating on the Russian Front, while the Afrika Korps was forced to retreat as far as the Bizerte beachhead.

Hitler called in King Boris of Bulgaria, the "*Conducator*" Antonesco of

*Minutes of the meeting of January 11, at the OberKommando der Wehrmacht. U.S. Nuremberg Archives no. I.342 P.S.

94

Rumania, and Admiral Horthy, regent of Hungary. Laval was also notified by Schleier on April 28 that Hitler wanted to see him. Schleier would take Laval to Salzburg on the twenty-ninth, and they would proceed to Berchtesgaden on the thirtieth. When Schleier turned up, he was with the arch-collaborationist Fernand de Brinon. During the plane ride, the two men worked on Laval, stressing the need for France's total participation in the Reich's war effort. Laval sidestepped their remarks, using gestures to create the impression that the altitude had affected his hearing.

The next day, two cars escorted the travelers to a plane whose wings were decorated with red, white, and blue pennants. Laval understood from this that Hitler was trying to show him a degree of consideration, no doubt to soften him up for the heavy demands to come. Laval was right: Hitler wanted France's full contribution to the German war effort in order to "remake" Europe. Hitler wanted the French to help in the rapid manufacture of 10,000 planes and 20,000 tanks. But Speer, the Reich's minister for armament, to whom productivity was of the highest moment, had paid close attention to Bichelonne's presentation of December 1942. Bichelonne had stressed the point that the French worker performed much better when in France than when deported to Germany. Speer the producer was about to win out over Sauckel the recruiter.

While the discussion continued, each side clinging to its postiion, an idea was forming in Laval's mind. Since Hitler had spoken of "remaking Europe," Laval would present his own conception of Europe, a conception that had ripened slowly since he was in charge of French foreign policy before the war. It was undoubtedly then that the words he was to address to the French people on June 5 shaped themselves in his thought. After making that speech, he telephoned Babut, the editor of his newspaper *Le Moniteur du Puy-de-Dôme*, and asked him to print the text.

As far as material needs are concerned, nations will have to help one another and merge their economic interests so that the needs of each may be satisfied without resorting to competition and violence, as has been too often the rule in the past.

A new Europe will be an enduring one if the germs of revenge can be exterminated forever. In the past, peace was the result of compromise, of an equilibrium, or of coercion. The European peace of the future will have to be the result of associations and harmony.

In the sphere of mores, culture, and politics, each country's individuality will have to be respected. No country will be permitted to impose its customs, its religion, its regime, on other countries. But one thing is certain: all these regimes will have one thing in common: they will have a popular base.

Everywhere labor will have the importance it should have, for without this no political institutions can have validity, lacking as they would the strong support of the masses.

Laval was well ahead of the speakers and delegates who advocated "The Europe of Nations" at the various postwar congresses sponsored by Churchill and other heads of state from 1947 through 1949, when the Council of Europe set up a Consultative Assembly at Strasbourg.

THE LAVAL–SAUCKEL TUG-OF-WAR CONTINUES

The last face-to-face encounter between Laval and Hitler had ended in a draw, or rather in a point advantage for Laval, since the latter had not given in but convinced his opponent by sheer argument. The outcome had greatly upset Brinon, who wanted to satisfy the Führer's demands for male and even female workers.

The next day, Brinon announced the "failure" of the discussions to Déat and attributed their negative outcome to Laval. Déat entitled his editorial of June 4 in *L'Oeuvre* "After Mégève, Vichy Must Be Shut Down." A month later, the Francistes (a Fascist group founded by Marcel Bucard) joined Sauckel's men and plastered the walls of Paris with enormous posters urging, "Get rid of Laval!"

But that was a minor worry compared to Laval's anxiety regarding Sauckel's visit. He could picture the Gauleiter's anger and frustration at the hurdles put in the path of his third raid on French labor. In the meantime, the census of those born in 1920, 1921, and 1922 yielded the figure of 715,000 men, of whom 52,000 were unfit and 418,000 exempted (302,000 farmers, and 116,000 policemen, railroad workers, and miners). Theoretically, there remained 245,000 men available. But on April 15, 81,000 had left for Germany, and 7,000 had been sent to build the so-called "Atlantic Wall" at the Todt yards, reducing the number of available men to 157,000.

The Germans saw the number of "their" French workers decreasing daily. To mislead them further, Bichelonne set up the "work card," which certified that a man was working in France or medically exempted. All men who could not show a reason for exemption must submit to a medical examination and were to be sent to Germany. The occupation authorities tried to lay their hands on the 715,000 who had been counted, in order to satisfy Sauckel's demands.

At that very time, an official report from these same authorities noted that "all of France is conspiring to protect its youth."* During the spring of 1943,

---

*Report from Hemmens to Ribbentrop (in the author's possession).

the available young Frenchmen literally melted away, escaping deportation by means of false identity cards, altered work cards, false certificates of employment, medical dispensations, and false assignments to exempted firms. At the end of May, 21,000 were sent instead of the 120,000 demanded by Sauckel.

The Gauleiter insisted that a memorandum be issued on June 1, instructing "field Kommandanturs to ensure the recruitment of workers by any means necessary." On May 30, 31, and June 1, 5,200 from the "Youth Construction Sites" were sent to Germany; on July 1 and July 2, 9,554 more. In all of July, only 36,000 men would leave for Germany.°

Sauckel, enraged, took this as a personal insult. His inability to fulfill the goals he had announced to Hitler hurt his pride, and he was particularly angry with Laval, whose "elastic defense" he could not outwit. On August 6, Sauckel was in Paris to present new demands. Unverifiable rumors spoke of 300,000 men and 200,000 women. For seven hours Sauckel asked Laval for workers, and for seven hours Laval offered legal texts. Once more Laval had gained a few months' time. On August 9, Laval met with the regional prefects in Vichy to work out a continuing, silent, efficient resistance to Sauckel's demands.

Seeing himself hopelessly thwarted, Sauckel sent a secret report to Hitler, also on August 9:

> The French President of the Council of Ministers has strongly rejected the broader plan for the recruitment and the hiring of 500,000 French workers who were intended for compulsory labor in Germany before the end of 1943. The discussion lasted more than six hours. Laval was not able to offer truly solid reasons for his refusal. He keeps himself completely aloof from groups such as Doriot's and Bucard's. He has even had a falling out with them and wanted their dissolution. Laval's barely disguised refusal to carry out the task of sending significant contingents of workers to Germany puts the German ability to fulfill its purposes within the Reich in a very embarrassing position. I therefore felt compelled to address the following letter to the German chargé d'affaire and Ambassador (in Paris), party-member Schleier.

Sauckel had written to Schleier begging him to bring Laval to reason, and he incorporated that letter in his report to the Führer:

> After having reflected calmly and coolly, I must inform you that I have completely lost faith in the good faith and goodwill of the French prime minister. His refusal constitutes purely and simply a sabotaging of the fight for life against Bolshevism undertaken by Germany. This time, moreover, he made the worst possible impression upon me, espe-

---

°Edward Homze, *Foreign Labor in Nazi Germany* (Princeton, N.J.: Princeton University Press, 1967), pp. 177–200.

cially toward the end of our discussion, by his completely baseless and incoherent statements in answer to my clear and precise questions.

I am asking you to inform him that an immediate reappraisal of his stubborn refusal is his only chance to erase this bad impression, for I shall transmit the entire truth about his current methods to the Führer. I also noticed that the French ambassador, de Brinon, was most unfavorably impressed by the attitude of his prime minister.

Heil Hitler! Your Fritz Sauckel°

This letter shows Sauckel's naïveté. Having experienced Laval's strength of will, did Sauckel really believe that a "reprimand" from Schleier would change Laval?

Meanwhile, after his discussion with Hitler in April Laval was convinced that Speer's concern for productivity would outweigh Sauckel's stubborn desire for the deportation of French workers to Germany. Laval won permission for Bichelonne to negotiate with Speer at the beginning of September, and his reasoning proved accurate: under the new agreement, a large percentage of French factories were put under special protection, their workers safe from Sauckel's demands.

Bichelonne executed this mission with great success. The protected factories *(S-Betrieb)* would not be compelled to manufacture arms; they would produce consumer goods. And part of the production would be reserved for French use.†

During this period, millions of men and women of all the satellite and occupied countries of Europe were being dispatched on Sauckel's orders to forced labor in Germany. By involving Backe, the German minister of agriculture, and Speer, Laval halted the deportation of a productive segment of the French population. He enabled these people to work on their home ground, to work so that France might continue to live.

Recognizing that the number of French workers leaving for Germany was insignificant, Dr. Elmar Michel, director of the Economic Division of the German military administration in France, announced in 1943 that the Division would abandon its requests for more workers "in recognition of the efforts of the French government and in deference to the needs of the French economy."

Nevertheless, Sauckel redoubled his efforts to "recruit." Even though Hitler had sided with Speer on the deportation issue, he did not oust the fanatic Nazi, the old comrade-in-arms that Sauckel had been. So Sauckel not only continued to speak out against Speer's S-Betrieb, which in the spring of 1944 accounted for more than 10,000 factories, but he also continued to battle for

°Nuremberg Archives, ref. 5780/366/43.
†The reader can judge what hundreds of thousands of workers in the 14,000 French factories classified as S-Betrieb owed to Laval, Bichelonne, and Speer by consulting the excerpt from Speer's speech to the Gauleiters of the Reich (Posen on October 6, 1943) which is reprinted in Exhibit F.

his policy of "recruitment." Here he had an advantage over Speer, for unlike him, Sauckel made frequent trips to Paris.

He had no difficulty in pursuing his effort to draft workers, because the German government in 1943 had issued only a memorandum to stop recruiting, whereas only an official agreement between the two countries would have fully guaranteed its validity.

To strengthen his position, Sauckel called French Nazi sympathizers to his aid. He organized groups, drawn primarily from Jacques Doriot's Parti Populaire Français, and sent them around to recruit, arrest, and denounce workers to the German authorities. Laval had protested earlier to the embassy against this Doriotiste, pro-German police and had succeeded in having it partially neutralized. But in August 1943, Doriot, eager to please Sauckel, organized a parade of his followers along the Champs-Élysées in an effort to intimidate Laval and Laval's supporters.

On his side, Sauckel tried to force Laval's hand by arresting several high officials. Laval made his invariable strong protest and would not budge from his position. Sauckel demanded the deportation of 30,000 young men from the "Youth Construction Sites." Laval refused. At the end of September 1943, Ritter, Sauckel's representative in Paris, was assassinated. The SS made mass arrests in Paris. But on October 7, Bichelonne obtained Speer's agreement to grant amnesty instead of arresting the resisters, who had just been hired by the S-Betrieb. And simultaneously, Backe saved peasants and other agricultural workers from deportation, over Sauckel's protests.

PÉTAIN'S BLUNDER

Looking to the possibility of Germany's defeat, Pétain cherished the dream of giving back to the French people the sovereignty it had delegated to him in July 1940. He hoped for a return to the French Republic after four intervening years of "the French state." Although Pétain spoke of this from time to time, Laval preferred to avoid the subject. The marshal, encouraged by some of his aides, worked on his grand design in secret.

On November 13, he summoned Laval and read to him a new constitutional act intended to effect his plan. He also announced an imminent meeting of the Chambers of the National Assembly under the presidency of Jules Jeanneney. The representative of the Reich in Vichy was notified.

The marshal addressed the nation in the role of repository of sovereign power, the supreme and sole responsible leader. He made no mention of Laval. To initiate a change of Constitution in a country under the heel of an occupying power and to do so without directly informing the Reich were dangerous decisions. Laval feared the consequences he foresaw.

The day after the message, Abetz announced that he would visit Vichy. He arrived that same morning, bringing a word from Ribbentrop that he was to transmit "urgently" to the marshal. It was an indictment of the marshal; Ribbentrop accused him of never having meant to collaborate, of having favored the machinations of the "Anglo-Saxon faction" within his entourage, and of issuing a major decree without informing the German government.

After the indictment, the verdict: the Führer, would not tolerate the act or its intention. The security of the German army required a complete change in French policy. Henceforth, all bills, all decrees, would be submitted to the German government for prior approval. Those hostile to the Reich and now in the marshal's entourage would have to resign; committed collaborationists would replace them in the government. Ribbentrop then indicated that should Pétain wish to resign, the Reich would do nothing to dissuade him.

After some hours of reflection, the marshal was prepared to yield. In his reply he agreed to take on Darnand, whom he admired for his performance in the two wars; but he protested against including Déat in the government. Abetz, understanding the predicament, declared that he would leave it to the good faith of the head of state, giving him as much time as necessary to decide this last, thorny issue.

Lucien Romier, who had given the marshal the idea for the whole unlucky scheme, succumbed to a heart attack on January 5. On January 9, as Pétain left the funeral services for Romier, the marshal learned of the death of Colonel Bonhomme. The old man was strangely indifferent to the loss of one who had served him for so long and who had given up everything for him. Pétain made only one remark about him to me. "We must turn the page and not think about it anymore," he said. "Now we must only think about France's misfortunes." I was disconcerted by the serenity in those blue eyes, the freshness of that face, with its pink complexion, across which eighty-seven years had passed without leaving the slightest wrinkle.

Tracou, an energetic prefect and good diplomat who had just been named director of the Office of the Head of State, wanted to go to work discreetly and bring about a rapprochement between Pétain and Laval. I was not surprised, therefore, by an instruction from Pétain before my leaving for Paris: "Tell your father-in-law to come to see me every day and help me to get out of this nasty situation."

I knew all about this "nasty situation": its name was Renthe-Fink, the German minister instructed by Ribbentrop to keep an eye on Vichy. The marshal had spotted it, too: "This Renthe-Fink bothers the hell out of me." He went on without a break. "Is Josée still angry with me?"

An embarrassing question. "Less so, marshal."

Tracou took me aside in the hallway of the Hôtel du Parc: "From now on," he said, "there will be a more equitable distribution of the burden, which until now your father-in-law has carried almost entirely on his shoulders."

On January 10, the "collaborationists" held a rally in Paris to protest against the Vichy government. The followers of Doriot, Déat, and Bucard packed the meeting hall. I, too, was there, in dark glasses and hoping to be inconspicuous. Behind the podium hung a giant portrait of Pétain, draped in a tricolor ribbon, with the slogan "Down with Bolshevism." Everyone rose when Doriot entered in a German uniform, with a single decoration on his jacket—the Iron Cross. Déat and Bucard followed, but Doriot was the darling of the crowd, which chanted: "Doriot to power! Doriot to power!"

In the speeches that day, not a word was said about either de Gaulle or Pétain. Laval and the Vichy government were the punching bags the orators tirelessly assailed. Déat painted Laval as the "wait-and-see" politician, the nostalgic lover of the Third Republic, the protector of former members of Parliament, of Jews, and of Freemasons.

Doriot called for an end to Laval's government: "While blood is flowing in the East for the defense of Europe, the Government that betrays simultaneously the marshal and the Führer's crusade against Bolshevism must be eliminated." Sixteen thousand voices responded: "Laval to the wall! Laval to the wall!"

The stamping of feet on the stands raised a cloud of dust that entirely filled the hall.

Some weeks later, Laval told us that the Allied landing on the French coast would probably take place at the beginning of summer. A few days afterward, von Rundstedt and his staff came to Matignon to ask Laval to accelerate defense preparations. Seven departments on the Mediterranean coast were to be put under the same type of occupation as the North Atlantic zone, and the English Channel coast as well as the Mediterranean were to be evacuated. The inhabitants were to be brought to the Massif Central.

Laval told him it would be impossible to settle these 600,000 people from the north and south in an area already overflowing with refugees. Bichelonne supported Laval, detailing the insurmountable technical obstacles that such a massive transfer would entail. Von Rundstedt retreated; but the game was not yet won. Laval asked Jean-Marcel Lemoine (freshly added to the Ministry of the Interior so as to "cover" Darnand and Lacombe) to draft a "plan of refusal" for presentation to von Rundstedt's representative.

All prefects were alerted. They would have to fight to protect their populations, town halls, police stations, and hospitals from any invasion by the Todt organization, which had built the Atlantic wall, or by units of the Wehrmacht. Laval planned the eventual defense of the Camargue, which the Germans would want to flood, and of the northern industrial zone. Meanwhile, Cathala was to try to save Provence; Bichelonne, to maintain rail transportation and prevent thefts of locomotives and railroad cars.

The German military situation worsened daily, and Sauckel, despite the failure of his attempts to recruit forced labor since 1942, resumed his demands once again. On March 1, he declared before an assemblage of high officials in Berlin:

My program has been destroyed. The French think they will no longer be carried off to Germany. It has gone so far that all French prefectures have received general instructions not to satisfy my demands, since even the German authorities are arguing among themselves whether or not Sauckel is a madman. In the past two months, we have only brought 4,500 Frenchmen to Germany, which is nothing.

After complaining that it was the existence of too many "protected" factories that kept him from carrying out his mission, he concluded with a dire proposal:

How, then, can I be in charge and obtain forced labor from France? There is only one solution: the German authorities must cooperate among themselves, and if the French refuse to act in spite of all their promises, we Germans must use a particular case to set an example— if necessary, execute a prefect or a mayor who does not submit to the rules. Otherwise, there will not be a single Frenchman in Germany.[*]

Two weeks later, Sauckel arrived in Paris demanding an interview with Laval. But Laval had left the capital for Vichy to meet with the regional prefects. Enraged, Sauckel sent Hitler a secret report on March 17, 1944:

My Führer

The program of recruitment of workers for 1944, which I have set up according to your instructions and with your approval, was intended, among other things, to supply 1 million French workers. Only if we obtain these Frenchmen will it be possible for our goal of 4,050,000 recruits to be met.

The organizational measures required for the mobilization of these forces was taken, as far as my part is concerned, during the latter months of 1943. But the realization of my plan is now meeting with serious difficulties that go beyond my competence and that I must submit to you, asking you respectfully to make a decision.[†]

The "serious difficulties" amounted to an accusation against Speer, who, by favoring the creation in France of 14,000 protected factories, removed them from Sauckel's influence and thus "fixed" 1,440,000 workers on French soil. The Gauleiter added that more than 4 million Frenchmen (railroad and transportation workers, farmers, miners, members of the Todt organization, construction workers, naval employees, employees of the Wehrmacht, of the Waterways and Forest Administration, and the police) were actually benefiting from "unacceptable measures of protection."

[*]Archives of the Chief U.S. Counsel of War Crimes in Nüremberg.
[†]Ibid.

To improve his chances, Sauckel also asked Ribbentrop to pressure Abetz so that the latter should have Vichy install Déat in the government as minister of labor. The Gauleiter, whose brutish ways were matched by his incredible naïveté, took at face value Déat's words: "If I were minister of labor, Frenchmen would leave for Germany by the hundreds of thousands!"

In the end, Abetz called on Laval and outlined the situation. If Laval did not accept Déat, Ribbentrop was certain to recall Abetz immediately. Abetz urged Laval to accept Déat and then try to "neutralize" him.

So Laval "took" him. But since a regular ministry of labor had not been in existence for a long time, Déat found himself at the head of a phantom ministry, without officials or records. The only organizations over which he might have exercised jurisdiction—the National Relief, the S.I.P.E.G.,° the Prisoners, the Veterans, the Red Cross†—were withdrawn from the scope of his duties by Laval. Pétain, whom Tracou had apprised of the maneuver, gave his consent.

Laval could do no more than frustate the intentions of the occupying power in a country about to become a battlefield. Systematic bombardments preceded the landing: Paris-La Chapelle (640 dead), Fives-Lille (510), Rouen (850), Tours (130), Orléans (275), Lyon (610), St.-Étienne (870). As always in a climate of panic and disarray, there were cases of looting and violence (livestock stolen, farms burned, farmers killed), which the real resisters, those who faced the enemy, were the first to denounce.

These resisters had Laval's sympathy to such a degree that he never tolerated the slightest criticism of their behavior. He employed two assistants at the Hôtel Matignon in Paris, André Guénier and Marcel Guillaume, who spent almost all their time intervening with the German authorities on behalf of resisters who had been threatened or caught. Laval went further: at his printing press of his *Moniteur du Puy-de-Dôme*, more than 100 of the 255 employees were resisters with false papers and false identity cards.

APRIL 25 IN PARIS

On April 23, 1944, Paris and its suburbs were again heavily bombarded, leaving many dead and wounded. General Brécard, chancellor of the Legion of Honor, and the Prefects Bussière and Bouffet telephoned Vichy to request

---

° Interministerial Administration against the Effects of War

† For a history of the National Relief, the S.I.P.E.G., and the Red Cross, see Schedule G of the Appendix.

that Pétain attend a mass for the dead at Notre Dame. Abetz agreed to Laval's conditions for this service: no Germans were to be in uniform at Notre Dame, no Doriotistes, Déatists, or other Francístes. Monsignor Suhard, archbishop of Paris, and Pierre Laval alone would receive the marshal in front of the cathedral.

The head of state, escorted by his motorcycle guards, arrived early in the evening of April 24 at the prefecture of Melun. Dozens of children clung to the metal railing of the courtyard. Pétain went toward them and teased them with the tip of his cane: "You look as if you were in a cage!"

"Yes!"

"Well, my children, I want you to know, we are all in a cage!"

These words were repeated all over town.

The next morning, Pétain arrived at the Hôtel de Ville and proceeded through dense crowds to Notre Dame. Monsignor Suhard led Pétain to the choir. Then the entire government followed, except for Déat. The doors were opened wide, and the crowd surged in, huge, anonymous, deeply moved— a Paris crowd. A few handkerchiefs furtively wiped away a tear here and there; they belonged to the relatives of the first victims to be identified.

The archbishop turned to Pétain: "May God preserve the world from the ruin toward which it seems to be rushing. Marshal, we are grateful to you for having come to pray with us here, under the vaults of this cathedral, which has seen true Christian and French valor."

During the ceremony, the crowd outside had kept on making its way toward the doors of the cathedral, and when the marshal came out under the porch, he was acclaimed by a sea of humanity: it was his first greeting from the people of Paris.

A lunch was given at city hall and then a meeting of the municipal and departmental councillors and the officials of the prefecture. Laval guided the marshal as he made the rounds of the tables and talked to various persons. Outside, the Rue de Rivoli, the Avenue Victoria, and the *quais* were made dark by the masses or clusters of people on the ground or perched on rooftops. Suddenly, the crowd began to chant, "Up on the balcony! Up on the balcony!"

When Pétain and Laval appeared there, an immense roar went up, followed by the "Marseillaise," sung as if by a single voice from the throats of thousands. When silence finally returned, the marshal spoke.

"Today is my first visit to you. I hope to come again later, and then I will not have to notify our keepers. I shall be without them, and we shall all be at ease. See you soon, I hope."

The cheering increased; the shouts merged: "Long live Pétain! Long live Pétain! Long live Laval!"

Only then did my thoughts turn to Josée's absence and its cause. The thirteenth of December seemed far away. The two men in front of me clearly shared the same emotion. The marshal was surely telling himself that Laval was indeed his strongest support, the best in protecting and defending to the end whatever could still be protected and defended.

Time cover story on Laval as the Man of the Year, January 1931. Reprinted by permission from *Time* magazine.

In New York City with Mayor Jimmy Walker and Albert H. Wiggins

At the White House in 1931. Mrs. Hoover, Josée Laval, President Hoover, Pierre Laval.

With Chancellor Brüning in Berlin (Sept. 1931)

With Mussolini in Rome for the signing of the Agreements (January 1935)

Laval as Prime Minister defends his foreign policy aimed at Hitler in a 3-day debate, December 27–29, 1935.

At the French Foreign Office (1935). The back row: Laval, Eden, and Benes.

In Moscow with Stalin for the signing of the Pact with Russia against Hitler's rising threat. Molotov sits behind the desk.

With Litvinoff at the League of Nations after Germany began to rearm

Mme. Laval and her daughter arriving at the Versailles Hospital after Laval's near-assassination, 1941

In Vichy with Marshal Pétain

Last meeting with Hitler. From left to right: Dr. Schmidt, Laval, Hitler, Ciano, Goerring.

Sauckel, the "Slave Driver," in the lobby of the Ritz in Paris

Prisoners of War returning from Germany on the coach: "Thanks to you, Laval!"

In court: "I am willing to be the victim of a judicial crime, but I won't be an accomplice to it."

THE ALLIED LANDING

On June 6 at 4:30 A.M. news of the Allied landing reached Sauckel, who promptly drafted a letter to Abetz:

> The long-awaited invasion has finally begun. I am asking you urgently to obtain by ten o'clock tomorrow morning the signature of the French prime minister on a decree of mobilization of the class of '44 [those reaching military age in that year]. Under no circumstances will I accept any dilatory evasions.°

The letter arrived at 6:15, but Abetz did not call Laval at Châteldon. He waited for Sauckel's departure for Hitler's general headquarters and did not get in touch with Laval until ten o'clock.

As he had done two years earlier, on June 22, 1942, with his speech including the famous "I wish," Laval again "took on every risk to enable France to have her chance." Laval rejected the German demand. That afternoon and the following day, he sent telegrams to all the regional and departmental prefects, to the generals Martin and Perré (commanders, respectively of the gendarmerie and the military police, ordering them to oppose any collective or individual departures for Germany.

The struggle between Laval and Sauckel ended with victory for Laval, two months before the liberation of Paris.

In this protracted exhausting scrimmage, Laval's health was impaired. Bichelonne, who also fought night and day on two fronts, knew that he was suffering from an incurable illness. He was arrested and deported to Germany with Laval and died several weeks later, far from home, on the operating table of a German hospital. Before leaving, his consolation was to know that, together with his chief, he had succeeded in saving hundreds of thousands of French men and women from work deportation.

In his cell in Fresnes, as he was preparing his defense in the hope of making his voice heard, Laval summarized his conflict with Sauckel:

> When, on August 17, I was forced to leave Paris on the order of the German government, conveyed to me by the German ambassador in the presence of the SS, I declared that I was giving up any exercise of my powers and functions. It was then, as the Germans withdrew, that

---

°See Exhibit G for the complete text of this ultimatum (Sauckel to Abetz, June 6, 1944) and two excerpts from Nuremberg documents corroborating Laval's own ultimatum.

raids were carried out in our eastern provinces and that entire populations of French villages were deported to Germany for forced labor. France thus experienced for a few weeks the methods the Germans had applied for years throughout Europe, including northern Italy. That was the system we would have long endured in France if I had not negotiated, discussed, acted, and spoken as I did to thwart, blunt, and brake the aggressiveness of Sauckel and his army of manpower recruiters.

My crime, then, consisted in protecting several hundreds of thousands, or rather millions, of French men and women, who, had it not been for the government's action, would have certainly been deported to Germany. My crime was to obtain the release of 110,000 prisoners after Hitler himself had given the order that not one more prisoner was to be released.

On June 5, 1942, before the American landing in North Africa and the active organization of the Resistance, I was faced with an order from Sauckel requisitioning the entire French work force (men and women) for work in German factories. Twenty million French people were then working in factories and fields, and there was nothing to prevent the Reich from "helping itself" to this forced labor, as it was doing in Poland, in Holland, in Czechoslovakia and elsewhere. Between June 5, 1942, and July 30, 1944, 2,060,000 were demanded of France. Under the terms of Sauckel's order, these demands were unilateral, that is to say, without counteraction. By my efforts and those of the government and of the administration, the following balance sheet was established on July 30, 1944, after more than two years:

Departures

From June 5, 1942, to July 30, 1944—*641,500* (this figure makes no allowance for the tens of thousands of prisoners on leave, who remained in France after the expiration of their two-week leaves).

Counteraction

Returned prisoners, *110,000* (100,000 peasants, 10,000 medical workers).

Prisoners changed into "free" workers: *250,000*

April 15, 1943: beginning of the two-week leaves for prisoners who became "free" workers.

October 6, 1943: *Departures for Germany are suspended,* except on a direct-exchange basis, with the number of French workers in Germany remaining constant. It did not then exceed 400,000.

June 7, 1944: *the departures finally came to an end.*

As I come to the end of this summary, it is proper to note that the number of workers who left for Germany always remained smaller than that of liberated prisoners. The number of workers in Germany, including volunteers, never exceeded 670,000. After October 16, 1943, when I obtained the suspension of departures, it decreased steadily. The number of prisoners, which totaled about 3 million at the time of the armistice, dropped to 2 million after the massive liberations of the *Frontstalags* (harvest of 1940) and to 1,050,000 during the years 1941, 1942, and 1943.

All the other countries in Europe—Belgium, Holland, and Poland, etc.— were subject to drafts of men and women from between fifty to eighty per thousand of the total population, while the number for France, (without of course, counting the returned prisoners) was 13 workers per thousand of the population.

Can there be a stronger refutation of the accusations brought against me in the indictment? If what I state for the other countries in Europe is true—and it can easily be verified—what better justification can there be for the existence of a French government during the occupation?°

Beginning in May, the bombardments became ever more deadly. The landing was nearing; the Wehrmacht was preparing to confront the Allies. German demands became ever harsher. In this tragic situation, Pétain and Laval shared a difficult task. The head of state, whose advanced age and other circumstances kept him from going into the thick of the fray, visited the towns that were hardest hit by aerial attacks. By his presence, he brought comfort to the wounded who crowded the hospitals. In Nancy, Dijon, Lyon, and St.-Étienne, the people gave him the same moving reception as they had done in Paris.

Laval had to divide his energies between Vichy and Paris. He resisted the pressure of the occupying power as well as those of the Rassemblement National Populaire (R.N.P.) and the Parti Populaire Français (P.P.F.). This resistance was to be dramatically shown immediately after the landing. He began by refusing to follow the "advice" of the Parisian collaborators to move to Paris with the government. Without notifying the Germans and to prevent reprisals by the Wehrmacht against the civilian population, he announced to the world: "France is not in the war!"

He reaffirmed this position during a meeting of ministers on July 12, when he declared: "Only a few madmen are against me, and even they are hardly eager to fight." He replied to one attack only, namely, Admiral Platon's, who had written to his brother, "When France is being ravaged, I find it painful that the head of the government can declare that we are not at war. This man deserves not to be shot, but to be hanged—and he will be!" Laval responded with serene objectivity: "Platon is a brave soldier. He has to his credit a glorious part in the war—the defense of Dunkirk. But he should not get involved in politics."

°*Laval Parle*, pp. 128–130.

The head of the government was striving not only to protect the lives of the French civilians; he was also out to protect industrial property, which the Wehrmacht would have liked to appropriate for its own use, or failing that, to destroy by means of a scorched-earth policy.

LAVAL AND HERRIOT ARRESTED

After the Allied landing, the days of the Vichy government were numbered. Since Laval's declaration of neutrality on June 6 and his injunction against any departures for Germany, the Reich could only view the head of the government as an enemy. Foreseeing his imprisonment by the Germans, Laval did not want to leave France in a political vacuum. He hoped to reestablish the Republic he had put to sleep so that its caretaker might defend France more effectively from the demands of the occupying power. Laval had in fact, taken care to specify that the important committees of the Chamber of the Senate could, if necessary, meet at a moment's notice. He had, in effect, maintained the legal continuity of the Republic.

What remained to be done was to bring it back to conscious life by convening the National Assembly. For this he needed the agreement of Edouard Herriot, the president of the Chamber of Deputies. Herriot, one of the great figures of the Third Republic, had retained the confidence of the majority of the parliamentary groups. Living under German surveillance in Maréville, near Nancy, Herriot was a true resister. He was the man of the hour, the right man for the change of government, to which Laval intended to give the solemnity it deserved. But it had to be done quickly.

On the morning of August 9, Laval began by convening the members of the Municipal Council of Paris, presided over by Mr. Taittinger, and those of the Departmental Council of the Seine, presided over by Mr. Victor Constant. He informed them of his intentions, and after being assured of their agreement, he had a communiqué published on the following day, August 10, in which he said that he had "given his colleagues the reasons for his return to Paris and told them of his desire to remain among the people of Paris."

On Friday, August 11, he saw a steady procession of former members of Parliament at Matignon, some of whom had just left a semiunderground existence. All of them agreed with Laval. That evening he received the eighty-seven mayors of the Paris *arrondissements* and suburbs, a majority of whom had been elected as Socialists, Communists, or Radicals. He presented his plan, whose keystone was Herriot's return. At the close of the meeting, the "87" unanimously adopted the following resolution:

> The members of the Union of Mayors of the department of the Seine wish to express to Prime Minister Laval, head of the government, the assurance of their affectionate and faithful friendship. They further assure him of their entire confidence in his proposed action, being persuaded that in his love for the wounded fatherland, he will find the safe path on which to lead the country to its revival. Being deeply devoted to his person, they are happy that by their cohesion they are able to set an example of unity and discipline, while their sole ambition remains service to their country.°

Meanwhile, at Laval's request, Abetz had arrived. Laval asked him to allow the convocation of the National Assembly, as German defeat was clearly inevitable. Abetz telephoned Ribbentrop and then gave Laval his consent.

After that, it was a race against time. The next morning, in Maréville, Laval saw Herriot, who agreed to the plan. The two arrived at the prefecture of the Seine on the morning of the thirteenth. Laval ordered the premises of the president of the Chamber, still occupied by the Germans, vacated immediately. On Herriot's advice, he tried to get hold of Jeanneney, the president of the Senate, in Grenoble. At the same time, he negotiated with the Germans and Swedish Consul General Nordling about the protection of Paris. On August 14, he prevented the destruction of the central power stations, and on the fifteenth, he received Abetz's assurance that the Wehrmacht would be under orders not to defend the capital.

But Laval had not reckoned with Déat and Brinon. During the morning of the sixteenth, Laval got a telephone call from the prefect watching the two men: they had left for Germany, but not before Déat had seen General Oberg, to whom he had denounced the "treason" of Laval and Herriot's project. The SS chief had immediately informed Himmler, who according to the prefect, ordered Herriot and the members of the French government arrested.

At eleven that evening, the prefect of the Seine notified Laval that the German police had just arrived at his prefecture with orders to return Herriot to Maréville. Laval went at once to city hall, where he argued with SS Captain Nosek against the arrest of the president of the National Assembly. Then he telephoned Abetz, who joined them without delay. Laval and Herriot protested indignantly.

Laval put his protest in written form and handed it to Abetz. Herriot did the same. These were letters of desperation, written in the slim hope that the ambassador would succeed in persuading his government to reverse its deci-

°See Exhibit H for the full text of the August 11 resolution and its eighty-seven signatures.

sion. It was agreed that M. and Mme. Herriot would spend the night at the prefecture and would see Abetz again at Matignon the next day.

On August 17, at 12:30 P.M., Abetz arrived for lunch, dismayed. He could only confirm the orders from Berlin, already being carried out. Herriot and Laval were prisoners. After lunch, President Herriot would be transferred to the prefecture of the Seine. Laval and the government were to leave that evening, Eastward bound.°

Before leaving, Laval managed to send a letter to Pierre Taittinger and Victor Constant, in which he expressed his gratitude and confidence in them, adding, "In the perspective of history, my role and my love for France will be better understood."

I went immediately to city hall. The prefect of the Seine took me into his apartment and whispered, "There is a side exit downstairs that leads to the sewers and through which they could easily escape." I entered the drawing room, gave Herriot a few books, and offered him my last cigar. He thanked me and said, "Your father-in-law and I have not always agreed. But the other day in Maréville, we did, so as to convene the National Assembly. He has the right to explain himself before the elected representatives of the country. It was even his duty to do it, and now, here we are in this mess."

I answered him in a low voice. "There is a side exit that is not watched, and I propose, with the prefect's agreement, that you both escape with me through the sewers. I will hide you in Passy in a little flat that an American let me have in case of need."

He looked at me in silence for a moment; then he alternately raised and lowered his right and left hands, as if weighing the pros and cons. Finally, he shook his head and whispered "I must follow my fate," then pulled me to him and embraced me.

SIGMARINGEN, MONJUICH: LAVAL BETRAYED

Josée and I were in danger of spending the last days of the occupation in a German prison, followed by incarceration in a French one. We had to disappear as quickly as possible. We found refuge with our American friend Seymour Weller, whom I had helped to become a naturalized Frenchman

°In 1947, Josée wrote an account of this last meal at Matignon; it will be found in Exhibit I.

before the war and who had generously offered to hide Herriot. We did not know if there was a warrant out for our arrest, and our great worry was not to add to Laval's grief a possible radio announcement of his daughter's arrest. Still, I decided to keep in touch with my office and arranged for meetings with a colleague.

The winter went by without any news of the internees of Sigmaringen. We were unaware even of Ribbentrop's decision to punish Laval by deporting him to Silesia. When he heard of Ribbentrop's order, Jacques Guérard got in touch with the sculptor Arno Breker in Düsseldorf. Angered, this friend of Speer's rushed to Hitler's headquarters, where he saw Bormann, who obtained the annulment of the order from his chief.

On May 8, the Germans officially surrendered. Paris, however, had been liberated since the Battle of France of August 24, 1944. At that time, General de Gaulle and his provisional government (formed at Algiers more than a year before) had assumed power, unopposed.

During the first days of June, the radio and the newspapers announced the arrival and "provisional" internment of Laval in Spain. He and Mme. Laval, along with Gabolde, the minister of justice, and Bonnard, the minister of education, were put in the Monjuich fortress, which overlooks Barcelona. On June 22, a Spaniard knocked at my father's door and handed him a brief message, without envelope, written in Laval's hand:

Monjuich Fortress   *Tuesday, June 5, 1945*

Dear General,

You have heard of my situation on the radio. I don't know where the children are: in Paris? In the United States? Perhaps even in Italy, as someone told me.

I am waiting for an answer by letter on which you will decide together and which will tell me whether I can return home right now or whether I should postpone my return. This is advice I absolutely need; you will supply it on the basis of information you have. I will act as you advise.

We were very unhappy in Germany. Our thoughts were constantly with all of you. My wife and I want you to know all the love we feel for you; we kiss all four of you.

Signed: *Pierre Laval*

P.S. Many kisses for my little Josée and my little Bunny. Your mother is brave, she sends you all many kisses.

This note took twenty-two days to reach my father. We immediately got together with two Spaniards: the painter José-Maria Sert, a friend from the time I opened my office and whose lawyer I was, and Carmen de la Torre, counselor at the Spanish embassy. The latter agreed to transmit my father's answer to José Felix de Lequerica, the former Spanish ambassador in Paris and in Vichy, who had become Franco's minister of foreign affairs.

Dear Prime Minister and friend,

Clara and I were very much moved by your letter of June 5, which we only received on June 27! A few weeks ago, one of your faithful servants, who was deported along with you, arrived safely in France with his comrades. After having been very well received at the head-quarters of one of the American armies in Germany, he came to see us. From him we learned of the difficult ordeal you have undergone and of your moral and physical suffering. What a joy it is for us to think that at least the latter has come to an end! The children have not stopped thinking of you since that sad evening almost eleven months ago when you were taken away from them.

You are asking me for advice. Should you stay where you are for a time or return to France immediately? The answer is clear to anyone watching France every day. You should stay there and wait for the day when those who defended the country inch by inch during the hard years of the occupation will be able to speak freely without being automatically condemned.

The advice I am giving you, in all certainty, is the same that all your friends from the Palais would give you. Nothing is more significant than the vain protest raised solemnly and unanimously with the government several months ago by the Council of the Order of the Bar of Paris against the illegal courts of justice, with partial jury members, and the regular suppression of the rights of defense.

This is also the advice of all your political friends who wish you well and who are silently and powerlessly watching the campaigns of defamation on the radio and in the press. Newspapers today have received permission to defame you but not to defend you. It is their duty to write that Pierre Laval worked for Germany. They are not permitted to show, with the aid of proof, that when faced with Germany's ever-increasing demands, the head of the government, his colleagues, his prefects, defended France's patrimony and her interests.

Finally, it is the advice that all your colleagues, whose faithfulness and loyalty to you are touching, would give you. All of them are waiting for the day when passions will have calmed down a little and it will be possible for you to give an accounting of your administration.

I have spoken of your possible return to some American friends who have come back to Paris. They are saddened to find our country in its present state and hope for an early improvement. All of them have said that for you to return now would be sheer madness. Those who have returned after an absence of five years are beginning to under-stand the intent of your effort to help France survive, and for the past few weeks I have had the impression that America, which did not understand the aim of your policy, is beginning to have its eyes opened. The United States is perceiving the danger of Soviet expansionism. Once again, you saw too far ahead too soon. In 1935, when you saved peace abroad by a wise policy of economic adjustment, you were right again too early.

I forgot to tell you that my brother, the ambassador, agrees with me. So stay in Spain for a time and try to keep up the courage, the patience, and the calm that you have never lacked.

You remember our conversations when I spoke to you about the Moroccan War; my only disagreement with Lyautey was about the Spanish business. I always thought that our policy should be based on agreements with our neighbors, which accounts for my conversations with Primo de Rivera in Larache and in Fez, when he was commanding the troops of Spanish Morocco and of Sanjurjo. I have not changed my mind. I know of your friendship for Spain, whose language you have spoken since your youth, and something tells me that the day will come when you will be as happy to have enjoyed Spanish hospitality as Spain will be to have offered it to you.

All four of us embrace you affectionately

A. de Chambrun

My father was wrong about the value of Spanish hospitality. Lequerica, Pierre Laval's presumed friend, intercepted the letter. Laval was to learn its contents only in Fresnes, when Josée came to see him. General de Gaulle demanded that Laval be immediately handed over to French "justice." Franco acceded to the request, ordering Laval brought not to the border of France, but to the exact spot from which he had left Germany. This spot happened to fall in the American-occupied zone. A few hours after his arrival, Laval was turned over to the French police, who seized his luggage and all the documents that I was to discover twenty-seven years later at the Palais Soubise. Early in August, he was jailed in the political section of Fresnes, whereas Mme. Laval, who could be accused only of being the wife of her husband, was put with the common criminals. She was freed a few days before the beginning of her husband's trial. Shortly after the incarceration and during Pétain's trial, the press, under orders from Minister of Justice Teitgen, announced that the pretrial hearings of the "Laval affair" would begin in September and continue into October.

For Josée to see her father, she needed a permit. The request had to be presented by a lawyer to the court. Josée went to the president of the bar, Poignard, who chose Jacques Baraduc. He had graduated second in his class, and he suggested to the president of the bar and to Josée that he join forces with the first ranking of that same class, Albert Naud. Several days later, Yves-Frédéric Jaffré joined the defense team.

Every evening after his return from interviewing Laval in Fresnes, Baraduc wrote down notes, which were typed in my office the next day. Every day I gave him those that I dictated myself for him and for my father-in-law.

Almost immediately after the trial, Baraduc published a summary of his notes in the form of a book entitled *Dans la Cellule de Pierre Laval (In Pierre Laval's Cell)*.° The collection of our notes, his and mine, makes it possible to follow exactly the unfolding tragedy of Laval's "trial."

THE JUDICIAL CRIME

Tuesday, August 21. Mr. Bouchardon (the first examining magistrate of the High Court of Justice) received Mr. Naud and Mr. Baraduc. "The pretrial hearings will be unavoidably long," he told them. Mr. Béteille, his assistant, added that the first and second interrogatory examinations would take place on September 6 and 25, and predicted that the hearings would take up October and November. He handed them a "Schedule of the Investigation" divided into three parts: "Origins of the Betrayal," "Consummation of the Betrayal," and "Execution of the Betrayal." This plan included a minimum of twenty-five hearings. Only five took place.

Wednesday, August 22. Baraduc related to Laval his visit to Bouchardon and Béteille, and gave him the schedule. "That's fine," said Laval, "but I don't believe in it. They are in a much greater hurry." After a moment's scrutiny, he added, "Get me a copy of the indictment as quickly as possible. They may be able to criticize my methods, but they can't reproach me for my motives."

Thursday, August 23. In the first interrogation at the Palais-Bourbon, Mr. Bouchardon read the conclusions of the report prepared by auditors concerning Laval's finances. He accused Laval of having purchased a town house, the Villa Saïd, in 1925 and le *Moniteur du Puy-de-Dôme* and Radio-Lyon in 1927, when, according to the auditor, he had no private means.

Mr. Bouchardon continued: "Today, your net worth is 57 million (570,000 francs in today's currency). Would you like to explain?"

"What's your auditor's name?" Laval replied.

"Caujolle."

"Well, he's a fool!"

Then Laval corrected errors of dates and figures, while M. Bouchardon lowered his eyes.

° Paris: (Editions Self), 1948.

Laval clasped Baraduc's arm: "As far as the *Moniteur* and Radio-Lyon are concerned, I bought the larger part of the shares of these companies with a loan." From an apparently empty briefcase, he drew out a worn-looking piece of paper—the loan form. He read it, folded it up again, and put it away. "You see," he went on, "I was so little disposed to undertake these transactions that when some people suggested that I buy a radio station, I told my friends that I didn't need it. I already had one in my dining room. Radio-Lyon, Mr. President, was a very bad deal in 1927. But that's how I am. I always like what looks as if it might fail."

The stenographer did not take anything down. Mr. Bouchardon did not say anything. He smiled a few times. Then he began to ask questions about the annexation of Alsace-Lorraine by the Germans, the law concerning Jews, the persecution of Freemasons, manpower, the scuttling of the fleet. It would have been impossible to reply to everything in one hour. Laval, ever ready to explain, replied invariably, "I will answer you by memorandum."

Baraduc pointed out to him the danger of such promises. The examination could not be carried on by correspondence. Laval promised to limit his written answers to explaining the sources of his investments.

Friday, August 24. Laval met with Baraduc. "The method of questioning used yesterday shows that the decision has been made to move ahead fast. Do you want me to tell you the scenario? There will be neither examination nor trial. I shall be found guilty and eliminated—before the elections!"

He showed so little emotion he might have been speaking of someone else. After a moment, he added, "This, after all, is not a matter for a justice of the peace! Bouchardon shows me a memorandum dated 1943, dealing with manpower, and he asks me whether I signed it. That is perfectly meaningless! If it has my signature, it's clear that I signed it, and there's no need to question me to find that out! What is needed is to examine the political conditions that led me to sign it. But to do that you need a real investigation. Administration officials must be questioned. Those who saw me live and act must be questioned.

"I have a good memory; that's clear. They're always talking about my memory. But I don't have any papers left. They have taken everything away. And when I ask to get in touch with my ministers, they refuse my request!"

Saturday, August 25. Laval handed Baraduc a note referring to Thursday's questioning: "A hurried trial like mine cannot be just. It has all the appearance of a formality to ratify a verdict already reached. That is what we must try to prevent.

"Did I tell you," he added, "that during the occupation Bouchardon asked me to intervene in behalf of his son?"

Laval was completely surprised when Baraduc mentioned the name of the deputy whom Bouchardon had asked to present that request.

Thursday, September 6. That afternoon, Mr. Béteille questioned Laval about his policies toward the Jews. The magistrate seemed to wish to postpone long explanations. He said as much by the end of the questioning, making it look as if Laval's answers had caught him off guard. The judge also made an odd mistake. Mentioning the law of May 8, 1942, he added, most likely to stigmatize it, "A law which bears your signature and which created the 'General Office for the Jewish Question.'"

Laval replied that this bureau had been created in 1941, when he was not in the government.

"It's not to the point that the organization was created earlier," answered Mr. Béteille.

"If it's not to the point," replied Laval, "why do you stress it?"

Friday, September 7. During a long discussion at home, my wife told Baraduc that she had been secretly approached by Mr. de Chevigné, the editor of a strongly progovernment newspaper, *Carrefour.* She returned greatly disconcerted from the encounter. The newspaper had proposed that if Laval agreed to reveal to them what he alone knew about the actions of the French Communist party and of Edouard Herriot, the trial would be postponed. Furthermore, if Josée did not wish the newspaper to use the information, the reporter would "vanish," and the documents would simply be put quietly on General de Gaulle's desk.

Josée retorted that she had surely not been asked to come and discuss an offer of that sort, which there was little chance would be accepted. "Your father," the editor answered, "will perhaps not say no. He might be glad to establish a link between his cell and the outside world, no matter how thin the thread."

Baraduc submitted the proposition to Laval; he did not have the chance to finish speaking. Laval looked at him furiously, and changing the confidential tone his voice usually assumed in the visiting room of the prison, he shouted, "What do they take me for? If that's how it is, you can tell them I won't say another thing. If they don't want to help me for the sake of the truth, let them stay away. I don't need them. And I won't lean on anyone— anyone, do you hear—in order to save myself."

Saturday, September 8. Béteille questioned Laval about the "Légion Tricolore." Obviously, the part played by Benoist-Méchin was in question. Laval tried to explain, then asked that Bousquet be questioned: "You would then learn a lot about what you refer to as my sympathy for the L.V.F.!° Please believe that the dislike was mutual!"

Béteille stared into space, but Laval looked directly at him. "Bousquet would tell you how he had to ensure my security with respect to certain members of the L.V.F. But he won't tell you if you don't ask him."

As always, at the point where the hearings were touching the most delicate subjects, the recording clerk put his pen down.

"God, how intelligent you are!" Béteille exclaimed.

"Oh!" Laval answered ironically, "it has nothing to do with my intelligence. We've gotten beyond that. Anyway, believe me, if I were as intel-

°Legion of French Volunteers against Bolshevism.

ligent as all that, I wouldn't be here—standing before you!" Laval smiled broadly at his questioner: "It's you, Your Honor, who are intelligent. You are a great magistrate. You have always been a great magistrate. You were a great magistrate at Riom."°

"At Riom I was coerced!"

"Of course you were coerced. You are always being coerced, and I certainly hope that today you are not questioning me voluntarily!"

Tuesday, September 11. Beginning with the brief question period on legal exceptions, it became clear that the schedule of the investigation was no longer being followed, nor were the assurances that had been given respected. The questioning speeded up in an alarming way.

After Laval had said, "Of course I signed that law!" he at once requested that Bousquet and Dayras, the secretary general of the Ministry of Justice, be questioned. He recalled Heydrich's dire demands and how Bousquet had succeeded in rejecting them. Béteille did not interrupt. Laval dictated directly to the recording clerk until six o'clock, when the judge deferred the remaining explanations to another day. Laval had reached the events of December 1942 and his refusal to permit the transfer of political prisoners to the occupied zone.

Wednesday, September 12. From the newspapers, the lawyers for the defense learned that the hearings had been terminated.

Thursday, September 13. Laval is taken in a police car to the public prosecutor's office, Rue Boissy-d'Anglas, in compliance with a summons of Examining Magistrate Ma, in charge of the "case" of Mme. Laval.

The judge, much embarrassed, asked "Monsieur" Laval to make a deposition about Mme. Laval by dictating to the recording clerk. Fearing a possible change in the wording, my father-in-law replied that he preferred to write down his "testimony." The judge said he had no blank paper except what was reserved for the record of the proceedings. On Laval's insistence, he left his office to ask for orders from the Ministry of Justice. The decision, finally made and transmitted, gave the judge permission to let Laval have pen and ink and some paper. On the spot he composed a moving, six-page sketch of Mme. Laval and her behavior during the occupation.

I have inserted this sketch in Exhibit K, having obtained it in circumstances that are themselves suggestive about the events under review. After Laval's death, I had asked a divisional commissioner—the same one who had procured a passport for me to go to England in 1947—to copy those pages from Mme. Laval's dossier. He found the dossier, but it contained only her discharge papers. In 1954, Judge Ma, forced to leave his position, came to ask me a favor and offered me in return these pages, which he had "kept as a souvenir of the prime minister."

° The place where the last leaders of the Third Republic and two of its generals were tried as responsible for the defeat of 1940. Pétain, who had instigated the trial in 1942, thought it best to cut it short, with no verdict rendered, because the defense implicated him in the defeat.

Saturday, September 15. It was rumored that the government had ordered the sudden closure of the investigation. Tuesday's questioning had been halted only because of the lateness of the hour, and Béteille was supposed to resume the following week. Was it conceivable that an "investigation" that had not even begun could be closed?

Laval did not believe the news was likely. "But," he added, "where there's smoke, there's fire—and there does seem to be a lot of smoke!"

Sunday, September 16. Nothing confirmed the rumor. Baraduc found Laval very calm. He had worked during the night and written many pages in reply to the indictment.

Monday, September 17. Complete silence from the Palais-Bourbon. No further summons to court.

Tuesday, September 18. The press announced the closure of the examination. Laval could not stop whispering as he read the newspaper, "That's awful! That's awful!" He smoked constantly, and his darting glances frightened us. He was looking for an answer to the unanswerable, for an exit where none existed.

In spite of all indications, Baraduc tried to reassure him by telling him that he had received no official notice and by reminding him that Tuesday's examination had not been completed.

Wednesday, September 19. Both Naud and Baraduc received letters from the High Court, signed by Counsellor Schnedecker. The press had been right: the investigation had been suddenly broken off and closed without notice to the defense:

HIGH COURT OF JUSTICE

Paris, September 18, 1945

Dear Sir:

In a letter dated today, Chief Justice Mongibeaux has requested the Investigative Commission to adopt a new schedule of investigation. In the absence of Mr. Béteille, the president and I have been charged with the responsibility for proceeding with the investigation.

I therefore have the honor of informing you that your client, Pierre Laval, will be questioned next Thursday, Friday, and Saturday at 2 P.M. at the Palais-Bourbon. There is, moreover, reason to assume that another interrogation may take place on Saturday morning, September 22, at 9:00 A.M. at the Fresnes prison.

Please accept, dear sir, the expression of my highest regard.

Signed: *Schnedecker*

Béteille had gone on vacation, as he had said he would. Did the prosecution suppose that the defense could be prepared in a few hours? Naud and

Baraduc wrote to Bouchardon, protesting against the suppression of all relevant facts and declaring that if the rights of the defense were not accorded proper respect, they would ask the president of the bar to relieve them of their duty.

As Baraduc was about to leave on that day, Laval detained him: "I forgot to tell you the most important thing. Do you know what I've just found out? It seems that I intervened with the Germans in order to save Teitgen's father. Yes, Minister of Justice Teitgen's father. I didn't remember it: before 1944, the name Teitgen didn't mean anything to me. But now I remember what I did.° So there it is—Bouchardon asked me to save his son, Teitgen his father, and today they reproach me for not having fled with the others to North Africa!"

Thursday, September 20. President Gibert questioned Laval about the Antilles and certain telegrams to Admiral Robert. Gibert, reported as being hostile to Laval, was very courteous. Nevertheless, one of his remarks irritated Laval, who threw his glasses down on the table: "Look here, you are a bunch of incompetents. I am sorry to say this, Mr. President, and I am not attacking you personally. But really, you are a bunch of incompetents. If my case were being investigated by political men, I would never be asked the kinds of questions you are asking!" After a pause, which showed how tired he was, he added, "You know, Your Honor, your profession is something you can learn; mine is too. You are a learned magistrate, but an ignorant political man."

Then Schnedecker questioned Laval about the merchant marine. When Baraduc asked to be permitted to consult the file containing the charges (which had never been given to the defense), the magistrate gestured vaguely. Baraduc insisted. "Impossible," said Schnedecker, "the file is in Béteille's safe, and Béteille took the keys with him on vacation."

Saturday, September 22. Early in the morning, Laval wrote to the minister of justice to protest against the unexpected closure of the investigation. "I do not fear justice when it is based on truth. I ask that a bright light be turned full upon my person, my policies, and my actions."

At nine o'clock in the Fresnes library, Schnedecker interrogated Laval about the flight of enemy planes over the free zone. None of the relevant telegrams put before Laval bore his signature. But it appeared that one of them was signed by General Revers, chief of staff of the army of the armistice. Laval leaned back toward Baraduc: "No word to the press! That name would really cause an uproar!"

° Note by Baraduc: "The appeal was made by Mr. Georges Prade, in the name of Mr. Amaury, the present director of the Agence Française de Presse and of Mr. Yves Fournis, the son-in-law of Mr. Henri Teitgen. Though Pierre Laval was unable to prevent Mr. Teitgen's deportation, he at least succeeded in protecting him from the military tribunal of Nancy, where his death sentence was considered a foregone conclusion" (*Dans la Cellule de Laval* (Pans: Self), 1948, p. 88). See also Prade's deposition, the Hoover Institution, no. 283.

The investigation continued from 2:00 to 6:00 P.M. in Gibert's office. Laval was questioned only about the fate awaiting Max Dormoy's murderers and the attack against Menthon on the shores of the lake of Annecy. Laval was not in power at the time of Dormoy's murder in Montélimar. But in connection with this tragic event Laval evoked the death of Mandel, who had been a minister of the interior and a friend of Laval's. "Can you understand, Your Honor, that on the evening when this horrible crime came to light, my wife and I wept? A friend had been shot down!" He reminded Gibert that he had saved Menthon's father. "If I saved the father, it was not in order to plot the stupid attack against the son. What is more, those are not my ways."

Gibert came to the end of his questions: "But all that is really of no importance in your case."

"If it's of no importance, why question me about it?"

Baraduc wrote in his notebook: "During this entire 'investigation,' everything loses its importance as soon as Laval has answered the question!"°

At 6:00 P.M., tired and irritated, Laval raised one last protest and insisted that it be entered on the record. He reminded the court that although accused of plotting against the internal security of the state, he was not questioned about his role in the National Assembly. And although accused of complicity with the enemy, he was also not questioned about Montoire or about all his negotiations with the German government. He ended by asking for "the natural right to defend himself that belongs to every accused."

He rose up, collected a few papers, and in a muffled voice, added, "Really! I've never seen anything like it: it's the accused who keeps asking that everything be brought out in the open!"

Sunday, September 23. Baraduc tried to compose a first list of witnesses. Next to each name he wrote Laval's brief appraisal of the witness. Laval listed as many opponents as friends. He expected the truth from all of them. "After all, when I shall look them in the eye . . . ," he began.

He was thinking of all those whom he had warned of danger, whom he had helped, protected, saved. Some were old socialist comrades; others, various people of note. Suddenly, he changed his mind. "Cross all that out! I'm not going to defend myself like a subprefect." His face lit up. "I don't want to *defend* myself. I want to *explain* myself. I want to justify everything I have done."

While asking him not to use it right away, Laval gave Baraduc a note:

Witnesses? That's an essential matter; we discussed it yesterday. General Denain, very important. The son of Cachin.

Warn Le Troquer that I will call him in order to testify that I advised him by telephone to leave the region—I knew the Germans were looking for him; that I promised him to ensure Léon Blum's

°Baraduc, *Dans la Cellule,* p. 97.

safety, that I had his secretary freed immediately when she was arrested in Châteldon. Inform Sadoul that I will have him called as a witness.

Monday, September 24. Laval was gloomy, convinced that after the sabotaging of the investigation, the sabotage of the trial itself would follow. He handed Baraduc a set of answers that settled the manpower question and asked that I have them copied in my office as quickly as possible.

Friday, September 28. Baraduc told us, "The prime minister is not in good spirits today."

Sunday, September 30. The investigating commission of the High Court, wanting to justify the sudden closure of the investigation, wrote that "under the terms of Article 270 of the Code of Criminal Investigation, it did not appear that research could be pushed further with any hope of obtaining results offering greater certainty."

"That's straight out of Molière!" said Laval in a tone of complete detachment.

Mme. Laval, released from prison the previous Tuesday, wrote to the minister of justice:

6B. Place du Palais-Bourbon   *September 30, 1945*

Mr. Secretary:

On August 17, 1944, Prime Minister Laval was deported to Germany, and I followed him into exile. After I arrived with him in Paris, on August 1, I was imprisoned in Fresnes and kept in solitary confinement until last Tuesday.

I am now happy to the extent that I have been able to see and embrace my children and I have only one further wish: to be with my husband and to watch over his health, which I have had to do for years.

I would be deeply grateful to you if you were to permit me to join him in his cell as soon as possible.

I wish you to believe, Mr. Secretary, in my most sincere sentiments.

Mme. Pierre Laval

On Monday morning, I took the letter to the Ministry, Place Vendôme, but Teitgen did not answer it.

Tuesday, October 2. The immediate start of the trial ("before the elections") was announced. Laval finished his notes hurriedly. Late at night, he replied to the capital charge of "having humiliated France."°

°The reader will find these last pages reproduced in Exhibit N.

Wednesday, October 3. Early in the morning, Laval was transferred to a temporary prison for the duration of the trial. He wanted to remain in Fresnes or to be housed in the Palais de Justice in the outbuildings belonging to the First Chamber, as the marshal had been. He was refused.

Baraduc met with hostility. His visitor's permit was checked; he was told that it was not visiting hours and that lawyers did not have special privileges. As he continued to object, his name was entered on the register near the door, and he was given a number on a metal counter: "If you want to get out again, don't lose it!" The remark seemed just barely ironic: it was not a prison but a dungeon.

At the bottom of a dark little staircase, Baraduc ran into Laval, preceded by one guard and followed by another. He regretted leaving Fresnes, but he did not complain. Instead of the two cells he had been promised, he had only one, which was dark and had no table.

As he headed toward the visiting room, he realized that he had forgotten to bring down two bundles of documents. He naturally tried to retrace his steps, but the guards stopped him. They insisted that nothing be brought to the visiting room. Laval threw his briefcase on the floor: "Don't tell me that I have the right to defend myself! Don't say that you intend to judge me! Just say that you intend to put me away like a dog!"

The guards, embarrassed, went back upstairs to get the files, and together with Naud, who had just arrived, all went to the visiting room, a windowless place that led to the main hall through a glass door. The transom in the upper part was open, so that the three guards on duty could follow the entire conversation. They did not let the three captives out of their sight. Naud and Baraduc were indignant, but Laval calmed them down.

"Don't say anything. You can see there's nothing to be done. If that's how it is, that's how it is."

When his lawyers gave Laval some pâté wrapped in dough, a guard opened the door to say that it was not permitted.

"Have some!" said Laval.

That did it: they all shared.

At 1:00 P.M. Naud and Baraduc met Laval again, at the Supreme Court of Appeal in the hall of the civil court. At 1:30 P.M. President Mongibeaux was to select the jury by lot.

The jurors were to number thirty-six. Eighteen were to be "resistants" and the remaining eighteen were to be drawn from among fifty members of Parliament, expected to be present at the drawing. But when the High Court convened, only nine such members were present, and the Ministry of the Interior spent a couple of hours fetching, by messenger, enough others to constitute a jury. As no drawing of lots took place for this group, this appointment of jurors was illegal.

"Gentlemen, we will meet tomorrow at 1:00 P.M. for the Laval case." The chief justice added, "If necessary, we will meet mornings, afternoons, and evenings, but everything will be over before the elections."

Before nightfall, Naud and Baraduc stopped by the jail. Laval was not surprised by the rush of events. "Didn't I tell you what the scenario would be?"

Thursday, October 4. Naud and Baraduc wrote to Chief Justice Mongibeaux to say that they would not appear in court and asked the president of the bar to relieve them of their duties. They arrived at the jail at 9:00 A.M. and found that Mme. Laval had preceded them.

The departure for the session was announced, and police gathered at the door, but Laval, with a quiet yet decisive motion of the hand, asked them to wait. Mme. Laval pulled out his shirt cuffs, and while Laval continued to talk, she combed his hair. With a movement of the head, he resisted the comb. He had never looked younger.

They left the visiting room. Nuns and guards lined the hallway. He moved forward among his guards not as if he were being hustled, but as if room were being made for him to pass. Before getting into the little police car, he bade his lawyers a moving farewell. "Oh, to be in Auvergne!"

In the evening, the proceedings were reported to Baraduc, who commented:

> Mornet [the prosecutor] maintained that "an investigation that has been going on *for five years* is not a sudden investigation," adding, "Laval's case does not need to be investigated."
>
> Chief Justice Mongibeaux appointed us ex-officio. Five minutes later, he wondered why we had not submitted to his order.
>
> Who notified us? Nobody.
>
> "Everything is being done in a race against time."[*]

Mornet, by way of introduction to his indictment, had just summarized the activities of the Vichy government when Laval replied: At the time, you were all under the orders of the government, all of you who are judging me, you magistrates, and you, Mr. Attorney General! You may condemn me, you can kill me, but you have no right to treat me without respect.

"The law and *force majeure* compel me to appear before you as an accused. But even if my body is in chains, my soul is free. I want it to be known, and I shall prove it, that I have worked and suffered for my country. Then justice will be done."

During the hearing, various members of the jury insulted Laval. Mr. Demusois called him a "double-dealer." Mornet broke in: "I will not tolerate this unseemly attitude any longer," but the warning was not addressed to Demusois. It was addressed to Laval, who had just stated that he loved his country.

At the end of the session, but before it had been adjourned, an unidentified

[*]Ibid, pp. 125–6.

member of the jury asked that a young man who had applauded Laval be arrested: "Like Laval, he deserves twelve bullets in his body."

The chief justice issued no contempt orders.

Naud and Baraduc were shocked to learn that at the opening of the case, when several jurymen who were members of Parliament did not answer their call, the court sent two cars to the provisional National Assembly to gather "volunteers" in order to condemn Laval.

Friday, October 5. Poignard, president of the bar, wrote to Naud and Baraduc: "You must continue to perform the task I assigned to you, no matter what difficulties you encounter in having the rights of the defense respected." The two lawyers informed Laval. Naud read the submissions, that is, the defense motions, he had hurriedly prepared. Laval approved them.

At the court, all the cameras focused on the side doors through which Laval was to enter. He arrived amid an explosion of flashbulbs and sat down. Naud and Baraduc developed their submissions. The court retired to deliberate upon them. The lawyers accompanied Laval to the room in an annex reserved for him and there met Mme. Laval and Josée. A guard remained present during their conversation.

Baraduc had still not recovered from his surprise. As he left the courtroom, the attorney general's secretary came up to him. "Mr. Mornet has asked me to inform you that the file of the charges will be at your disposal every day."

Baraduc was about to thank her when he had asked for clarification: "Every morning?"

"No, in the afternoon."

"You mean during the trial?"

She left, apparently confused.

Baraduc remembered that before seeing her at the session, serving as an aide to the prosecution, he had seen her in Béteille's office, an aide to the investigation. He was no longer surprised, for it was clear that the prosecution and the investigation were one and the same. One woman's face in both connections had made it clear.

Naud arrived, bringing a bit of evidence that Mornet had just given him: a magazine cover where Hitler's hand could be seen shaking another. Laval, laughing, looked at it closely: "Not mine!"

After an hour's recess, the bell emptied the antechamber. The submissions of the defense had been rejected. Argument and rebuttal would continue. Laval explained the constitutional acts in a quiet and brilliant exposition, interrupted by personal remarks. The session drew to an end. Naud and Baraduc accompanied Laval to the little staircase that led to his floor. Once again, Baraduc admired "the bearing of a free man, despite the guards he was led by."[*]

Saturday, October 6. Laval had asked that the proceedings of the trial be

[*]Ibid, p. 133.

published in the *Journal Officiel,* pursuant to the constitution of the Third Republic. This had been done in the famous Caillaux trial. Pétain's trial had also been reported, but despite the demands of the defense lawyers, Laval's request was denied.

A kind of gut burst of feeling effected a change in favor of the prisoner. The crowd had seen the members of the jury abandon their supposed impartiality as judges; it had heard the insults directed at Laval. It had particularly admired Laval's lightning-fast answers to his accusers. He was to remain master of himself and of repartee until the end.

Mornet expressed regret that Laval had not been arrested immediately after the liberation, quickly condemned, and executed. He did not use "executed," but "conviction followed by you-know-what."

"That would have deprived me of the pleasure of listening to you," put in Laval.

When the chief justice asked Laval who had kept him at the marshal's side, he himself went on: Those who did have a name; it was the Germans; it was Mr. Abetz."

"I understand you, *sir,*" responded Laval. "You find it preferable to answer yourself the questions you put to me."

"*Sir.*" To Laval, Mongibeaux was no longer the chief justice but just a man. Then, standing in the center of the hall, he shouted: "Above you, sir, above all of you, above me, there is justice and truth."

"Justice will be done,"shouted the members of the jury in protest. They stood up at their benches and hurled insults. The uproar was at its loudest, but Laval dominated the uproar and concluded: "Yes, 'justice' will be done, but the truth will live on."

The chief justice suddenly adjourned the sitting. Laval, taken to a nearby room, smoked calmly. He asked his guard, "And what do *you* think about all this? Am I dealing with judges? Have you ever seen anything like it? No?"

It was again rumored that the sitting would not be resumed. An hour later, it did. What would the chief justice say? Everyone was frantic with curiosity. But he said nothing. No mention was made of the insults. While the jurors took their seats, Mongibeaux threatened the public with ejection and arrest. Then, dropping his questions about plotting against the internal security of the state, Mongibeaux suddenly asked Laval to respond to the accusation of conspiring with the enemy. "I give you permission to speak."

"No," Laval answered, "the insulting manner in which you have questioned me and the demonstrations that certain members of the jury indulge in prove that I am about to become the victim of a judicial crime. I do not want to be its accomplice. I prefer to say nothing."

Mongibeaux, seated rigidly at his table, called for further witnesses for the prosecution. The usher informed him that there were no witnesses. Amid laughter, the session ended.

Laval had just returned to his retiring room when a guard summoned him to appear before the High Court on the order of Mongibeaux, failing which, he was to be taken there by main force. Laval wrote out an answer, weighing every word:

I have been put in a situation that makes it impossible to present my defense. Not only has no thorough investigation been undertaken, but I have become convinced that I am not faced with real judges. The insulting manner in which I was questioned by the chief justice, the threats and the invectives hurled at me at various times by certain members of the jury, prove, as I declared in open court, that a judicial crime is in the making.

The chief justice thought it his duty after asking me a question to answer it himself in terms I consider outrageous. Jurors calling me "pig," or telling me "you'll have twelve bullets in you," "in two weeks, you won't yell so much," have demonstrated unequivocally that they are not taking part in a work of justice.

The revolting prejudice and partiality of the proceedings have not allowed me to present my defense. The High Court, acting as if it feared the truth, will condemn me, but it will not have judged me; I leave to that court the entire responsibility for its decision. The judgment that I am refused here, I shall await from public opinion and from history.°

The sitting resumed without either the accused or his lawyers present. While President Lebrun testified, Laval was speaking quietly with his wife and Josée. It was the last time he was to see them.

Monday, October 8. Laval very calmly received Naud and Baraduc. Was he to be taken back to Fresnes? Would he be taken to the hearing by force, as was threatened on Saturday? He could imagine every kind of possibility. "Because," he said, "they're capable of anything."

A guard came in to tell Laval that the session would start at 1:00 P.M. and that he was ordered to attend. Laval repeated his answer of Saturday. The guard, leaving, excused himself for having disturbed him. "Not at all," Laval replied in a polite, indifferent tone.

Shortly before noon, President Ausset informed Naud and Baraduc that Minister of Justice Teitgen urgently wanted to see them. They were immediately taken to the minister's office; there Teitgen offered them his cigarettes and his congratulations. "I really want to congratulate you; you do honor to the bar, and it is not the first time in history that the Paris bar is thus signalized. I can't say the same for my magistrates!" And without even asking them to keep it confidential, he went on to say that Mongibeaux had agreed to preside at the High Court if, in return, he were to be made chief justice of the Supreme Court of Appeal. "Before turning to him," the minister added, "I had asked seven counselors; they all declined. I put a lot of

° Ibid, p. 138.

the blame on the jurors who insulted Mr. Laval: I can assure you they are people with whom I will never shake hands again."

Nevertheless, he believed it both in France's best interests and Laval's that the adversary proceedings continue. "I may say that the examining magistrates were much impressed by Mr. Laval's answers. Think about that and about the following proposition: if Mr. Laval agrees to take his place again at the sessions, I give you my word that the jurors will stop insulting him and that the trial will proceed in the atmosphere of decorum that is desired. Furthermore, I will instruct the attorney general to give you immediately the file of the charges in its entirety."

Baraduc and Naud thanked the minister for his goodwill, but Baraduc immediately added, "Even if the jurors have nothing but smiles for us from now on, it will not induce us to believe in their impartiality. They have definitively revealed their thoughts and their decision. Mr. Secretary, a true trial can only be held before a different set of judges." Teitgen looked at him as if disappointed that the flaw in his argument was so apparent, and he raised his arms to heaven.

The two lawyers left the ministry to report Teitgen's proposition to Laval: the resumption of the trial under promise of calm ensured by the government.

"No such thing is possible," Laval cut in. "Go tell that president that I don't want to see him any more. Let them investigate my case, let them change my judges, and then I will explain myself."

Mongibeaux received Laval's refusal dryly and, with the backing of the attorney general, insisted on his conditions. Baraduc reminded Mornet that the incidents he pretended to deplore would surely never have occurred had an honest investigation preceded the trial. As the attorney general maintained that the investigation had been amply sufficient, Baraduc watched him being caught in his own trap. "Do you realize, Mr. Attorney General, that in order to demonstrate the dishonesty of the 'changing of the guard,' you put words into Laval's mouth that he never uttered?"

"You surprise me."

"We can prove it!"

Unemotionally, Mornet replied, "It's possible. You know, I've been conducting this investigation since 1940. I had a little notebook, and every day I took down what I heard on the radio from London. So it's possible that I made a mistake in the sentence you mention. It's possible." Naud and Baraduc returned to tell Laval what they had learned about the sessions he had missed. After the depositions, Mornet had asked that certain affidavits be read. The clerk obeyed, but the prosecution had erred: the documents dealt with Pétain. The audience, which had gone to sleep, woke up to laugh at this.

"Poor fellows! Poor fellows!" muttered Laval.°

°Ibid, pp. 143–8.

Tuesday, October 9. At five o'clock, the verdict had just been handed down. Baraduc went to the jail.

"Death?" asked Laval.

"Yes."

Laval displayed no emotion. With his elbows on the table of the visiting room, he sat smoking. He asked for a piece of paper and began to write.

"Please give this to my wife and daughter. And get the text of the verdict by tomorrow." In a low voice, he added, "My morale continues excellent."

THE LAST DAYS

Wednesday, October 10. Baraduc entered the cell in the block where the condemned await death. Laval sat on his bed, smoking. He was dressed in the special cape, the *robe de bure* worn by convicts before execution, and he was shackled.

"Not bad, my tuxedo." His voice sounded detached. He did not complain of having to sleep in chains and was grateful that he had been allowed to keep his own underclothes. Over a silk shirt he wore a tricolor scarf.

A guard told him to go to the visiting room. He walked with small steps. The chain dragged noisily on the floor.

"It reminds me of sack races," he whispered.

What was to be done? Present a petition for mercy? The idea had not entered Laval's mind. The only thing he wanted was that the government quash the conviction and order an honest investigation and a trial before real judges. With this in mind, Naud and Baraduc wrote to de Gaulle:

General:

As the lawyers appointed for the defense of Laval, who was condemned to death by a decree of the High Court of Justice on October 9, we have the honor of requesting the favor of a meeting with you.

We wish simply to set forth the conditions under which this verdict was rendered and to ask you to consider declaring a mistrial, a move that can henceforth come only from your authority.

Please accept, general, the assurance of our high and respectful consideration.°

°Ibid., pp. 158–9.

At Josée's suggestion, Baraduc sought the aid of François Mauriac. But Mauriac warned his visitor about the limits of his supposed influence.

"De Gaulle had promised me that he would pardon Brasillach. Did you know that?"

"Yes."

"Well, you can see for yourself—"

Baraduc no longer insisted that Mauriac speak to the general, but he did urge him to write an article. "For Laval?" asked Mauriac.

"In connection with Laval's trial, on the question of the rights of the defense," Baraduc replied.

Mauriac hesitated. "I am not free to write such an article."°

Thursday, October 11. Naud and Baraduc turned to Léon Blum.

"I understand that you are looking for every possible support to obtain something like a quashing of the verdict by the government," he said. "But I don't see what I might suggest to the general. I also doubt the effectiveness of my trying. But I authorize you to make my opinion public. It is explicit: the trial, as it was conducted, is a scandal and a mistake."

Blum was shocked to hear that Laval had been put in chains. "Who could have ordered that?"†

In the evening, Baraduc saw Laval, who asked him to take a little walk with him in the hall, as if he did not notice his chains. But the chains were there.

Deprived of the right to see his wife and daughter, Laval entrusted Baraduc with various brief messages for them. "They are full of courage in the face of their misfortune," he said, turning his head aside slightly to hide a few tears. He took off his glasses. "Dear God, how my eyes hurt tonight."

Friday, October 12. Laval handed over all his papers to Baraduc. "You see, I've seen how things are done here. When they take someone to be executed, they sweep up everything in his cell, wrap it up, and none of it is ever seen again. I would like my notes to be made into a book. You can no longer save my life, but you can save my memory. That's more important than life to me."

To the end, he maintained a calm and lofty look. Never a complaint, never a fear. "One must stand up to misfortune," he said.

At six o'clock, Naud and Baraduc, accompanied by Mr. Patin, director of criminal affairs, entered Clemenceau's office, now occupied by de Gaulle. The general, standing near the door, received them without a word. He sat down at his desk. They remained standing for a few moments and then, without being asked, sat in two available chairs.

Naud broke the silence by explaining to the general how the trial had been conducted. De Gaulle lit a cigarette. Baraduc described the investigation.

°Ibid., pp. 160–1.
†Ibid., pp. 166–7.

The general moved toward the door, opened it, and after a quick handshake, closed it again without having uttered a word.

Patin, who had remained in the general's office, came out a half hour later and told them that de Gaulle wanted to consult Teitgen but cautioned them against raising their hopes. Naud and Baraduc entertained no hopes. Before receiving them, de Gaulle had announced at a press conference that Laval's case would not be reviewed.°

"Mauriac is a friend of Teitgen's," Josée told them, and suggested that they call upon him once again. They went immediately to his house. Mauriac agreed to write to Teitgen.

> *Mr. Minister of Justice and dear friend:*
>
> Please excuse me, for I am writing at the entreaty of Laval's daughter and of his lawyers, who assure me that it is up to you to overturn the sentence. It is not for me to present to you, a jurist, the reasons for preventing his execution.
>
> I simply want to tell you that if I were in your place, I would not hesitate for an instant. In the eyes of the world, this case must be decided in the light and the serenity of true justice.
>
> But you do not need to be given advice at such a solemn moment. You are among those who will reflect deeply at such a time. May God inspire you and enlighten you, dear friend!
>
> Please excuse my extreme audacity and accept my deeply devoted sentiments.
>
> *François Mauriac*

The letter was delivered by official government plane.

At nine o'clock, the lawyers returned to the Place du Palais-Bourbon, where they met Mme. Laval, Josée, and my uncle, the ambassador, who in spite of the lateness of the hour, called the private secretary of the British ambassador, Duff Cooper. He asked for a meeting, which was granted to him on the spot. He began by telling Cooper, "I will remind you of everything England owes Pierre Laval."

Saturday, October 13. In the morning, Laval welcomed his lawyer: "I will imitate the Chinese when they address their last greeting to the world." With his right hand raised, he slowly, deliberately, gestured good-bye.

In the afternoon, Baraduc found him talking to the guard about the potato crop. Laval seemed so interested that Baraduc felt he had intruded. But Laval came up to him, smiling. While he lit a cigarette, his face took on a worried look.

°Ibid., pp. 173–4.

"Do they execute people on Sundays?"

"No."

"I do not want them to disfigure me. I grant that right only to the earth."

Sunday, October 14. Josée appealed to Monsignor Chevrot, who wielded some influence over the general. The prelate immediately wrote to Miss de Miribel, de Gaulle's secretary:

Dear Miss de Miribel:

I entreat you to receive Mme. de Chambrun and to do everything in your power to have General de Gaulle listen to her. It is impossible that you do not agree that Laval's trial was a sham. It must be begun again seriously. Pierre Laval must be tried.

If you care for General de Gaulle even a little, stop him from approving a miscarriage of justice.

I thank you in advance for everything you will attempt in order to permit Mme. de Chambrun to see the general, and in case this should prove impossible, to inform the general yourself in all urgency.

Please accept, dear Miss de Miribel, the expression of my most devoted sentiments.

Monsignor Chevrot°

Baraduc went to Fresnes before breakfast. "Here," said Laval, "this is for you, this for Naud, and this one for Jaffré: you may read it." And as Baraduc put these letters of farewell in his pocket without reading them, Laval handed him a general farewell, which he had entitled "During the Vigil for the Dead."

It was not enough to prevent me from speaking; it was also necessary to prevent me from writing. Why get rid of me so fast, when I was already chained and in prison? Even so, nothing will keep the French people from realizing that there has been an attempt to hide something from them.

I had nothing to fear from an open hearing. I had asked for the proceedings to be published in the *Officiel* so that the French people might know the charges and my replies. I was turned down. Now they *know* there was an attempt to hide the truth. France is not liberated, because she is not allowed to know the truth.

I feared nothing, for I would have dispelled and disposed of all the complaints that were on the books. I would have undone the ugly stories one after the other. I was always fought with lies, and I would have nailed the lies. I, who was misrepresented so that I might be hated,

° A copy of this letter is in the possession of Mme. de Chambrun.

would have emerged as a man who presents himself with an open face, one whom all my enemies know for what he is, one who is feared, and whose voice they wanted to silence.

I was represented as cunning and crafty, whereas I have always fought with the pure, simple intelligence of a man of the people.

I was always represented as an enemy of the people, whereas those who know me are aware that it is the people I have always defended.

I go to my eternal rest. My conscience is at ease. Remorse will perhaps torment those who did not know me, who besmirched and tortured me. It will certainly one day weigh down those who had me assassinated. I pity them, but I do not hate them, because the hatred that inspires their actions has never lived in my soul.

I weep for my family, to whom I am causing pain.

For my country, which I love, I wish happiness and the freedom that has been torn from her. She will find them one day, together with another morality and other leaders.

I await and accept death with serenity, for my soul shall survive. I prefer death to chains.

                                                                    P.L.°

At two o'clock on October 14, the telephone rang in Baraduc's office. "Sir," an anonymous, courteous, and grave voice began, "tomorrow, at exactly eight o'clock, make sure to be in front of the high gate of the Palais de Justice. A car will take you to Fresnes." Naud received the same call. The two went to see Josée.

She understood as soon as she let them in and spoke the words they dared not say. But she recovered herself and wanted to fight to the end. She asked the two men to take her to Miss de Miribel, who promised to plead yet again with de Gaulle. The lawyers then drove on to Fresnes, where the warden of the prison met them. "Above all," he said, "don't tell him that it's tomorrow."

As Laval welcomed his counsel, he stared at Baraduc. "You look awfully tired!"

"No, but I'm worried that I don't know anything anymore."

Laval understood. "Shall I see all three of you?" In the deserted hallway, he shook their hands and with a last smile said, "See you tomorrow."

Monday, October 15. Before the Palais de Justice the little group gathered, silent. The secretary of the High Court pointed out to each person his car, and the long line, like a funeral procession, headed toward Fresnes, which had been declared "out-of-bounds" since seven o'clock.

Mornet, his back bent, stayed on the threshold of Laval's cell. Baraduc and Naud went in. Laval looked at them for a long time without saying anything. Then he pulled the bed sheet up to his face and suddenly swallowed the

°This letter is in the possession of Mme. de Chambrun.

contents of a vial and of a tin box of Azym powder,° which he then threw at the feet of the attorney general.

Mornet left. Laval's body shook with a death rattle. Baraduc took his hand. The torso, above the sheets, was racked by convulsions.

Dr. Paul declined to give an opinion, and while he called for the interns of the central infirmary, raised Laval's arm. No reflexes. The poison seemed to have acted with lightning speed, and the medical man believed death imminent.

Baraduc noticed an open letter next to some sealed envelopes: "To my lawyers in order to instruct them; to my executioners, in order to answer them."

Laval in his note announced his suicide. He did not want to die under French bullets. He was going to resort to the Romans' quietus. He asked that neither his lawyers nor his guards be suspected. He had had the vial for a long time. His coat and his briefcase served alternately as a hiding place.

While they read, an intern arrived and declared coldly: "He can be revived." Mornet approved, and the pumping of the stomach began in the presence of an indignant nun, who whispered, "Is that what I'm here for?"

Mornet and Bouchardon, who had phoned the Ministry of War, returned and announced that Laval would be executed on a stretcher. "Impossible," said Dr. Paul. "The law forbids the execution of anyone not in a condition to make disclosures."

They had forgotten.

About six o'clock, Laval whispered, "I did not want to die by French bullets." At eleven o'clock, the doctors confirmed that Laval was "saved." The chaplain leaned toward him. "Mr. Prime Minister, this may be the moment to pray for absolution."

Laval dressed himself despite terrible waves of nausea. Little by little, his strength returned. He asked for his comb. Baraduc having offered him a mirror, Laval, with a completely sure hand, parted his hair. They looked in his suitcase for his white tie, the last one.

At noon, Laval refused an offer to be carried on a chair or to be held up by guards. "I have my lawyers to help me."

As he passed through the door, Naud and Baraduc each took an arm. The prison van waited below the steps. Laval got in without help. As Baraduc moved near him, he pulled on his sleeve. "Please tell my wife and daughter that my last thoughts were of them. Please tell them also that I did not suffer. They won't believe it, but it doesn't matter."

The van brought Laval to the place of execution, a spot between two poplars. He got out of the prison vehicle as if he were getting out of his own car.

"Where are the magistrates?" he asked, and repeated the question in a very clear voice. Mornet and Bouchardon appeared from behind the hearse and faced Laval. They removed their hats, as if before the dead. Laval

---

°Made from unleavened bread and used to mask the unpleasant taste of certain drugs that must be taken by mouth.

looked at them for a moment. "Honorable Magistrates, I merely wanted to tell you that I pity you for having agreed to carry out this task." He was still looking at them, but they did not look at him. "You wanted to have this spectacle," he added. "Well, see it through to the very end."

It was only a few steps to the knoll, to the execution post. He took these steps deliberately, neither slowly nor quickly, and leaned against the post. "Don't go too far off," he said to his lawyers. "I would like to look at you as I die."

Everything happened very quickly.

"Aim!"

"Vive la France!" shouted Laval.

"Fire!"

Laval slid to his knees, his face to the ground.

The sergeant major fired the coup de grace.

The whole prison shouted, "Murderers!" and "Long live Laval!"

On the eve of his supreme trial, Laval had written a letter "for little Bunny," which I could not make up my mind to open: against all hope, I was still hoping.

And then, during the cruel night that followed, I had perforce to open it.

What a revelation! It was not a message of misery, but one of courage and hope:

October 12, 1945

My dear Bunny,

I don't want to leave you without telling you of my deep affection, without embracing you. I leave Josée with you. Continue to love each other dearly. What you did for me, for my defense, will bring you luck. Josée must not let herself be discouraged. My thoughts will always be with her and with you, because my soul will survive. Be strong in adversity, my little Bunny. I love you very much.

I kiss you and hold you close to my heart.

Pierre Laval

Kiss your parents for me; they have been so good and have acted so worthily.

On the eve of his execution, Laval had written to his family. Mme. Laval took the secret of this last confidence to her grave. Mme. de Chambrun has permitted me to reproduce two excerpts from her father's letter to her, a letter she and I cannot forget:

I shall disappear from this world, to be intermingled with the earth, which consumes us all, but my soul will survive and never leave you.

I shall be always with you and your mother, so that you may not lose courage. Do not think of avenging me, I beg of you. But since you have no cause to be ashamed of me, you will be able to defend my memory. Do it calmly, without wrongheaded passion, but with the certainty that when things have straightened themselves out, I shall find a place in the hearts of decent people again. Keep your heads up in this misfortune. All of France now knows that I was prevented from speaking and from defending myself. Later on, the country will want explanations, an accounting. They did not want to listen to mine. Let my sacrifice at least help those who have been unfairly convicted and sentenced or who live under the threat of it. They, too, only wanted to help our country when it was suffering.

If there is a heaven, we will all meet there again; for tonight, alone, I will speak to God. He will understand me, this God of my childhood. Before I die, I shall find him again. I hate no one. I only pity those who persecuted me. Feel as I do—hatred is not a worthy feeling. Promise me to be strong; you must stand erect under misfortune, as I shall know how to stand erect tomorrow in the face of death. I want you to be able to be proud of your father to the very end.

APPENDIX

INTRODUCTORY NOTE

A few days before his death, outlining the pattern of his defense, Laval wrote: "There is no area [of national life] as to which I cannot prove conclusively that the occupation would have been infinitely more deadly and cruel had I not been there."

Since no defense was ever presented at the mock trial, I have gathered some of the facts and figures relating to five important economic activities, three aspects of social life (education, health, and security), and five groups of persons.

These statistics are followed by fifteen Exhibits (A–O) consisting of official documents referred to in the text.

SCHEDULES

A.   French Assets, Public Savings, and the Franc

B.   Agriculture and Food Supplies

C.   Organizing for Industrial Production: Facts and Figures

D.   Energy: Coal and Fuel Substitutes

E.   Transport and Communications

F.   Health and Sports

G.   Welfare: Facts and Figures

H.   Education and Culture

I.   War Prisoners

J.   Protection of the French Workers in Germany

K.   Protection of the Civil Service (Prefects)

L.   Protection of the Law Enforcement Personnel

M.   Protection of the Jews and Freemasons

(See also material inserted in the text, pages 80–85.)

EXHIBITS

A. The First Document

B. The Second Document

C. The "Dossier Laval"

D. The "I Wish" Speech

E. Address by Pierre Laval to the Mayors of Cantal at Vichy, November 9, 1943

F. Extract from Speer's Address to the Gauleiters, October 6, 1943

G. The Sauckel–Laval Showdown

H. Resolution of the 87 Mayors of Paris and Vicinity

I. The Last Luncheon with Pierre Laval

J. Extract of Laval's Speech to a Delegation of Artisans

K. Sketch of Mme. Laval by Pierre Laval, Written on Thursday, September 13, in the Chambers of the Examining Magistrate of Mme. Laval

L. The Questioning of Mme. Laval by the Examining Magistrate, September 7, 1945

M. Telegram from the Files of the Office of Chief of Counsel for War Crimes

N. The Last Words Written by Laval in His Prison Cell, in Answer to the Accusation That He Had "Humiliated" France

O. *The Sorrow and the Pity*, a film

SCHEDULE A

French Assets, Public Savings, and the Franc

Situation at the Return to Power of the Laval Government—April 1942

France had a creditor encamped on her soil, and a huge claim resulting from the armistice treaty (in the negotiation of which Laval did not participate). The Wiesbaden Diktat of August 22, 1940, imposed on France the unbearable levy of 400 million francs a day to cover occupation costs, payable in advance every ten days. The amount was reduced to 300 million a day in August 1941. As a yardstick, compare:

1941: total budget of France	150 billion
German levy	169 billion

Pierre Cathala, minister of finance, a friend of Laval's who had helped him set up the French social security system in 1930, had a triple task:

1. To resist the ever-increasing demands of the occupying power.

2. To prevent the collapse of the currency.

3. To have the taxpayers share the burden equally.

Resistance to the Occupying Power

Cathala organized what was called "la résistance administrative." It consisted in quibbling and using legal artifice to gain time, to fend off threats, and to dole out cash so as to protect tangible assets otherwise sure to be confiscated.

Examples:

1. *August 1942:* The French government made a formal demand for reduction of the costs of the occupation—delaying tactics.

2. *November 1942:* After the Allied landings in North Africa, France was totally occupied. The Germans attempted to place a "counselor" in the Ministry of Finance. The minister, Cathala, flatly refused and threatened to resign with all his staff. The Germans withdrew their demand.

3. *December 1942:* The Germans increased to 500 million a day the occupation costs. The government succeeded in delaying the application of the new levy until the summer of 1943.

4. Laval and Cathala stubbornly refused to deliver any part of France's gold and foreign currency reserves, as well as the securities and valuables belonging to individuals on deposit in bank vaults.

5. The director of the treasury, Jacques Brunet, was arrested in August 1943, freed after Laval's and Cathala's violent protests, and reinstated by Laval at the head of the treasury. A few months later, two high functionaries at the ministry, Georges Pebrel and Adéodat Boissard, were arrested.

6. *August 8, 1944:* Just before the Allied armies entered Paris, General Michel subpoenaed all the bank directors, ordering them to surrender a large part of the assets in their hands. The minister of finance ordered the head of all the banks to disobey. At the time of the liberation, not one share of stock or bond had been surrendered.

7. The gold of the Bank of France, of which the Germans had continuously claimed the return from North and West Africa, was never

transferred. The entire gold reserve of 84.6 billion francs shown in the balance sheet of the Bank of France in 1940 appeared for the same amount on August 31, 1944.

8.   The Ministry of Finance blocked all sales of real property and the purchase of shares in French corporations by foreign nationals so as to prevent German organizations from acquiring French real or industrial property (four exceptions: Havas (news agency), Francolor, the Société Vinicole de Champagne, and the Mines de Bor).

Defense of the Franc

The enormous sums paid over to the Germans for occupation costs created a growing danger of inflation. The government might have been tempted to resort to increasing the money supply, thus wrecking the economy. The Germans would have been the only beneficiaries, for they would undoubtedly have resorted to seizing solid French assets in lieu of cash.

The Laval government undertook, instead, to wage a long-term war to maintain stability:

1.   By increasing taxation and reducing the French budget of 1943 by 10 million over the previous year.

2.   By increasing from year to year the national savings accounts of the people and the short-term financing of expenditures by treasury bonds at low rates of interest.

This practice had been initiated during the First World War (1914–18). Poincaré's treasury bonds were then called defense bonds. Poincaré had said, "When the amount of currency exceeds the needs, the surplus automatically takes refuge in the purchase of defense bonds."

Thirty years later, Laval and Cathala did the same, with success. The treasury issued more than 400 billion francs in such bonds and reimbursed more than 300 billions. The "dépôts à la Caisse d'Epargne" (public savings) rose to 90 billions by the end of 1940, 119 by the end of 1943, and exceeded 130 by the end of March 1944.

As a result, the old 3 percent perpetual loan rose to par during the last couple of months of the occupation. This enabled the first de Gaulle government to issue the "emprunt libératoire" at the same rate of 3 percent and to convert into the 3 percent loan the three loans at higher rates issued in 1917, 1918, and 1932, thereby saving approximately 100 billion francs in interest payments.

Between 1940 and 1944 the dollar only rose from 43.80 francs to 49.53 francs and the pound from 176.62 francs to 199.78 francs. The franc began to lose value rapidly only after the liberation.

An Equitable Tax Burden

Income tax rates were sharply progressive. Above 400,000 francs, the rate reached 70 percent. The offices and officers of the Wehrmacht protected French black market profiteers, who sold them food and goods at high prices, but despite continuous German efforts to keep this market going, proceedings against profiteers were started all over France on the charge of raising prices contrary to law. Profits and penalties produced billions of revenue for the state.

After the landings in North Africa and despite German opposition, the government paid the salaries of all officers and noncommissioned officers fighting in North Africa and Italy under General de Gaulle and General Juin. The payments were made to their families in France.

For four years, despite continuous German opposition, the government managed to raise the salaries of workmen in the factories. As a consequence, the attraction of going to work in Germany for higher pay was much reduced.

The expert on financial matters, Mitzakis, in a book published after the liberation, *l'Evolution Financière de la France Entre 1936 et 1944 (The Financial Evolution of France Between 1936 and 1944)*, states:

> Despite the dangerous inflation of the public debt and the increased circulation of currency resulting from the enormous cost of the occupation, the year 1943 was marked (incredible as it may seem) by a notable improvement in the credit of the state and its fiscal system, as well as by an encouraging increase in the national revenue.[*]

SCHEDULE B

Agriculture and Food Supplies

The situation in May–June 1940: farmers and farm laborers were fleeing toward the South in carts, cars, and tractors. Entire villages were abandoned. Cattle roamed free, dying of thirst, sometimes shot at by the German troops. The harvest was at a standstill.

Livestock, 1940–44

For four years, a tough Prussian, Dr. Reinhardt, acted as a "dictator" for the German minister of agriculture. Four determined, competent, and energetic French ministers of agriculture successively waged a continuous battle to fend off his demands for food, cattle, etc. Caziot, Leroy-Ladurie, Bonna-

[*]See *France During the German Occupation*, Hoover Institution (Documentary Series), vol. 1, (1958) pp. 69–132.

fous, and Cathala wore themselves out in the struggle. But their staunch resistance placed France in a unique position after the Allied victory: of all the countries occupied by Germany, including Germany itself, France was the only one to show almost the same number of horses, cows, oxen, bulls, sheep, and pigs as before the war began. The following figures are the official statistics:

	1939–1940	December 1945
Horses	2,114,705	2,256,878
Mules	89,257	86,506
Oxen, cows, bulls	14,380,550	14,273,082
Sheep	7,696,003	6,631,807
Pigs	5,011,155	4,386,443°

°Official records of the war years, French Ministry of Agriculture, supplied to the author in 1981.

These results were made possible by:

1. Organizing in time for the harvest the return of 3 million refugees, farmers, farm workers, and men and women who came back from the free zone to their homes in the occupied zone immediately after the Armistice.

2. The return of half a million war prisoners, mostly farm laborers, about to be sent to Germany from the "front stalags" in France.

3. The continuous pressure of the French government and police against the unlawful slaughter of cattle for the French and the Wehrmacht black markets.

Immediately after the armistice it became imperative.

First, to prevent starvation of the overpopulated southern "free" zone. During his first talk with the German ambassador, Abetz, Laval obtained the release of the French war reserve (in the suburbs of Paris) of 3 million metric quintals of wheat.° On July 20, trains and trucks began to rush this supply to Bordeaux, Limoges, Toulouse, and Marseille for massive distribution in the free zone.

The second need was to save the 2 million draft and plow horses and thoroughbreds. The Reich wanted the former for its farms and the latter for its national stud (Altefeld). A general order of requisition had been issued. To enforce it, the German army occupied and blocked production at the large factory of Duclair, where practically all the nails for horseshoes were man-

°One quintal equals 100 kilograms (220 bushels).

ufactured. Minister of Agriculture Caziot° rushed there and obtained the resumption of production, while Laval obtained from Abetz the repeal of the requisition order.

The third urgent need was to put an immediate end to the seizure of the best stallions. Three—Pharis, Bubbles, and Biribi—had been taken immediately. The only way to prevent the seizure of several thousand foals, young and old race horses, and stallions, was for the government and the stewards to reopen the numerous race tracks all over France. This was done as early as October 1940 and continued despite three attempts by the SS to close them.

The official statistics of the Ministry of Agriculture for the years 1930–1944 show the number of stallions and mares and the number of yearlings born on the stud farms, mostly in Normandy:

	Stallions	*Mares*	*Yearlings*
1939	274	2,597	1,252
1940	246	2,455	1,181
1941	225	2,195	1,054
1942	225	2,048	997
1943	260	3,128	1,762
1944	300	2,885	1,815

Increased production of livestock and farm products would not have been possible without the enactment of laws for the development of farms and breeding, and without making accessible to farmers underdeveloped land in certain regions of France such as the Provence:

1. The Law of December 21, 1940, made possible the modernization of the "rural habitat."

2. Several laws protected and developed individual and family farming by (a) organizing small farms and (b) parceling out larger areas.

3. The Law of July 5, 1941, organized agricultural education and assistance, etc.

4. In 1942, a law created the Crédit Agricole which was to become the national bank for farmers.

The Battle Against German Levies

This subject would warrant a book. Each June, from 1940 to 1944, Reinhardt served his list of demands on the French minister of agriculture. As

---

°With the knowledge of Pétain and Laval, Caziot organized the camouflage of French war equipment in the French state forests (Forêts Domaniales).

the Germans were retreating from Russia and the grain fields of the Ukraine, the levies increased. Here, for example, is the "bill" for the period July 1, 1943, to June 30, 1944:

	Amount (tons)
Food grains	800,000
Feed grains	600,000
Animals for slaughter (weight before slaughter)	200,000
Fats	35,000
Potatoes	400,000
Dried vegetables	10,000
Fresh vegetables	124,000
Cheese	15,000
Fruit	105,000
Hay	450,000
Straw (of which 100,000 tons to be oat straw)	400,000

Upon receipt of such summons, Bonnafous or his predecessors would refuse the levy as a whole and in detail. Then they would go to Vichy to consult with the prime minister.

Thereafter, endless discussions would begin at the Hôtel Majestic in Paris between Reinhardt and Bonnafous and his staff.

To gain time, the minister would request the appointment of experts. Weeks would go by, and then the slow deescalation would begin. In the particular year 1943–44, the meat levy was lowered from 200,000 to 145,000 tons—final "offer": "Do you accept?" asked Reinhardt. "I have to ask President Laval." The final figure was 135,000 tons. Then the delays began in the deliveries. Ultimately, the Germans received 126,000 tons.

After fifteen months of resistance, Bonnafous fell ill, and Cathala and Chasseigne took over his role.

How Paris Was Fed During the Battle of Normandy (1944)

June 20–21: The heavy Allied bombardments completely cut all railroad lines leading to Paris from the Northeast and the South.

June 22: The Moulins de Paris (the wheat center for Paris along the Seine at Brie-sur-Seine) was bombed out. Trucks and barges on the river and canal were destroyed. No wheat could come to Paris.

June 26: Reinhardt demanded the reduction of the daily bread ration from 350 grams to 300. Laval and Chasseigne refused.

June 27: Laval stayed in Vichy to avoid meeting Sauckel, having given the order on June 6 that no French worker could leave France for Germany. Laval phoned Chasseigne in Paris, asking him to make an appeal over the

Paris radio to the farmers for their cattle and wheat reserves and to the bakers of Paris to remain open on Sundays. All complied.

This is how Chasseigne described what was done to organize the food supply for Paris while the battle was raging less than one hundred miles away:

> After the landing, I decided to reorganize the Normandy region and to draw as much as I could from the zone near the fighting. The Germans wanted to evacuate only a part of the cattle, the basis of the herds, keeping the remainder to feed their forces. I sent to that region a superintendent accompanied by a delegation from the (Paris) slaughter yards at La Villette. Their task was to corral all the herds behind the front and bring them by road from the battle area to Paris, the stages of this journey having been planned and coordinated. In that way, 6,500 head of cattle reached Paris in July and over 10,000 in August. Some came during the fighting. Paris lived on its own supplies until the beginning of September. Here again, it should be noted that many of those in the convoys were killed by machine-gun fire. It should also be noted that among the cattle it had not been possible to evacuate or drive off, more than 100,000 head were killed by bombardments.

August 9: Laval left his home town of Châteldon (twelve miles from Vichy) at 4:00 A.M. He reached Paris at 10:00 A.M. and met Cathala and Chasseigne and the préfets of Paris, Bussière and Bouffet, at his Matignon office. He announced that he would remain in Paris to pursue three objectives:

1. With Chasseigne, Cathala and Bouffet, to guarantee that the population of Paris was fed until the arrival of the Allies.

2. To prevent the Germans from destroying Paris, its bridges, plants, power stations, etc.

3. To call, if possible, a meeting at the National Assembly (Senate and Chamber).

Each evening, he held a meeting on food supplies. Some of the reserves released: wine, fruit, vegetables, cheese, butter (August 11–16). Early each morning, Laval and Chasseigne checked the arrivals from the east and the suburbs.

August 16: Laval and Chasseigne prepared for the provisional government that would succeed them an inventory of all the reserves of basic supplies—bread, milk, meat, and the rest.

August 17: Laval was arrested. While he was deported by the Germans, Chasseigne, who had escaped, put in the hands of one of the heads of the resistance, Georges Monnet, a three-page memorandum prepared with Laval:

STATE SECRETARIAT FOR FOOD SUPPLIES

Paris, August 18, 1944.

SITUATION IN PARIS, AUGUST 17, 1944.

BREAD

According to estimates prepared by the National Cereals Offices, M. Fadier, and M. Mayer, director of the Moulins de Paris Company, this was the situation yesterday: in the bakeries, about a four-day supply; in the mills about thirteen tons of wheat, which is theoretically blocked but for which I have given a release order; making a total of seven or eight days' supply.

Daily arrivals amount to about 50 percent of needs. These might increase a little after the departure of the Germans and the end of their levies.

A new difficulty arose this morning. Because of the short supply of electric current, many bakeries have less bread available than usual.

I summoned the representatives of the bakers and proposed that until August 27, 1944, all rest days, including the weekly rest day, should be suspended. As compensation, bakery workers will receive daily one bottle of trademark wine, paid for from the special food account, and one meat ration.

I had been begged to reduce the bread ration, but I did not wish to do so, believing that bread is the chief food available at the present time to the poorer classes.

The three pages that followed gave an inventory of the entire reserve of food supplies that the provisional government of de Gaulle would find immediately available on the liberation of Paris.

The document ended:

I have prepared this inventory in order that those who come after us may take note that in spite of the difficulties of transport during the last three months, I have left them supplies with which they can get through the most difficult period, that which will come immediately after the occupation of Paris by the Allied troops.

I add that, on my order, the president of the National Cereals Office sent out three inspectors to the Allied lines in the west charged with the duty of following the troops and making a census of the cooperatives, so that as soon as Allied troops have entered Paris, the plan for the transport of wheat, at present directed toward the departments east of the capital, may be immediately turned in the other direction.

SCHEDULE C

*Organizing for Industrial Production: Facts and Figures**

Situation at the Armistice

One of the most serious consequences of the disaster of June 1940 was the determination of the Reich to take entire control of the economy in the occupied zone. Around Lille, they began setting up through their *Warrenstelle* industrial centers to allocate raw materials, hire labor, etc.

The French manufacturers immediately turned to the French government. Not only did they accept, but they demanded, that the state act as guardian and defend them and their corporations against the German military administration.

The immediate result was the Labor Law of August 16, 1940 (La Charte du Travail). Its purpose was to:

1. Free the economy from the stranglehold Germany was trying to secure over France by forcing the occupying power to negotiate.

2. Protect French industry further by keeping the allocation of raw materials and the control over labor in French hands.

By the end of August, thirty "manufacturing" committees had already been created with the help of technicians within industry. Their number was to reach 200, many of which were still functioning years after the liberation. (See Schedules D and E.)

In every large factory, a Comité Social d'Entreprise (Workers' cooperative committee) was created, to be all-inclusive for each factory. The powerful French C.G.T. union (5 million members in 1936, mostly communists) had fallen to pieces at the declaration of war, when Hitler and Stalin, being allies and invaders of Poland, were alike enemies of France. The Comités Sociaux d'Entreprise took the place of the C.G.T. and other unions. Their delegates were elected by secret ballot. By December 1943, 6,000 committees represented more than 3 million workmen.

SCHEDULE D

Energy: Coal and Fuel Substitutes

Situation Before the War

In 1938, France produced 40.8 million tons of coal—two-thirds of her needs. The last third was imported from Poland and Germany. The coal beds

*Ibid, pp. 198, 135, 138–185, 186ff.

of Lorraine, in the heart and in front of the Maginot Line, produced 7 million tons, no longer available after the declaration of war in 1939.

In May 1940, the German blitz invasion stopped the mining of the large coal beds in Nord and Pas-de-Calais and the vital imports from Belgium, Holland, and England. These had in the interim taken the place of those from Poland and Germany, as well as the shortfall caused by the loss of the coal from Lorraine.

On November 9, Aimé Lepercq, who was later arrested by the Germans (May 1943) and became de Gaulle's minister of finance (1945), headed the coal industry (Comité d'Organisation des Houilles). His two aims were:

1. To prevent extortionate German requisitions (in fact they never exceeded 4 percent of the total production) and to prevent the deportation of miners, employees, and supervisors to Germany.

2. To protect future long-term production by exploiting second-grade fields and reopening mines of second quality that had been closed before the war.

These measures caused a lowering of production and an increased financial burden on the state. Investments were made with a view to building the necessary equipment for the opening of mines in 1945, 1946, and 1947. These investments in future production were double those of 1939.

Protection of the Miners

During the winter of 1940–41, 2,400 miners, employees, and supervisors, who were war prisoners, were liberated. The next year, Laval, struggling against Sauckel, obtained from Speer that all miners would be exempted from the draft of the 1942 and 1943 classes destined to work in Germany— so long as they were in the employ of the coal mines. This would permit 48,000 "résistants," Jews, and young men in fear of arrest by the SS to be drafted in the mines of the north and southern center of France between June 1942 and June 1944. By the end of May 1942, a total of 250,000 were working in the "industries" (168,300 actually underground mining, as against a total of 211,500 in 1939, of which 140,700 were in underground mines).

A special food allotment was made for the benefit of miners, and their salaries were increased by percentages higher than the average of all other salaries. The level of 78.5 percent above 1939 in January 1944 was far in excess of the rate of inflation.

Production

	Amount (tons)
1941	43,737,000
1942	43,908,000

Amount (tons)

1943	42,468,000
1944	Calculated on the basis of the first six months: 40,600,000

The total output was recorded in the central Office de Répartition du Charbon, which controlled distribution. Not a ton could leave the mine for a French or German destination without being checked by the distributor. This procedure made French or German black markets impossible.

Priorities and Percentages

First priority: Public utilities, railroads, gas factories, electric plants and coal mines, which together consumed 38.4 percent of this energy.

Second priority: Industries in the two zones. They obtained 32.06 percent.

Third priority: The public consumed 19.5 percent (instead of 26 percent in 1938).

The German army, including the navy and the Todt Organization, received an average of 4 percent, that is, 1,545,000 tons.

In effect French coal was consumed essentially in France and in North Africa, which could not be supplied from its usual sources and which received 550,000 tons in 1941 and 630,000 tons in 1942.[*]

Fuel Substitutes

Between the two world wars, no extensive study of substitutes had been undertaken. It was difficult to conceive of a defeat and an enemy occupation, followed by a blockade that would deprive France of the oil reserves of the British Empire. Certain quantities of alcohol had nevertheless been conditioned, because the importers were obliged to supply alcohol as an offset to their imports of gasoline.

As early as July 1940, the government began to tackle this problem with the object of:

1. Converting as many cars and trucks as possible into gas-driven vehicles.

2. Producing the largest quantity of charcoal and gas from France's forests. The navy released for this purpose all the iron and corrugated

[*]Statistics assembled by Roland Fabre, former secretary-general, of the Houillères et du Comité d'Organisation de l'Industrie des Combustibles Minéraux Solides. The Hoover Institution, no. 263, vol. 1, pp. 265 ff.

iron sheets from the naval depots and dockyards. The Service des Eaux et Forêts organized in all the state-owned forests the production of charcoal and gas. Private forest owners leased their woods and forests to qualified corporations.

In the years 1940–42, 210 industrial corporations were set up that produced in one year the equivalent of 317,000 tons of gasoline. During the same year, more than 150,000 licenses were issued to cars and trucks using charcoal gas.

Increase continued in 1943, during which year the total of gasoline substitutes amounted to about one-third of France's consumption of gasoline between June 1, 1938, and June 30, 1939.°

SCHEDULE E

Transport and Communications

Situation at the Armistice

In an attempt to delay the German advance, the corps of engineers of the French army destroyed practically all the railroad bridges north of the Loire River while thousands of German bombers were attacking railroad stations, freight yards, and junctions. During the forty-day blitzkrieg, the total amount of destruction exceeded that of the four years of World War I.†

During the first few days after the armistice (July 1940), the food situation in Paris was catastrophic. Only two trains, using a single track, came from the South. Most of the canal locks had been destroyed, and transport by road was scarce.

The top priority was to avoid what was happening in Belgium and Holland, where the German Eisenbahn Direktion had immediately seized control of the entire railroad systems of both countries. The president of the French national system, Le Besneray, and the French government were able to block the general take-over by the Germans. Until V-Day, the French kept full control over their railroad system, while a small staff of the Eisenbahn Direktion (not admitted to the central building on the Rue de Rome) was housed at 13 Boulevard de la Gare. They coordinated the timetables for the German military trains and convoys between France and Germany, with the schedules of the French passenger and freight trains.

32,278 meters of partly destroyed tracks *(brèches)* were mended.

1,260 railroad buildings were partly or totally repaired.

Hundreds of switches and switchlines were reconditioned.

°See *France During the German Occupation*, pp. 347–60.
†See the technical report by the S.N.C.F.; "La Reconstruction des Ouvrages d'Art de la S.N.C.F. Juillet 1940–Juillet 1942" (Library of Châteldon), 381 pp.; only 28 copies.

Hundreds of kilometers of telegraph lines and hundreds of electric pylons were repaired.

By the end of 1941, the S.N.C.F. had on its payroll 463,400 staff, employees, and workmen, and the total length of railroads in operation was 41,457 kilometers. The annual receipts (in francs) were:

1941	25,440,000
1942	27,548,000
1943	36,739,000
1944	26,295,000

Number of passenger trips:

1941	511 million
1942	579 million
1943	685 million

Amount (in tons) of goods carried:

1941	98,000,000
1942	102,000,000
1943	93,000,000

Finances

The S.N.C.F. operated at a slight profit in 1941, 1942, and 1943, as against deficits in 1936, 1937, 1938, and 1939. The equipment in operation during this span consisted of:

10,172 steam locomotives

766 electric locomotives

420 self-propelled electric railway coaches

17,600 passenger cars

198,300 freight cars.

The yards and works built, in 1941, 110 heavy locomotives of the 141 P Mikado type, capable of exceeding 100 kilometers per hour, and they continued to modernize engines and passenger cars.

Like the miners, all the 463,400 employees and workmen of the S.N.C.F. were exempted from labor in Germany. The exemption applied to the classes that reached twenty-one years of age in the years 1941–43. The entire personnel was given the status of men mobilized by the French government.

Posts, Telegraph, and Telephone (P.T.T.)

June 1940: During the exodus of refugees, thousands of postmen fled with their families, and 18,000 were made prisoners of war by the Wehrmacht. Many of these last were subsequently released.

Under the Hague Convention, the occupying power can take control of the entire postal and telegraph system in the occupied country. But the French government was able to retain control over the central telephone building in Paris and the central exchange offices of the large towns. (Postal service, telegraph, and telephones were unified under one ministry.)

After August 1, an unlimited number of postcards could be sent between the occupied zone and the southern *"zone libre."*

War damage was considerable. More than a thousand buildings were destroyed or severely damaged. Sixty central buildings were completely destroyed, and 440 needed repairs; 250 kilometers of wires had been destroyed along the railroad tracks, and many cables were made inoperable.

July 1940: Massive mailings of letters and packages to the prisoners began. By the end of July, 300,000 letters and 45,000 packages left daily.

August 1940: Practically all the post office stations were opened, and by the end of the month, 85 percent of the employees of the occupied zone were back at work.

By the end of January 1941, practically all the damaged buildings had been repaired. Three collections and two deliveries of mail took place every day. At the end of the month, three airplane postal routes were created, and the repairs of the telegraph and telephone lines along the railroads were done simultaneously, by the workmen of the P.T.T. and the S.N.C.F., who were housed in "dormitory trains."

March 1941: Postal office cars were put on the long-distance trains where mail was sorted at night. Letters sent from Paris were delivered the next afternoon in Bordeaux, Toulouse, and Marseille.

May 1941: 6,200 postmen returned from prison camps; 11,700 remained in captivity.

January 1943: The Ministry of Food Supplies organized with the P.T.T. the sending of food packages up to 3 kilograms into large towns. The average shipments delivered in Paris exceeded 100,000 packages a day, that is, 300 tons of food supplies over and above the rations.

March 1, 1943: More than 1 million letters crossed each way from one zone into the other.

June 1944: When the Allied bombings began, the P.T.T. used gas-run cars for the delivery of mail and packages.

Protection of possible war material: When the general German withdrawal took place, the large stockpile of copper at Limoges, in the center of France, was dispersed and hidden.

August 10, 1944: The efficiency of the P.T.T. was immensely beneficial to the morale of the French people, who could communicate without restriction by letter, telephone, and telegram.

Merchant Marine

Before the war, two-thirds of French imports came by sea, and France's colonial empire was kept prosperous thanks to trade by sea with the homeland.

A clause of the armistice (June 1940) forbade any sailing or shipping from a French port without authorization from the Armistice Commission, then sitting continuously at Wiesbaden. Laval's first concern was to obtain a blanket authorization for shipments from the ports of the southern free zone: Marseille, Toulon, Port-Vendres. This was a difficult negotiation, as Pétain and Laval consistently refused to have German consuls in France's North African territories.

Admiral Auphan became the active head of the merchant marine. In July, two-thirds of the tonnage afloat (1,650,000 tons) was operated by fuel; 183 ships, totaling 619,000 tons, used coal. Navigation in the Mediterranean was dangerous, because of the presence of German and Italian mines and submarines. To stiffen the morale of sailors and fishermen, apprentice schools were set up and a law of September 16, 1940, provided that "any ship lost would be replaced, ton for ton, by the state."

As was true of miners, railroad employees, and other industrial workers, the 150,000 sailors and professional fishermen were exempted from labor in Germany when their classes were called up in 1941, 1942, and 1943.

The rotation of ships between Marseille and the French North African ports varied between sixty-five and eighty crossings per week, just about the average frequency before the war, with a larger average cargo per shipment:

	1940 (tons)	1941 (tons)	1942 (tons)
Wines	750,000	960,000	400,000
Phosphates and minerals	400,000	1,200,000	1,500,000
Cereals	230,000	350,000	200,000
Fruits	200,000	250,000	250,000
Miscellaneous	150,000	200,000	200,000
	1,730,000	2,960,000	2,500,000

Trade with Morocco became more sizable than before the war:

	1938 (tons)	November 1941– November 1942 (tons)
Cereals	121,000	135,000
Fruits	60,000	31,500
Meat, eggs, fish	19,000	20,800
Vegetable horsehair	3,450	16,600
Phosphates, minerals	200,000	230,000
Miscellaneous	100,000	70,000
	503,450	503,900

In two years, French Senegal shipped to France more than 500,000 tons of cocoa and peanuts and 10,000 tons of oil to Algeria. The other African colonies during the same period shipped nearly 500,000 tons of cocoa, coffee, bananas, palm oil, and wood. The Antilles exported to Casablanca (Morocco) and continental France 100,000 tons of sugar and 8,000 tons of rum; Madagascar and Indochina, nearly 200,000 tons of rice, meat, coffee, manioc, and sugar.

Official statistics show that without the peanuts of Dakar, the individual ration of oil in France would have been 50 percent less, and the production of milk (because of the lack of oil cake for the cattle) would have been 25 percent less.

Until 1942, the French merchant marine supplied North Africa with coal and manufactured products.

In 1941 and 1942 considerable military equipment was secretly stockpiled in North Africa and raw materials sent and camouflaged. In 1942, the Algerian and colonial army, headed by General Juin, would not have been so successful in supporting the U.S. Army in its landings and pursuit of the Germans in Italy without this equipment. General Juin himself, more than one-half of his officers, and 80 percent of his African soldiers had been released in 1940–41, thanks to the government efforts, from the German prison camps.°

SCHEDULE F

Health and Sports

Medical Services for the Military

In June 1940, the Medical Corps suffered severely from the blitz and the defeat. Within a few days of the armistice, its head, General Liégeois, immediately went to work and organized his headquarters at Clermont-Ferrand, then at Royat, a suburb. The government obtained from the German Armistice Commission the transfer to the southern free zone of the "Centers of Instruction and Studies."

In December 1940, the greater part of the stocks of surgical instruments, medicine, bandages, etc., escaped capture by the Wehrmacht and gradually found its way to the southern zone, where the entire medical corps was practically rebuilt. By December 1940, it constituted part of the French Army of the Armistice (100,000 men), stationed mostly in North Africa, outside the reach of the Wehrmacht.

Bacteriological and X-ray departments continued to function, and General Liégeois obtained the use of certain sections of the large civilian hospitals. In North Africa, the hospitals of Algiers, Tunis, and Casablanca continued to operate for the benefit of the army, with the assistance of 500 doctors and chemists.

In November 1942, the Wehrmacht invaded the southern zone as a result of the Allied landings in North Africa. A grave problem arose as to saving

°*France During the German Occupation,* pp. 305–338.

all the equipment, pharmacy, and bandages, and they were hidden practically overnight in civilian depots. Practically all the officers maintained their military status (rank and pay), and many volunteered to go to Germany to take care of the French war prisoners. Many of those who did not volunteer to go to Germany found their way into the Armée Secrète (Secret Army of the Resistance). Here are the statistics of the officers on the payroll of the military medical corps in June 1940 and July 1944:

	June 1940	July 1944 (approximate)
Doctors	14,583	12,700
Chemists	3,844	3,300
Dentists	1,868	1,700
Officers in administrative departments	4,114	3,500

The Civilian Ministry of Health

In April 1942, the Laval government appointed Dr. Grasset, a well-known physician, as minister of health to replace an undersecretary of state, because of the increased importance of health problems. Before his appointment, Dr. Grasset had presided for years over the Council of Physicians.

Medical supplies: during the first hours of the invasion of the southern zone, in November 1942, Laval and Grasset decided to transfer the custody of all medical corps stocks (worth several billion francs) from the Defense Department to the Ministry of Civil Health, which, in turn, organized the camouflage of these stocks all over the South of France. Ninety percent of the stock was saved from seizure by the Wehrmacht, which was in great need of these supplies to wage its war on two fronts. The transport of the supplies was accomplished with the connivance of the Red Cross, which lent its trucks for the operation. During the bombardments preceding and accompanying the battle of France, these stocks proved indispensable.

Dr. Grasset opposed every attempt of the Wehrmacht to requisition hospitals, psychiatric centers, clinics, and the like. All the stocks of alkaloids, opium, Pasteur vaccines, etc., were saved from seizure by the Germans, and the ministry continued to purchase from Spain and Switzerland essential medicine not made in France.

Sanitary Conditions in France from 1940 to 1944

1. *Epidemics*

   A typhus epidemic with fifty cases in Marseille as a consequence of the spreading disease in North Africa was rapidly contained by prophylactic measures.

   In 1943, a sudden rise of poliomyelitis was checked.

   Diphtheria and typhoid fever slightly increased in 1942–44.

Although undernourishment and overwork brought on cases of tuberculosis, deaths increased only slightly, from 140 to 170 for 100,000 inhabitants. Starting October 1943, the figures decreased.

2. *Infant Mortality*

Per 1,000 births

1940	80
1941	71
1942	73
1943	77
1944	78
1945	109

3. *Death Rate for 10,000 Inhabitants*° (death from natural causes and war casualties excluded)

	1940	*1941*	*1942*	*1943*	*1944*
Gross rate	183	174	168	160	176
Apparent increase in death rates as compared to 1939 (death rate in 1939: 155)	28	19	13	5	21
Actual increase in death rates due to the rotation of population starting in November 1942	28	15	9	1	17
Actual increase in death-rate percentages as compared to 1939	19%	10%	6%	0%	11%

°Ibid., pp. 889–900.
Figures published in the official publication *Population* for the quarterly period January–March 1946, p. 137.

Physical Training and Sports

1. *The Sports Program*
A vast sports organization was created under the name of Commissariat Général aux Sports, which organized programs of instruction in physical training in all schools.

In July 1940, Marshal Pétain appointed as high commissioner Jean Borotra, the former world tennis champion, a man of great competence and high principle. His assistant, Colonel Pascot, a former international player on the French rugby team, succeeded him in 1942. In 1944, Borotra was arrested by the Germans and deported.

Colonel de Maisonneuve and other officers were detached from the army, and while ostensibly performing their normal duties, their secret mission was to constitute, within the sports program, the nucleus of a secret army of officers and noncommissioned officers for the Resistance.

2. *Construction of Sports Facilities*
A top priority was the purchase, building, and equipping of sports grounds all over the country. The government subsidized 60 percent of the total cost. No government before 1940 had been as generous. On January 1, 1944, 10,335 grounds had been purchased, and thousands had been inaugurated or were nearing completion. In 1940, France had only twenty-three public swimming pools. On January 1, 1944, 250 had been opened for use, and more than 250 others were being built.

Youth camps (Chantiers de Jeunesse) were constructed in many areas, and extensive sports programs were developed under the direction of General Laporte Dutheil. His main task was to save the 33,000 young members of the organization from forced labor in Germany.

3. *German Opposition to These Activities*
Beginning in the summer of 1942, the Germans exerted more and more pressure to force the government to curtail the credits and stop the furnishing of materials, cement, stone, etc., for these programs. The aim was to increase the number of young men going to Germany. Laval told Colonel Pascot, the high commissioner: "Spend as much money as you can, use as much labor as you can. It will be that much money and men the Germans won't get."*

SCHEDULE G

Welfare: Facts and Figures

Secours National

1. *Origin*
This agency, created during World War I, took its motto from Pasteur's famous saying *"I am not asking you where you come from, nor your nationality, nor your name, but what is your trouble?"*

*Ibid., p. 877.

Its extraordinary achievements in 1914–18 were to be duplicated following the catastrophe of June 1940.

2. *Leadership*

Under the honorary presidency of Marshal Pétain, the guiding genius of this huge organization from October 4, 1940, until the liberation was Georges Pilon; his first deputy was Mr. Garric. These two exceptional men managed a budget of billions of francs, donated by hundreds of thousands of French men and women. Both worked day after day (and often night after night) for a salary of one franc a year, directing thousands of volunteers.

3. *Activities of the Agency*
   a. Assistance to all the refugees from Alsace and Lorraine in the southern zone.
   b. Assistance to all the Belgian and Dutch refugees who chose to remain in the southern zone because of their anti-German sentiments.
   c. Relief and assistance to elderly people in both zones.
   d. Organization and management in all towns, large or small, of workrooms where old and disabled people without adequate means received small salaries to make garments, knit sweaters and socks, repair clothing, etc.
   e. Shelter, help, and relief for those refugees forced to escape from their homes during the battle of France in 1944.
   f. Organization of canteens in schools. Vitamins and casein, sugar and biscuits, were distributed in addition to food. The making and giving out of these products robbed the Germans of thousands of tons of flour. These supplies were secretly obtained from Ministry of Agriculture and Food Supplies (see Schedule B). By January 1, 1941, more than 30,000 volunteers were already employed without pay by the agency, serving in every préfecture of the eighty-six departements of France (see Schedule K).

4. *German Hostility to the Agency*

The Germans were worried by the continuous expansion of the Secours National and opposed its activities as often as they could. A few examples:
   a. In 1942, the German police discovered in the northern part of France, near Lille, a large depot of several hundred tons of wool that had been hidden for more than two years. Laval immediately asked Pilon to act as if the entire stock belonged to the Secours National. In two consecutive nights, the stock was loaded in trucks of the Red Cross and Secours National and taken to workrooms of the Secours National in large and small towns of the occupied zone.

b. Attempts were made by the Germans to dissolve the Salvation Army, the Quakers, and the Secours for Spanish Refugees. In each case, Laval asked Pilon to absorb the three organizations, and they continued their work under different names within the framework of the Secours National.

c. In April 1944, the Germans requested the resignation of Georges Pilon's deputy, Mr. Garric. Laval received the representative of the German embassy in the presence of Mr. Pilon and said: "If he goes, I go . . ." Garric remained at his post until the liberation.

5. *Postwar Recognition*

In September 1944, General de Gaulle's provisional government changed the name of the Secours National to L'Entr'aide Française. It continued to take care of the repatriated war prisoners, deportees, and others.

Three years later, the president of the Republic, Vincent Auriol, conferred upon the Entr'aide Française the Grand Cross of the National Medal of Honor. The citation read as follows:

For more than ten years past, thirty-five thousand public-spirited volunteers and the regular personnel have given a unique example of their devotion to social aid and relief work and brought together hundreds of thousands of French people in their generous mission.

The S.I.P.E.G.*

1. The Third Republic created this organization at the beginning of World War II (September 1939). It continued after France's defeat (June 1940) by coordinating all the work undertaken by the five government agencies concerned with: Agriculture and Food Supplies, Industrial Production, Defense, Interior, and Health. Included in this last, of course, were the Secours National and the Red Cross. S.I.P.E.G. steadily expanded its activities until the end of the battle of France of 1944.

2. *Principal Achievements*

a. After France's defeat and the exodus of refugees to the South, from July 1 to October 30, 1940, the S.I.P.E.G. organized, in conjunction with the National Railways, S.N.C.F. (see Schedule E), the return of more than 2 million refugees in more than 2,000 trains using rebuilt roadbeds.

b. Fourteen million tons of gasoline were distributed in the free zone to facilitate the return of more than a million refugees who had fled from their homes by car.

*Service Interministériel de Protection contre les Événements de Guerre (literally: Interministerial Service for Protection during War Emergencies).

c. Giving aid and comfort in the resettlement of the several hundred thousand refugees who could not or would not return to their homes: Alsatians, Lorrainers, Belgians, Dutch, Spaniards, etc. S.I.P.E.G. records give the numbers of "registered" refugees as follows:

Refugees from the occupied zone choosing to remain in the free zone	16,871
Refugees from the prohibited zone (northern districts on the Belgian frontier)	125,528
Alsatians-Lorrainers	97,543
Foreigners	17,592
	257,644

These refugees received official cards as *réfugié secouru* and were listed in the labor office of each district. All received free medical assistance, clothing, and other necessaries.

The French Red Cross

The growth of this semiprivate organization parallelled that of the Secours National, so that the Darlan and Laval governments and their prefects had to give the Red Cross continuous protection from German attacks.

1. Financial and material aid came periodically from the Ministry of Finance and other agencies without the knowledge of the Germans. Both trucks and fuel were supplied by government agencies. Large quantities of medicine were secretly turned over by the Ministry of Health to the Red Cross. Certain drugs, only available in Spain or Switzerland, were purchased in those countries by representatives of the Red Cross and paid for with French government funds.

2. During the entire occupation, the American Hospital in Neuilly remained open and protected under the banner of the French Red Cross.°

SCHEDULE H

Education and Culture

Universities, Schools, and Libraries

1. The seventeen universities that functioned in France at the beginning of the war and all the *grandes écoles* (leading institutions for

° *France During the German Occupation*, pp. 900–14.

specialized subjects) maintained their courses of study and yearly examinations until the liberation. Practically all the incumbent deans and professors in the universities were confirmed in their posts.

A striking example was the case of the University of Strasbourg, in Alsace. The university administration and four of its colleges moved bodily to the town of Clermont-Ferrand in the free zone in November 1940, when the Reich proceeded with the de facto annexation of Alsace. The teaching continued in French, and as a sign of solidarity, the dean was appointed to the high office of secretary-general of the Bureau of Education in the Ministry of Education.

At the end of the war, the university returned to Strasbourg, and retrieved all its properties and privileges. This example is typical of Laval's concern for preserving in the universities and the *grandes écoles* the two fundamental freedoms of speech and thought. Despite strong, persistent German pressure, these freedoms were maintained.

2. Public schools: More than 100,000 schoolteachers who had fled the German advance in May and June 1940 went back to their posts after the armistice. Not only did they resume their functions and receive slightly better salaries than the average of other civil servants, but they were left entirely free to voice their opinions. As the Liberation approached, many of them joined the Resistance.

    On September 3, 1942, Laval addressed a large gathering of schoolteachers at the Hôtel du Parc in Vichy. The essence of his message was that France, despite her present hardships, had always played a major role in history and would be saved with their help. He also explained to those teachers his public speech of June 22.

3. Libraries: The main French libraries, including the American Library of Paris, which contained 100,000 English and American books, were successfully operated and maintained during the entire occupation.

Books and Publishers

While the publishers of the occupied zone had "agreed" with the Propagandastaffel in September 1940 not to publish books whose authors were Jewish, Freemasons, or "anti-German," and although the paper shortage permitted only limited printings, still, in 1942, 9,348 books were published in France (as against 7,705 in the United Kingdom during the same year).[*]

In December 1940, France's leading publishing house, Gallimard, was allowed to resume its activity. The publisher's internationally known periodical, *N.R.F. (Nouvelle Revue Française)*, came out again on December 1, 1940, and continued under Drieu La Rochelle's editorship until 1943, num-

[*] See G. Heller's book *"Un Allemand à Paris,"* Seuil, 1980, p. 32.

bering such contributors as Montherlant, Chardonne, Ramon Fernandez, Valéry (*La Cantate de Narcisse*, 1/1/1941); Eluard (*Blason des Fleurs et des Fruits*, 1/2/41); and Gide (Feuillets de Journal, 1/2/1941).

Up to 1942, the following works of importance were published in France: Arland (*Sur une Terre Menacée*, Stock 1941); J. de Baroncelli (*Vingt-Six Hommes, Récit de Guerre*, Grasset 1941); Benoist-Méchin (*La Moisson de Quarante, Journal d'un Prisonnier de Guerre*, Albin Michel 1941); Brasillach (*Notre Avant-Guerre*, Plon 1941); Chardonne (*Voir la Figure*, Grasset 1941); Fabre-Luce (*Journal de France*, 1940); Aragon (*Le Crève-Coeur*, Collection Métamorphose, Avril 1941), (*Les Yeux d'Elsa*, Cahiers du Rhône, 1941); Camus (*L'Etranger*, Gallimard, 1942); Mauriac (*La Pharisienne*, Grasset 1941).

It is interesting to note that one of Camus' masterpieces, *L'Etranger*, was published by Gallimard in 1942. The French publishers that remained open during this period were Gallimard, Garnier, Sirey, Grasset, Costerman, Denoël, Stock, Armand Colin, Flammarion, Hachette, Larousse, Mercure de France.

Theater and Film

1. *Theater:* In September–October 1940, the Germans, surprisingly, did not oppose the reopening of the theaters in Paris. But little by little even the four National Theaters (Opéra, Opéra-Comique, Comédie Française, and Odéon), which are normally managed by the government, fell, like the other Paris theaters, under the de facto control of the Propagandastaffel.

   The Germans delegated the task of supervision to two Frenchmen (Roger Capgras and Robert Trebor), who were soon distrusted. In the end, a committee of four talented artists—Baty, Dullin, Jouvet, and Jean Renoir—were, in effect, in charge of the theaters.

   The French countermove to the pressure of the Propagandastaffel was the creation on July 7, 1941, of a Comité d'Organisation des Entreprises de Spectacles (C.O.E.S), which managed to evade German control.

   The C.O.E.S. was at first run by the general manager of the Comédie Française, Jean-Louis Vaudoyer. He resigned early in 1942. In May, the general manager of the Odéon, René Rocher, succeeded him.

   The Germans were obviously opposed to the creation of the C.O.E.S., but Rocher succeeded in avoiding all incidents until 1944; even during the tense period of the first months of that year (bombings, shortages, etc.). Throughout, the C.O.E.S. functioned under the French government's responsibility.

   Evidence that the roster of theater productions was comparable in quality to that of the prewar years is suggested in the following list:

1941–42

Opéra and Opéra-Comique: Mozart (*Don Juan, L'enlèvement au Sérail*); Maurice Ravel (*Bolero*)

Comédie Française: Edmond Rostand (*Cyrano de Bergerac*); Shakespeare (*Hamlet*)

Odéon: Molière (*Le Bourgeois Gentilhomme*)

Atelier: Pirandello (*Vêtir ceux qui sont nus*); Jean Anouilh (*Eurydice*)

Michodière: Edouard Bourdet (*Hyménée*)

Madeleine: Sacha Guitry (*N'écoutez pas, Mesdames*)

Comédie des Champs-Élysées: Bernard Shaw (*Candida*)

Oeuvre: Paul Claudel (*L'annonce faite à Marie*)

Chatelet: Strauss (*Valse de Vienne*)

1942–43

Opéra and Opéra-Comique: Honegger (*Antigone*); Fauré (*Pénélope*); Richard Strauss (*Ariane à Naxos*)

Comédie Française: Montherlant (*La Reine Morte*)

Odéon: Sophocles (*Antigone*); Beaumarchais (*Le Mariage de Figaro*)

Sarah-Bernhardt: Shakespeare (*Richard III*); Sartre (*Les Mouches*)

Mathurins: Ibsen (*Solness le Constructeur*)

Michodière: Shakespeare (*Macbeth, The Taming of the Shrew*)

Renaissance: F. de Rojas (*La Célestine*)

1943–44

Opéra and Opéra-Comique: Verdi (*Otello*); Gluck (*Alceste*); Giraudoux (*Amphitryon 38*)

Comédie Française: Paul Claudel (*Le Soulier de Satin*); Molière (*Le Bourgeois Gentilhomme*)

Odéon: Feydeau (*Un fil à la Patte*); Lope de Vega (*L'Etoile de Séville*)

Atelier: Anouilh (*Antigone*)

Bouffes-Parisiens: Roger Ferdinand (*Les J3*)

Hébertot: Shaw (*Pygmalion*); Giraudoux (*Sodome et Gomorrhe*)

Michodière: Anouilh (*Le Voyageur sans Bagages*)

Oeuvre: Strindberg (*La Danse de la Mort*)

Sarah-Bernhardt: Calderon (*La Vie est un Songe*)

Vieux-Colombier: Sartre (*Huis-Clos*)

The principal achievement of the C.O.E.S. was to organize and regulate the profession as a whole, which had never been done before. The Enabling Act of December 27, 1943, was kept in force by General de Gaulle and is still the law governing the French theatrical world.

2. *Film:* The French film industry faced three major problems:
   a. Before the war, the Germans had established in France a strong producing corporation, Continental Film, which was aided by a large distribution network. These companies, heavily supported by the German authorities, made it difficult for the French cinema to carry on its independent work.
   b. A shortage of raw materials and services (plaster, electricity) also hampered production.
   c. Another blow was the prohibition against exports, which previously had amounted to 40 percent of the income of the French cinema industry. Exportation was now made a monopoly of the Germans' Continental Film.

   In spite of these difficulties, which at the outset appeared insurmountable, the French moviemakers produced 160 films between 1942 and 1944, and of such quality that in France they completely outmatched the films produced by Continental Film or made in Germany.

   Among the French films of those years were such outstanding classics as: *Le Corbeau, Les Visiteurs du Soir, Goupil Mains-Rouges, La Nuit Fantastique, Chiffon, Douce, Les Enfants du Paradis, Lumière d'Eté, Le Ciel est à vous,* and *Les Anges du Péché.*

   This result was due to the Comité d'Organisation de l'Industrie Cinématographique headed by Roger Richebé, Marcel Achard, and André Debrie. The government fully supported this Committee and also created a Direction Générale du Cinéma to protect the French against German competition in all its forms.

   Jacques Siclier, the film critic of the daily *Le Monde,* in his study of the cinema during the occupation (La France de Pétain et son Cinéma) concludes with this tribute: "The Organization Committee of the Cinema Industry not only enabled this industry to remain French but also fostered its financial and artistic development in spite of the German pressure and of the economic difficulties due to the war."*

SCHEDULE I

War Prisoners

Liberations

1. At the signing of the armistice, on June 22, 1940, more than 2 million French war prisoners had been captured.

*Ibid, p. 869–965.

2.   In July 1940, more than 500,000 French soldiers, mostly farmers and farm laborers, were liberated from temporary camps in France.

3.   In November 1940, an official treaty was signed with the Reich providing for the appointment of a French ambassador for the French war prisoners: Georges Scapini. The appointee was a former deputy from Paris who had been severely wounded in World War I.

4.   From July 1940 to 1944, 900,000 French prisoners were released by Germany through negotiation and without any *quid pro quo* given. Among the number were 20,000 officers (out of a total of 45,000) and *all* the veterans of World War I (approximately 400,000).

5.   During the first months of 1941, the Reich agreed to release fathers of four children or more; prisoners whose wives had died during their husbands' captivity; and all imprisoned sailors and railway and mine workers.

6.   Between July 1940 and July 1944, of the French prisoners who were severely wounded or sick, 120,000 were returned (as against only 1,200 British).

The Life of War Prisoners in Germany

1.   *Organization:* French war prisoners who remained in Germany were divided into so-called Kommandos, that is, small groups of fifteen to fifty agricultural or industrial workers.

2.   *Clothing and feeding:* From August to November 1940, feeding was insufficient for the industrial groups, especially those of the Ruhr, and clothing inadequate as winter set in. Packages from France could be sent in unlimited number until the end of December. After that, two packages per month were permitted (until 1944). In addition to the "family packages," the government also sent, during the four years, 97,825,146 kilos of food, 4,272,699 kilos of tobacco, 302,737 kilos of soap, and 18,715,110 pieces of clothing.

3.   *Health care:* In 1942, typhus spread in Germany, occupied Poland, and Russia. There, tens of thousands died. Professor Lumière and members of the Pasteur Institute were sent to Berlin and the prison camps with large stocks of serum. The deaths were limited to fewer than one hundred.

   Cases of tuberculosis reported amounted to less than 1.5 percent, as against 10 percent among French prisoners of war in Germany during World War I.

4.   *Pay:* The German lagermarks could only be spent in the camps and the Kommando groups, and no money could be sent back to families

in France. Starting in 1941, the French government obtained permission for the transfer to France of German currency from soldiers and officers alike.

5. *Correspondence:* By the end of 1940, no limitation had been placed on the number of letters sent by French families to their war prisoners. After that, one letter and two cards per month each way was the permissible limit.

6. *Religion:* The assignment of a minimum of one chaplain to every camp was obtained.

7. *Books and music:* Each month, 55,000 books were sent from France, 1,800 games, 1,800 musical instruments, and 2,500 recordings.

Assistance to War Prisoners' Families in France

1. A monthly allowance indexed to the cost of living was paid to the spouse of each prisoner, with a supplement for each child and relative. Thus, 24 billion francs were paid by August 1, 1944, in addition to the contributions from other, specialized government agencies.

2. A Central Committee of Assistance was established as part of the Secours National to help families in need through the distribution of clothing and medical aid, and the organization of holiday camps, social clubs, etc.

3. In each town, a Famille du Prisonnier came to the aid of prisoners' spouses and children. These organizations distributed in four years 1,610,000,000 francs' worth of coal, bread, meat rations, etc.

Legal Measures for Protection of War Prisoners

A coordinated group of laws and decrees was enacted to protect all the French war prisoners during their forced absence from their homeland.

1. No income taxes were to be levied on them.

2. All rents paid by prisoners' families were reduced by 75 percent.

3. All agricultural leases were prolonged until prisoners' return.

4. No claims against prisoners for commercial debts could be brought to court.

5. Job status in factories, farms, companies, etc., were maintained.

6. The rights of civil servants to promotion or increases in salaries were guaranteed, as well as pensions.

Returning Prisoners

Reception and relief organizations were created in Compiègne for the northern zone and Lyons for the southern. At Compiègne, the "record day" of March 20, 1941, became known as "l'Exploit": in one single day, 8,000 prisoners were fed and clad and given medical care, bonuses of repatriation, and railroad tickets to their homes.

In each of the eighty-six departments, a Maison du Prisonnier was organized and in the towns, comparable centers.

In Paris and Lyons, two Secrétariats des Camps acted as permanent liaison between the repatriated prisoners and those still in camps. They took care of transfers of funds, food supplies, etc.

Each prisoner on his return received a savings account, a gift of the state financed by the Secours National (see Schedule G). The total sum for this purpose exceeded 2 billion francs by 1944.

Toute La France, The War Prisoners' Newspaper

A German-sponsored propaganda newspaper called *Le Trait d'Union* (The Hyphen) was distributed in the German camps and expected to circulate among the prisoners' families in France. Laval refused it entry and distribution in France among the liberated prisoners. To check the action of the *Trait d'Union*, the government and repatriated prisoners created the bimonthly *Toute la France*, printed in the southern zone, not subject to any censorship and certainly no "collaborationist" propaganda.

The distribution across the frontier was made through an office in Paris that helped prisoners who escaped from Germany. The head of the Paris office, Michel Petitjean, was arrested on November 18, 1942, when the Germans discovered that he had built a huge "escape road," and he was condemned to 3½ years hard labor in Germany.

Escaped Prisoners

Thanks to Michel Petitjean's "road" and numerous others routes, approximately 80,000 war prisoners escaped between the armistice of June 1940 and the Allied landings in North Africa (November 1942). Most of them took refuge in the southern unoccupied zone. There they had been immediately demobilized and had been given jobs, many in the civil service. Laval obtained assurances from Hitler and General Keitel at the time of the invasion of the South (November 1942) that they would be considered as legally repatriated prisoners.

The D.S.P.G. (Direction des Services des Prisoniers)

Here are the statistics kept by the D.S.P.G., a part of the Defense Ministry headed by General Besson, who supervised with a large staff all the shipments leaving the region of Lyons for the camps in Germany.° The figures include shipments from the Secours National and the families:

Food	250,762,784	kilos
Tobacco	6,531,172	kilos
Soap	1,205,252	kilos
Clothing	18,715,710	pieces

SCHEDULE J

Protection of the French Workers in Germany

July 1940–December 1941—Volunteers

Before Hitler attacked Soviet Russia (1941), Hitler and Stalin were allies, and the real war had not begun; 200,000 French workers, some of whom were Communists with Soviet sympathies, had volunteered to work in Germany on one-year contracts for higher salaries than those paid in France.

January 1942–June 6, 1944 (D-Day)—Forced Labor

The relentless war between Laval and Sauckel began in May–June 1942 and ended only on June 6, 1944, D-Day, when Laval, by secret telegrams to each prefect and to the head of the French police, forbade *all* departures of French workers for Germany. In the late spring of 1942, the war in Russia reached its climax, and the Reich urgently needed more labor.

Hence, the *Decree of June 5, 1942*, signed by Hitler and countersigned by Sauckel: "All men and women between twenty and sixty-five in the European countries occupied by the Reich are subject to call for work in the Reich factories."

This sparked Laval's first major counterattack. He wrung from the Germans the absolute exemption from the decree of all women, farmers, and farm workers.

During the Laval-Sauckel war, Sauckel's demands totaled 2,060,000 men; 641,500 left France for Germany: 100,000 prisoners of war returned to France; 250,000 war prisoners became factory workers in Germany and were paid salaries and given fifteen-day furloughs in France each year.

From France, thirteen workers per 1,000 inhabitants worked in Germany. From Belgium, Holland, Romania, Bulgaria, and other occupied countries, the percentages varied between fifty and eighty-two workers per 1,000, the highest percentage occurring in Poland.

° Ibid, pp. 203–235.

Protection for the French Workers

The Hague Convention had not provided any protection for civilians compelled to work in an enemy country, and the D.A.F. (German Workers' Front) began to take charge of the French volunteers.

1. *The innovator:* In 1942, a dynamic and disinterested French engineer who spoke fluent German, Gaston Bruneton, devised a plan to protect the French workers and to counter the influence of the representatives of the German Workers' Front. Bruneton's plan was immediately accepted and backed by Laval, Lagardelle, the French minister of labor, and Bichelonne. Even Bruneton's enemies were later to give him the nickname "Saint Vincent de Paul." This crusader managed to build with the moral and financial support of the French government a unique social organization that functioned both in France and in Germany. All this began in May 1942 with the foundation of the Service de la Main-d'Oeuvre Française en Allemagne, of which Bruneton, its creator, became the chairman.

2. *The results:* The first results were limited by the work and propaganda of the German Workers' Front. In 1942, only seven of Bruneton's first representatives were allowed to travel in Germany.

   a. But month after month, the French D.O.F. opposed the German D.A.F. and gained ground and momentum. By October 1944, 11,000 French representatives were working and circulating in Germany, solving the variety of problems facing the French workers at all levels—organizing their housing, medical assistance, social activities, sports, and correspondence with their families in France. The French volunteer workers signed a two-year contract and had a ten-day furlough in France after the first year. Many stayed in France at the end of the ten days and went into hiding.

   b. Three "social departments" were set up in Vichy, Paris, and Berlin to coordinate all questions related to wages, housing, food, clothing, medicine, etc. Five distributing networks were created in Germany, and each depot had its own stock of goods, lorries, and workers. In a period of eighteen months, they distributed 280 freight cars of food and clothing.

   c. The organization took care of the professional training of young workers, thus preparing them for reinsertion into French life at the end of the war.

   d. After 1942, medical aid for French workers in Germany became a serious problem, and the German government readily accepted the presence of more than three hundred French MDs. Thanks to Bruneton's intervention, 70 percent of all French medical students who were conscripted in the two classes sent to

Germany were assigned to their worker compatriots and given the same status as German medical doctors.

e.   Perhaps Bruneton's most remarkable achievement was to set up two hospitals in Germany and obtain for them the right to own and manage their own stock of drugs.

f.   The D.O.F. provided sixty tons of cultural materials during its existence: books, records, musical instruments, and cultural publications.

g.   In France, the D.O.F.'s purposes were twofold: (1) To assist the workers' families and help them send food or clothing packages to Germany; (2) To obtain all conceivable assistance, financial and other, from French industries that dealt before the war with German concerns.

During the last weeks before Germany surrendered, Bruneton arranged for the take-over of his organization by the French Action Clandestine Committee. On his return to France, he was put under house arrest for several months and jailed at Fresnes for a year. He was finally acquitted by the notoriously severe High Court of Justice. After his death in 1962, his family made a few hundred copies of his memoirs entitled *L'Aventure d'Allemagne*. One copy is on file at the Hoover Institution under No. 378. It is today of great interest.[*]

SCHEDULE K

Protection of the Civil Service (Prefects)

Historical Importance of the Corps des Préfets

The reader should know that for nearly two centuries, the French prefects have been the permanent representative of the state in their capacity as heads of the départements or districts in a highly centralized country. The corps, founded by Napoleon, was designed to form a strong body of highly trained and qualified civil servants. With a very few exceptions, prefects always have been career men, like most of the ambassadors in the French foreign service.

During the Third Republic, prefects represented and spoke for *l'état* (the state) in its eighty-nine geographical districts. Each department had, in proportion to its population, from three to six subdistricts *(sous-préfectures)*. The powers of the prefects resemble those of U.S. governors, but with a stronger link to the central government. In France, not only do the prefects represent the prime minister but also each minister within the government.

<hr>

[*] Ibid, pp. 236–250; and Edward Homze, *Foreign Labor in Nazi Germany* (Princeton, N.J.: Princeton University Press, 1967), pp. 177–200.

Seventeen regional prefects act as liaison between the prime minister and the geographic regions, each of which comprises several departments.

The "Corps" During the Occupation

The responsibilities of the three grades of prefects were particularly taxing during the occupation. One-third of the corps of 373 men were arrested by the Germans and deported during the last two and a half years of the occupation (1942–44). All had stood in the front line of defense against the German authorities, protecting the population, homes, properties, food supplies, hospitals, schools, libraries, and other institutions of their country.

1. *Pétain's shake-up of 1940:* When France fell and Pétain formed his first government, he was influenced by the rightist members of his cabinet and took a step that had far-reaching consequences. It involved the replacement of practically all the career prefects by generals, admirals, and other officers plus some civilians, all conservatives, who lacked the necessary experience and training to hold these difficult positions. But the "purge" was intended to be one of the bases of Pétain's so-called Révolution Nationale, directed against the prewar, leftist majority.

   Laval, who had been minister of the interior during the years preceding the arrival to power of the Popular Front in 1936, had worked with these career prefects and was opposed to this shake-up. He used to say, "A prefect's job is one of the noblest in the world. To be worthy of it, one must be intelligent, have long experience, and a great deal of courage."

2. *The rebuilding of the corps:* Accordingly, when he returned to power in April 1942, Laval decided to rebuild and restore the authority of the traditional corps. He counted on it to strengthen the government's and administration's resistance to German pressure, which he felt was and would be increasing at all points.

   To accomplish this, he named as undersecretaries of state two young prefects, Georges Hilaire and René Bousquet, who, as heads of two important regions, the Aube and the Marne, had already successfully opposed the Germans. Both were members of the old Radical-Liberal party that stood between the conservatives and the socialists. In the winter of 1930, at the age of twenty, Bousquet, the youngest member of the staff of the prefect of the Tarn-et-Garonne District, had in his own person saved several lives by rescuing people from the catastrophic floods of the Garonne, where hundreds had drowned. He was made the youngest member of the Legion of Honor. As Laval's undersecretary of state for the police forces in 1942 and 1943, he waged an uphill battle against the head of the German police, General Oberg, and was arrested and deported (see

Schedule L). Georges Hilaire was Laval's direct representative as head of the prefectorial corps.

To understand how the Corps was rebuilt and their work restructured in 1942, those interested should read the account by Georges Hilaire, in collaboration with four leading regional prefects, two of whom were arrested and deported to Germany.°

Features of the Rebuilding Program:

a. Several of the new, noncareer prefects were maintained in their posts, when it appeared that they had been successful.

b. All the others were offered other posts in the administration with approximately the same salaries.

c. Before assuming office, each appointee, after seeing Laval, made a protocol visit to Marshal Pétain, who informed the appointee that the oath of allegiance to the head of state was no longer an obligation.

d. The few career men who had been dismissed in 1940 and who turned down jobs offered by Laval because of the risks involved were reinstated as prefects *"en disponibilité"* (i.e., inactive, but available for service) with regular salaries.

e. In 1943 and 1944, the wives of those arrested and deported by the Germans (one-third of the entire corps) continued to receive their husbands' salaries.†

SCHEDULE L

Protection of the Law Enforcement Personnel

The Police

1. *June 1940:* The Armistice Convention of June 1940 included a draconian paragraph with ominous implications for the police:

    The Reich exercises the rights of an occupying power. The French government will comply with the decrees resulting from the exercise by the Reich of these rights. To this end, the French administration is under the obligation to cooperate.

    Under such compulsion, French police officers and men balked at carrying out certain duties, and conflict became endless between the prefects and the German authorities, as well as between the French

°The Hoover Institution (documentary series): Chaigneau, deposition No. 219, Vol. 11, pages 393 to 419.
†See *France During the German Occupation,* pp. 427–537.

and German police forces, since their respective powers had not been defined.

2. *In 1942*, when Laval returned to power, one of the first steps he took was to attempt to lessen the pressure of the German police upon the French police and other administrators. He called on René Bousquet, a former prefect filled with energy and courage, to keep up opposition against General Oberg, and his first assistant, Colonel Knochen, heads of the SS in France.

In June 1942, Bousquet began his stubborn fight against Oberg. He finally obtained for the French police a *modus vivendi* based on four principles:

a. The German police were to ensure the security of the German army.

b. The French police were to ensure the security of the French territory and the protection of the French population.

c. The French police were not to be compelled to designate hostages, and persons arrested by the French police were not to be subject to German reprisals.

d. French persons guilty of offenses not directed against the German army were to be liable only to the French courts applying French law.

Time after time, the prefects and their representatives invoked this *modus vivendi* in their endless arguments with the Germans, and thousands of French nationals thus escaped German arrest. Many French police officers and inspectors were arrested by the Germans because they stubbornly applied the Bousquet-Oberg agreement. René Bousquet himself was arrested and deported to Germany in 1944.

The Gendarmerie

This old corps, comprising the Garde Républicaine of Paris and the (national) Garde Républicaine Mobile, helped to handle and care for the millions of refugees at the time of the German blitz.

During the occupation, they ensured the security of the roads and railways and the protection of the civilian population and the farms. They denounced to the prefects the black market dealings of German officials and of the Wehrmacht and played a considerable part in the relief of the victims of the bombardments that went on during the battle of Normandy, after June 6, 1944.

The Mobile Guard

This group comprised 19,000 men and was classified as part of the Army of the Armistice—six regiments in France and three in North Africa. When the southern zone was occupied at the time of the Allied landings in North

Africa, Laval ensured the continued existence of the Mobile Guard, transferring it from the Defense Ministry to the Interior Ministry, under the command of General Perré. Its main task was to counterbalance, if not to neutralize, Darnand's Germanophile "militia."°

SCHEDULE M

Protection of the Jews and Freemasons

August 13, 1940: A law inspired by the rightist members of Marshal Pétain's cabinet, particularly the minister of justice, Alibert, ordered the dissolution of all "secret associations." The law was, of course, specially aimed at French Freemasonry, whose members were now excluded from most public offices.

November 10, 1941: Another law created a Special Commission, which permitted a few ex-Freemasons to retain public office under two conditions: (1) persons who had broken off their Masonic association at some time before 1940; (2) persons who had served the state with distinction and had sworn allegiance to the new regime (Marshal Pétain).

April 1942: Laval, once more in power, vigorously opposed the application of the anti-Masonic laws and decrees. His first step, on August 19, 1942, was to appoint and direct, as head of the government, a special commission for the "civic rehabilitation" of Freemasons. He named as president of the commission Maurice Reclus, a member of the French Academy and a liberal member of the Conseil d'Etat, the highest court of administrative justice. Admiral Platon, a diehard anti-Freemason, denounced Laval's policies to Marshal Pétain. Laval forced Platon to resign from the commission, which restored the rights of more and more applicants.

The Freemasonic mayors who had been demoted were reinstated in their towns, and the Association des Maires de France and the Union des Maires de la Seine were able to reconvene.

August 1942: The mayors of all the cities of France held a meeting at Vichy, and Marchandeau, mayor of Reims and a Republican as well as a Freemason, was reelected president of the association.

The long deposition by Maurice Reclus concludes:

I am very proud of having been placed in a position in which I could save Freemasons from persecution, and I am greatly indebted to Pierre Laval for having permitted me to fight for this just cause.†

For the facts and events relating to the Jews in France, see pages 80–85.

°Ibid., Vol. 1, pp. 555, 571, 597; Vol 2, pp. 1556, 1657.
†Ibid, p. 651.

EXHIBIT A

The First Document

First document in the batch of papers shown to me in Paris by Clark Denney in December 1947 and found again in the files delivered to Mme. de Chambrun and me by Captain Ullman and Lieutenant Dufeld of the Information Control Division, American Military Justice, Nüremberg:

THE REICH AIR MINISTER SUPREME COMMANDER OF THE
AIR FORCES

Attention: The Chief of the Air Armament
Az. 66 Nr 26719/40 (LF.3).

Express letter

Berlin W.8
Leipzigerstrasse 7.
9 December 1940.

Re: The inclusion of French aviation.
Ref.: Nr. Pol. I. Lu. 2543/40—November 28, 1940.
To the Ministry of Foreign Affairs of the Reich, Berlin.

By my letter of October 21, 1940—Az. 66 Nr. 2022/40 (LF 3 111)—I have already stressed the importance from the standpoint of our armament policy of my request for the transfer of the management of the shares of stock belonging to the French state that represent its interest in aviation corporations.

The negotiations show that an intolerable slowing down is taking place, as for each measure of any importance the French department in charge of state participations [in industry] must refer to the main shareholder, which is the French government in Vichy.

Meanwhile, the government proceeds with changes in personnel within the companies without informing in advance the German administration of these changes. We have the impression that the French government intends to reorganize the companies in which it has these participating shares or to transfer blocks of shares into other hands.

All this makes me fear that the execution of my orders by the corporations in which the state has an interest will be compromised.

Under no circumstances can I accept the dilatory measures proposed by the French government on November 18, 1940, to the German economic delegation of the armistice.

I must, on the contrary, firmly maintain my demand that the shares of stock which the French state possesses in all aviation firms be transferred to me.

Please convey my demand upon the French government and insist upon its execution as rapidly as possible.°

(*signed*)
Udet

EXHIBIT B

The Second Document

Second document in the batch of papers shown to me in Paris by Clark Denney in December 1947 and found again in the files delivered to Mme. de Chambrun and to me in Paris by Captain Ullman and Lieutenant Dufeld of the Information Control Division, American Military Justice, Nüremberg.

Paris, January 8, 1943

Memorandum

Re: The Franco-German plan of aviation construction.

After the demobilization of the French army, the French delegation informed us by a memorandum of December 23, 1942 (v. Del. W. No. 8099) that military manufacture would be stopped and submitted proposals for a change in the program of Franco-German aviation construction.

Meanwhile, the Reich Air Ministry ordered the transfer to Germany of certain airplane construction factories. This decision was transmitted to the French, government by a letter of the Supreme Western Command, dated December 29, 1942 (v. Del. W. No. 20).

In order to preclude probable French protests, the text of the French memorandum of December 29, 1942, was transmitted by a telegram of December 28, 1942, to the Wilhelmstrasse, with the suggestion that a memorandum be delivered to the French government pointing out that by virtue of the change in the situation, the Franco-German program of construction of aircraft should be considered terminated.

In a conversation with General Feldmarschall von Rundstedt, President Laval stated on January 11, 1943, that the French government could not accept the German injunction. He proposed instead that more orders be given to the French industry and that, if necessary, some equipment would be transferred from one plant to another, but in France.

°See *Baraduc Les Archives Secrètes du Reich,* pp. 77–78.

By letter of June 4, 1943, the delegation informed Feldmarschall Milch that the Franco-German program of aircraft building would cease.

The French government has maintained until now its position of refusal.°

> *Minister Hemmen*
> Director of the Economic
> Services in France

EXHIBIT C

The "Dossier Laval"

How I obtained access, in 1970, to the "Dossier Laval," collected by the prosecution and kept from Laval's defense lawyers, and how I was authorized in June 1971 to add five folders to the eight cartons of documents. The folders and cartons will be released to the public in October 1995.

After Laval's death, the eight cartons constituting the so-called Dossier Laval had been transferred from the attorney general's office to the Archives de France, to be kept in complete secrecy for a period of fifty years from Laval's death (October 15, 1945, to October 15, 1995). I knew that the German files and the statements of hundreds of French witnesses to Laval's actions during the occupation (filed at the Hoover Institution) and the documents in the archives of our Foundation at Châteldon contained the answers to every charge of the prosecuting attorney general, Mornet. Nevertheless, I wanted to be certain that these "cartons" did not contain any accusation or document so far unexplained or unanswered.

In November 1967, I asked the minister of justice, Mr. Louis Joxe, for an appointment and brought with me the following letter:

> *November 10, 1967*

Monsieur le Ministre,

On August 22, 1945, in the middle of the summer judicial vacation period, the defense lawyers of President Laval, Jacques Baraduc, Albert Naud, Yves-Frédéric Jaffré met him for the first time.

The day before, they had called upon President Bouchardon and M. Béteille, the examining magistrate. Both told counsel that the case

---

°Ibid., pp. 79–80. Laval's refusal concerning the transfer of equipment to Germany was "maintained" until the liberation of France; and the Germans never received the shares of stock held by the French state in the French nationalized aviation corporations.

would be a very long one, as it involved a long period of the life of the nation. They added that two examinations would take place in September and that the pretrial hearings would continue in October and November. M. Béteille handed them a schedule calling for a minimum of twenty-five hearings.

Only four ever took place. On August 23 and September 6, 8, and 11. The fifth hearing was interrupted owing to the late hour and was never resumed.

Two of the sacred traditions of the bar were then violated: the defense lawyers were denied access to the documents of the prosecution and denied the right to call witnesses. Under these scandalous circumstances, the president of the bar urged the lawyers not to appear in court, and the trial took place in the absence of Pierre Laval and his defenders.

Twenty-two years have gone by.

Jacques Baraduc is dead. Naud has been seriously injured in an automobile accident. Mme. de Chambrun and I have a legitimate concern in wishing to have access to the dossier of Pierre Laval's case.

We have entrusted M. Jaffré with the task of examining this dossier at the Archives de France. We will, of course, bear the expenses pertaining to the making of copies or photostats.

I beg you, therefore, to grant our request and to instruct the director of the Archives de France to give M. Jaffré access to the dossier so that he can carry out his assignment.

M. Joxe told me he would present my plea to M. Pompidou (prime minister in General de Gaulle's government), whose private secretary called me to arrange for an appointment. She told me our meeting would be the last on M. Pompidou's agenda on that afternoon.

I had not met Mr. Pompidou. Like Laval, he came from Auvergne. His first words expressed admiration for Laval's courage and intelligence; two qualities, he added, that do not always go together. He referred to what he termed *"le scandale judiciaire"* and assured me that some way to grant Josée Laval's plea would be found. A couple of weeks later, I met again with M. Joxe, who gave me the good news. Permission was granted not to M. Jaffré, the young assistant of the two defense lawyers, but to Mme. de Chambrun, with the possibility that she might delegate me to act for her. Pompidou and Joxe thought that my presence at the Archives de France would attract less attention than Josée Laval's. They thought it preferable for me to wait until the quiet summer vacation period to begin my work. In May, the so-called student rebellion began, and it was only on August 16, 1970, that the secret and final arrangements were ready for my first call upon Mr. Cézard, chief custodian in charge of classified documents. His office was on the top floor of the beautiful seventeenth-century Palais Soubise. He greeted me cordially, and made clear the exceptional character of this authorization without precedent, which involved his own responsibility.

Opposite his office on the other side of the stone-walled corridor was a huge room in which, with the help of his secretary—they were the only inhabitants of this top floor—Mr. Cézard had placed on a large table eight cardboard boxes, with pads, pencils, and paper clips. He told me that our two doors would be kept open so that I could call on him or his secretary at any time.

I opened the cartons and made a quick survey of their contents. My indignation increased as my inspection progressed. I found batches of pages written by Laval for his defense during the eight months of his captivity at Sigmaringen, dealing with the armistice, his meetings with Hitler, Ribbentrop, and others. All his papers had been confiscated when he was arrested on his return to France. He had been permitted to keep only his watch.

The cartons also contained old Laval family papers, letters, and documents that had no relation to the occupation. They had been seized—stolen—from the two Laval homes in Paris and Auvergne, after the arrest on August 17.

When I showed all this to M. Cézard at the end of the first afternoon, he expressed his surprise and told me that the seals on the cartons had been removed only that morning; neither he nor anyone else had seen the contents of the boxes.

I told him it would take me many months to copy the papers that interested me. I added that the only practical solution would be for me to have the assistance of at least two secretaries. M. Joxe was consulted by telephone, and it was agreed that two secretaries, Mme. Verle of my law office and Mme. Van Haften, my secretary at Baccarat, whom I would pledge to secrecy, would assist me. They came three or four afternoons a week, transcribed, dated, and signed the copies they made.

The secretaries copied all the protests by Darlan, and later by Laval, that had been made to the Germans against the de facto annexation of Alsace. The attorney general knew, of course, that he had these in his files, but he denied their existence. I found and copied Laval's own will, which had been taken from him.

I discovered that the only record of the four and one-half pretrial examinations were not even typed but handwritten by a clerk, as in the days of the French Revolution, when the judges were in a hurry to condemn and execute.

On one folder containing some notes by Laval for his defense, written during his captivity, was this inscription in Mornet's handwriting: "Activity of Laval in Germany." These words proved that Mornet had suppressed not only the "evidence" in favor of Laval but Laval's own notes written for his defense.

After the strenuous afternoons during which I disappeared from my law office or from Baccarat without being able to tell anyone where I was going,

I had to work late to cope with the huge backlog of work. At the archives, I had been able to assemble notes of my own and copies of documents into five large folders, in two sets.

On June 25, 1971, one set was placed next to the eight cartons at the Archives de France, the other in the safe of the Fondation Josée and René de Chambrun.

On July 1, 1971, Guy Duboscq, general director of the Archives de France, officially acknowledged receipt of the five folders and confirmed that these would be released to the public at the same time as the Dossier Laval, on October 15, 1995.

EXHIBIT D

The "I Wish" Speech

M. Jean Anglade   *July 30, 1975*

Dear Sir:

I beg you to excuse my lateness in responding to your letter referring to a conversation between Alexandre Varenne and Robert Fabre about Laval's "wish."

Pierre Laval, like the immense majority of Frenchmen in June 1940, believed that the Germans would win. He continued to believe this possible up to the time when the Allies landed in North Africa.

Those who have criticized this "I wish" sentence, spoken only once, on June 22, 1942, and connected with a single definite fact, have always taken it out of context. I am sure that historians will attach particular importance to the relation of this text to its date—June 22, 1942—which preceded by five months the Allied landing in North Africa.

Gigantic battles were then taking place in the east, on a front that stretched from Petsamo to the Caucasus, between the Germans and the Soviets. In France, Pierre Laval had to face the threat of the SS being installed in the southern zone; to preserve France from a Gauleiter; to oppose the deportation of two million workers.° Sauckel's order had just been promulgated: "All men and women between twenty and sixty-five years of age in the occupied territories are requisitioned by the Reich for compulsory labor."

At the outset of the toughest negotiations of his life, Laval the statesman sought and found the lightning-rod words that would permit him,

---

°See *Laval Parle*, pp. 94 ff., for an account of the dramatic conditions surrounding his return to power in April.

even as he was taking the risk upon himself, to save millions of Frenchmen from deportation. Here are the words he so carefully weighed:

"Germany is struggling against communism. Gigantic battles are taking place on the east from Petsamo to the Caucasus. I wish for a German victory, for without it, communism will take over all of Europe."

What happened next?

The precise and prudent statement, which contained not the slightest denigration of the British or even the least reference to them, so angered Goebbels that he ordered the sentences before and after the "I wish" to be cut, reducing the text to: "I wish for a German victory." And the next day, the French information bureau in London performed the same amputation.

In the following month, Laval, after alluding to the "truncated" speech before the prefects and the Instituteurs de l'Allier, reestablished the truth by saying: "I went far from my purpose, as far as I could go, and so that you understand me correctly, I accept all risks myself so long as I can give France every chance."

Five months later, the Allies landed in Africa, and Pierre Laval refused the alliance offered by Germany. No one ever again heard a single word from Laval that could suggest—let alone state—that he wished for a German victory and a British defeat.

The one wish Pierre Laval never ceased to express throughout those tragic years was to keep France alive, and that wish was granted.

Before his lips had been sealed forever by the court that perpetrated the judicial crime of October 1945, Laval had testified about the "I wish" statement as a witness at the trial of Marshal Pétain: "Those words were of the kind that heads of governments, that ministers of foreign affairs, when goaded by circumstances, sometimes utter and find wrongly interpreted. But if those words were put in context, the context of the moment and of the reasons for their delivery, they would be better understood. You would be surprised if I were to quote to you, for example, a speech by Mr. Churchill discussing the Russians. You would be surprised again, if I were to quote to you, for example, a speech by Molotov addressed to the Germans."

Laval was referring to a speech by Molotov of October 31, 1939, that the Communists (and those who did not want to come into conflict with them) have kept under wraps for the past thirty years. Laval had the full text of this speech, along with other documents that were taken from him when he was imprisoned. I copied that text at the Archives de France among the mass of documents that the prosecution refused to make available to the defense. I extract a passage from it, which Laval would certainly have quoted and commented on at his trial. When the Soviets welcomed Ribbentrop on October 31, 1939, this is what Molotov said: "The national socialist conception can, like all political conceptions, be accepted or discarded; it's a question of political position. But everyone must know that one cannot annihilate a political doctrine by force and that one cannot dispose of it by a war. That is why it is irrational, even criminal, to pursue such a war with the goal of destroying Hitlerism, even if one camouflages this war under the cover of a war for democracy!"

Returning to the "I wish" speech and Laval's motives for its delivery, I may say that historians will read with interest the testimony of the witnesses who surrounded Laval on June 22, 1942. Here is part of the statement by Paul Morand, to whom Laval showed the text of his speech before reading it over the radio:[*]

> When I suggested to him a different formula to obtain the desired goal, he answered me: "Do you think I have not thought of that? Do you imagine that it would please me to see the Germans win the war? But I prefer to pay them in words instead of acts, because the cost is less high, because the cost is less high for France. A phrase like that can be worth the return of a hundred thousand prisoners. A politeness on the radio can permit me to refuse that brute of a Sauckel the workers whom he demands for Germany by the hundreds of thousands. Tomorrow, at Matignon, it is not you, it is I who must face Sauckel and Abetz and look them in the eye. As always, they'll talk to me of their 'sword.' My own 'sword' will be these words; I have no other."[†]

It was with this "sword" that Pierre Laval, during two long and terrible years, was able to confront the Germans and defend the French people and their welfare.

When he saw Hitler for the last time at Berchtesgaden, on April 30, 1943, Laval knew—he had only to look around him to be convinced— that Germany, under massive bombardments, was losing the war. Through the interpreter, Dr. Schmidt, he flung at his interrogator: "You wanted to win the war to create Europe. You had to create Europe to win the war!" That was his manner of saying to Hitler, "I no longer believe in your victory"; but he continued to plead, with all his power and to the very end, the case of his murdered country.

Even in front of his ministers, my father-in-law had to keep from disclosing certain confidential matters. If he had expressed any doubt about the outcome of the war to one or two of them in particular, his words would have been immediately repeated at the German embassy. . . . The Germans occupied all of France. They had ears everywhere, and an imprudent statement could have reduced his margin for negotiation to nothing. This margin shrank every day in the course of the interminable arguments by which Laval resisted ever more stubbornly

---

[*]Hoover Institution, no. 144.

[†]Rochat, general secretary for foreign affairs, had presented the same suggestion. See Hoover Institution, no. 22.

the measures that Germany's apprehension of military defeat rendered ever more imperious.

This is a rather long letter, but I so greatly enjoyed your book about Auvergne and the way in which you evoked the memory of him who so deeply loved his village and countryside that I wanted my answer to be as complete as possible.

René de Chambrun

EXHIBIT E

Address by Pierre Laval to the Mayors of Cantal at Vichy, November 9, 1943

During the occupation years, the governors, mayors, magistrates and higher executives were in the habit of coming to Vichy or the Hôtel Matignon to see Marshal Pétain or Pierre Laval. They felt the need of guidance in the midst of the contradictory propaganda that saturated France. Laval always received them and talked freely with them when he felt he could do so in confidence.

In order to avoid leaks, his words were not supposed to be taken down. But most of them were transcribed without his knowledge by a reliable stenographer.°

Dear Friends,

The words I have just heard have moved me deeply. I have often received delegations coming here from all over France, but nothing could warm my heart more than the speech of the president of the council of the Department of Cantal.

I come, as you all do, from Auvergne. That is to say, we are fellow Frenchmen through and through. No one from our region can help loving his country passionately.

Certainly I did not want war. I have too great a share of our peasant good sense to wish for war.

A country must wage war when it has been attacked; it has then the right and duty to wage it in self-defense. That has often been the case with France; it was true in 1914. But in 1939 we were not attacked.

A country may also wage war when it is hungry, in order to eat, but that was not our case. France was contented and prosperous, perhaps too much so, and failed to appreciate her good fortune.

°The text of this and seventeen other speeches is filed at the Hoover Institution under no. 221.

A country may also wage war to defend its honor, but our honor was not at stake in 1939. We did not fight when Germany annexed Austria. We did not declare war when she remilitarized the Rhineland. Neither did we do so when she took over Czechoslovakia.

We went to war for the Danzig Corridor. Today the whole world, the diplomats of every nation, acknowledge that the Danzig Corridor was a piece of crude bungling, the worst, perhaps, in the entire Versailles treaty. One can always divide a country in two pieces by force, and there was Germany on one side and East Prussia beyond, but knowing the history of mankind, it was inconceivable that a country, having regained its strength, should accept such a situation. At Geneva, the representatives of all the nations, even those most hostile to Germany, agreed that an amicable solution to this difficult problem had to be found. Yet it was for the Danzig Corridor that France went to war.

Many said we went to war "because of our obligations to Poland." Today I am speaking to men of Auvergne, and I know you will understand me correctly. If it were true that we were bound by treaty with Poland to declare war, the boldest might say to me, "Even at the risk of defeat, it was a question of our honor; we had to fight." Well, I shall prove that false, because we were not obliged to go to war for Poland.

I was the colleague and friend of Aristide Briand. He signed in 1925 the Treaty of Locarno, which guaranteed the eastern frontiers of France. This guarantee was subscribed to by England and Italy, also. On the same day, Briand signed a treaty with Czechoslovakia and another with Poland, and while the Franco-Soviet and Franco-Polish treaties were not included in the Locarno Pact, they were published the same day and in the same issue of the *Journal Officiel*. They were interconnected, and I frequently heard Briand in 1925 (Painlevé was then prime minister) report on his negotiations and the results he had obtained. He told us that the engagements he had entered into with Poland and Czechoslovakia were but the logical and natural result of those made by England and Italy regarding France's eastern frontiers. The treaties with Poland, signed by Millerand in 1921 and 1922, were annulled and superseded by the treaty of 1925.

At the time of the remilitarization of the left bank of the Rhine, when England refused to apply against Germany the clauses of the Locarno Pact, France's guarantee to Poland automatically lapsed. It was said or rumored that we have made other pledges to Poland, in addition to those in the treaty of 1925. There were said to be secret military agreements. Well, I ask you, you who represent the common sense of our region, such military agreements could hardly be kept secret from the prime minister, could they? Now in 1931, 1932, and 1935—I can tell you today—they were so secret that I never heard about them. *(Sensation)*

I am telling you this, my compatriots from Cantal, and someday, when at last I shall be able to speak freely, I shall tell it to the world without fear of contradiction.

I will go further. In 1939, when the Daladier government drew up the military budget, I felt a black foreboding that we should be drawn into the war if we voted for those appropriations.

I had no desire to deny the military their budget. Throughout my public life I have never refused appropriations for military purposes, because they were necessary and indispensable for France. There was no question of my opposing the measure when I asked to speak on that day. One or two of you probably attended that session. Those who did will remember it. I was greeted by the vociferous outcry of those who had for years consistently refused to arm France. Some of them are now in Algiers, expressing themselves very unjustly toward the man who, after all, is only the receiver in their bankruptcy.

To be precise, what was it that I wanted to ask the senators on that day? I wanted to ask them to convene in secret session and to vote against the declaration of war.

What does our constitution say? One thing that to me was vital and sacred: France cannot and should not declare war without the consent of Parliament. Neither the Senate nor the Chamber of Deputies was ever called upon to vote either for or against war. You Republicans, who respect legal procedure, do not ever forget what I have just told you: we went into this war illegally.

Had we had our secret session, what would I have told the senators? I would have told them, only in greater detail, for I would have had the time to speak carefully and at length, just what I have told you now. And I would have added something more; I would have said, "We are going to war alone and we cannot win." Then the Auvergnat in me would have gone on to say, "Does one go to war alone, in the certainty that France will have to pay with tragic suffering for her imprudence?" No! Isn't that the answer?

I would have said then that we were going to fight without modern bomber planes. I would have added, wrongly, that we had only nine modern bombers. The truth, which I learned later, was that we had none and that the nine I referred to were not received until two months after hostilities had begun, whereas Germany had three thousand modern bombers.

Germany and Russia had just divided Poland between them. We entered the war practically alone and lost it. Why? Because this war is not like the others; it is not in defense of the land of our fathers. It is not a war to defend our country. It is a war of passionate fanaticism in which ideologies contend against each other.

I am speaking in an ancient land of liberty, liberty lost for the time being but soon, I hope, to be regained; and I affirm that we went into this war for ideas that are not our own.

If Russia has communism at home, that is her affair, but let her keep her communism there.

If Germany has national socialism at home, that is her affair, but let her keep her national socialism there.

If America and Great Britain cherish antiFascist ideologies, that is their affair. But we of Auvergne, who are ignorant of fascism, who have never suffered the imprint of any race other than that of our own ancient province—no one can force us to accept those ideologies. We went to war, and our young men left, for the sake of ideologies, and not to defend the Puy-de-Dôme and the meadows of our Cantal.

All my life, as you well know, I have been an apostle of peace. I have been mayor, deputy, senator, and minister often; socialist I have always been and still am to the depths of my heart. The marshal once said that the conditions of our proletariat must be eradicated. How right he is! I have often been slandered and abused when I was best fulfilling my duty to France. I have known painful moments when some of those within the working classes, who had given me their esteem and friendship, were being robbed of that esteem and friendship because I would not subscribe to the schemes of those who were lying to them every day, who deceived them, and who, after disarming them, were leading them straight into war.

Women bear children, fathers struggle to raise them, and then, one day, a few politicians without conscience throw them into the crucible. That is why I hate war. It never pays. It has been proved that France herself, after she wins a war, continues to suffer.

Now, then, what is happening? Every morning, every day, every Frenchman listens to the radio and hears the dispatches. We do not like Germany over here, especially not in Auvergne. Our education has been all the other way. Most of our battles have been fought against her.

But life is hard, and the history of mankind is complex. The fact is that today, were Germany to be suddenly eliminated (believe me and remember what I am saying—I ask you to remember every statement), chaos would gradually overtake Europe. It would establish itself in Germany, in the Balkans, in Italy. Now I love my village; I love every stone of the place, and I do not want disorder to install itself there. I want to act in such a way that Germany will not be strong enough to crush us, so that Bolshevism may not suppress us. Do you understand me? That is the tragedy I live each day. Only yesterday I was in Paris and talked with the Germans until late into the night. They were not easy, those talks. They never are. You see, each day I try to do my utmost in order that we may have to endure only the minimum of damage, and when night falls, I often have the impression of being caught in a pair of pincers. I wonder sadly which, the Germans or the French, have caused me most suffering that day. Nevertheless, I never lose courage, for I have but one ambition, one goal, and only one, toward which I strive like a sort of sleepwalker: to do everything to save our country by reducing her sufferings each day, to act so that the land of our fathers shall remain in the hands of their children and so that that land may always be called France.

Now, you who are men of common sense, you who represent the pioneers among Frenchmen because you come from the high regions of our land, because you represent ancient Gaul, whence came the cries of hope and the salvation of our country, I ask you, even though you may not always understand me—we are not free, and I do not like to talk—as a matter of fact, I do not know why I gave away so much in confidence today—I ask you, when you are in your villages, to tell yourselves, no matter what happens or whatever I do, that I am doing it because I believe it is the way to rescue our country, to ensure peace, and to save the civilization in which we were born and in which we shall continue to live.

EXHIBIT F

Extract from Speer's Address to the Gauleiters, October 6, 1943

If under the pressure of imminent war the French government was not able to turn the nation's industry into an armament industry, I believe that our efforts will likewise not succeed in converting the French industrial plant into an armament industry. But in that plant we possess the means of obtaining extraordinary and uninterrupted reserves through the production of consumer goods. These resources will be exploited by the transfer of materials: for example, by the transfer of cellulose to the French textile factories. I fully realize that the exploitation of the French consumer-goods industry, to which France will agree on account of the advantages it will bring, will be profitable. These advantages chiefly consist in the fact that by the end of the war this consumer-goods industry will be working to full capacity, whereas during the same period our consumer-goods industry at home will have practically come to a standstill. Therefore, instead of the transfer of the armament industry, France will be sure to avail herself of this chance of producing consumer goods. The conferences with Bichelonne have shown this to be true. It is a great sacrifice that is being made by our fatherland, and by each Gau in particular, to submit to this radical change in its economic structure, which is still based on peacetime conditions. But I am of the opinion that if we want to win the war, it is we who have to make sacrifices in the first place.

EXHIBIT G

The Sauckel-Laval Showdown

Document A

At 4:30 A.M. on the morning of June 6, 1944, news of the Allied invasions caused Gauleiter Sauckel, the Reich minister of labor (also known as the

Nazi Slave Driver), to be abruptly awakened in his suite at the Ritz Hotel in Paris. He immediately wrote the following letter, which was rushed to Otto Abetz, the German ambassador.

Paris June 6, 1944

Dear Ambassador and Comrade Abetz:

The long-expected invasion has at last begun. Thus ends the period of procrastination against our labor demands, a procrastination that has been used to justify openly or tacitly the pretended impossibility of transferring manpower to Germany because of the alleged political disturbances that might result.

Now that the German soldier must again fight and pour out his blood in the Manche region, now that the battle may at any time spread to many other parts of France, all the pleas, all the arguments, of Laval can no longer have any weight.

The only voice that must be listened to and must be heard is that of the German soldier. In these decisive hours, I request you to demand that President Laval accede to a necessary act even though it will be manifestly painful for him to do so. He must sign the order of mobilization of the class of 1944. I do not want to be fooled any longer.

Consequently, I urgently ask you to arrange that, before 10:00 A.M. tomorrow morning, the prime minister of France sign the Decree of Mobilization of the class of 1944. And you will immediately report to me if his answer is no. I will not accept under any circumstances any dilatory tactics. All the technical measures are ready for the allotments to be furnished by each department, and the means of conveyance are organized as a result of our meetings.

Heil Hitler—*Fritz Sauckel*

During the trial of the Nazi war criminals at Nuremberg on May 30, 1946 (Sauckel was sentenced to death), this letter was read to him by the French prosecutor, Hertzog, who made him admit that it constituted an ultimatum served on Laval.*

Laval bluntly refused. He secretly ordered all the prefects and heads of the National Guard and "Gendarme" Corps to prevent any individual or collective departures to Germany.

Document B

A year after the hanging of Sauckel and the other principal war criminals, the trial of the other high officials of the Wilhelmstrasse (Von

---

*Sauckel Trial, Chief Counsel on War Crimes (French), Exhibit 822, May 30, 1946, pp. 102–3

Weiszaecker et. al.) *took place, and Otto Abetz, the German ambassador in Paris, was called as a witness in the case of Steengracht, the secretary-general of the Wilhelmstrasse. Examined on July 1, 1948, by Dr. Carl Haensel, the attorney for Steengracht, Abetz deposed as follows.*°

Question: The negotiations between Sauckel and the French government took place at the embassy, did they not?

Answer: Yes, that is what I have already said. For reasons of protocol, these negotiations would take place at the embassy, as the head of the French government personally took part in them. Laval had asked for this because he thought that if they took place at the embassy, I would side with him against Sauckel.

Question: Did Laval hope you would help him?

Answer: Yes.

Question: How did the French government react in the face of Sauckel's demands during these negotiations?

Answer: The French government offered obstinate resistance to the conscription of labor, except when it was on a voluntary basis. It seized every occasion to try and obtain matching exchanges, in particular, through the liberation of war prisoners. The government opposed the demands of Sauckel for conscription by proposing the creation of S [Speer] Betrieb factories in France, and the efforts in that direction met with some success.

Question: During these negotiations between Laval and Sauckel, what was the attitude of the embassy? Can you give us a practical example?

Answer: I will show you how one of these meetings took place.

Question: That is what we want to know.

Answer: It happened in the first days of 1944. Gauleiter Sauckel came to Paris to mobilize one million French workers for forced labor in Germany. He greeted me with these words: "You, Abetz, have organized the resistance of the German bureaus against the mobilization of labor. Today, I come to Paris carrying an order from the Führer, and a few heads are going to roll."

I answered: "My name begins with the first letter of the alphabet. I am perfectly willing to place my head, first, under the guillotine. I prefer to lose my life rather than consent to things disastrous for Germany."

I added: "If ever the Maquis† erects monuments in France, you will be entitled to the biggest one with this inscription 'To our principal recruiting

°See files of the Chief Counsel for War Crimes, pp. 10.684–85.
†Literally, the bush, meaning the underground Resistance.

agent, Gauleiter Sauckel. Gratefully, The Maquis.'" Herr Sauckel rose suddenly and left the room, slamming the door. General Blumentritt suggested that I follow him and shake hands. I refused. Thereupon, the general joined Sauckel at the Ritz Hotel. He did not succeed in getting him to come back.

We communicated thereafter by exchanging notes.

Question: Did he complain to Hitler about your resistance?

Answer: Certainly, because the next morning Ribbentrop telephoned and instructed me to support Sauckel's action.

Question: Do you remember from where Ribbentrop was calling—Berlin or the headquarters?

Answer: From Westphalia, the headquarters of Gross Steinort.

Question: Did you give in?

Answer: Not being able to resist openly, I used a stratagem. I approached Laval and made the suggestion that the French government propose to Sauckel the mobilization of four classes of young men, in France and with French staffs in charge. The groups would be stationed in France for a period of months, in camps, and after a time they could be sent to Germany. Satisfied, Sauckel left Paris.

What Pierre Laval and I had anticipated did, in fact, happen. The Armistice Commission set the plan aside, considering it was impossible to accept on the eve of a possible Anglo-American landing the presence in France of organized groups of one million workers with their French staffs. The discussions between Sauckel and the Armistice Commission on this point lasted until June, and this is how Sauckel, instead of receiving the one million men he had demanded, received none.

I want to add immediately that I performed this act of obstruction in agreement with the French government because I was convinced that it was my duty as a German to prevent the deportation of labor from France. My opinion in this regard was exactly the opposite of Sauckel's.

Question: Another question concerning the labor problem. Did you exercise a political or diplomatic pressure on the French government? We are referring to the year 1943.

Answer: On the contrary, I was always in agreement with the French government's view that forced labor was against the interests of France and Germany. That is way I backed the efforts of the French government to avoid the disastrous consequences of these transfers of labor that swelled the maquis. That is why I supported the Speer-Bichelonne agreement to increase as much as possible the amount of work done in France.

In his closing argument on the case, Haensel declared:

In July 1943 Speer made an agreement known as the Speer-Bichelonne Treaty, according to which production would be increased within France and no further workers should be transferred to Germany. This new method placed long segments of industries and plants under the protection of the Speer-Bichelonne treaty, to which Hitler gave his consent.

The prosecution presented the original minutes of a meeting presided over by Hitler (document 2305-121). During this meeting, Hitler attempted to get an exact picture of the mobilization of labor. The minutes show that the minister of foreign affairs had asked to be present, which Hitler refused. When Sauckel came to France to recruit a million workmen, the French government refused this request. Sauckel threw the blame for this on Abetz, stating that he had supported French Prime Minister Laval against the order. Sauckel went as far as to threaten Abetz with the death penalty. Whereupon Abetz resorted to the stratagem conceived by the French prime minister, and working together, they succeeded in outwitting Sauckel. He did not obtain one worker.

EXHIBIT H

Resolution of the 87 Mayors of Paris and Vicinity

On August 11, 1944, at 6:00 P.M., the 87 mayors of Paris and the suburbs met with Pierre Laval. He informed them of his plan to call a special meeting of the National Assembly. They unanimously expressed their confidence and passed the resolution translated on page 109. Here is the French original:

EXHIBIT I

The Last Luncheon with Pierre Laval

The following account is condensed from a reminiscence written in May 1947 by Josée de Chambrun, the daughter of Pierre Laval. It was the last meeting she had with her father before his arrest that same day by the German SS police.

The lunch took place at Matignon on August 17, 1944, eight days before the liberation of Paris and the installation of the de Gaulle government.

There are rare moments in life when every minute, every gesture, every word, remains forever engraved on the memory of those who lived them. Such a moment was the last meal that my parents were to have together on French soil.

Present besides my parents, my husband, and myself were President Edouard Herriot and Madame Herriot and the German ambassador, Otto Abetz. The purpose, as originally conceived by my father, was to arrange a special convocation of the former Chamber of Deputies, of which Herriot had been president, and the Senate, gathered jointly in a National Assembly, to arrange for the smooth transfer of legal power from Marshal Pétain's government back to the National Assembly. Abetz had previously assured my father that approval from Berlin had been obtained for such a transfer.

After an endless period of anguish, a painful page of the history of our country was coming to an end, and we were living this drama around that table with extraordinary intensity, for it had a specially powerful bearing on our lives and on the lives of those whom we loved. I might add that it was a marvelous summer day in that handsome old Hôtel Matignon [the official residence of French prime ministers], with its windows wide open on one of the most beautiful gardens in the world.

The Herriots and Abetz arrived together, and together they admired Matignon and its lovely grounds.

The lunch was good. Everyone tried to cover up the anxiousness of the situation with pretended lightness. Abetz began by asking if it was true that, in Lyons, Herriot's city, there was a statue dedicated to a "good German"? Madame Herriot then told us of the statue of a rich German merchant of the sixteenth century who had showered the city with good works.

More small talk followed. Then Herriot spoke out to express his indignation at what was taking place. He emphasized that no one had worked harder than he for a Franco-German rapprochement. He recalled the fact that despite strong opposition from French public opinion, he was a member of the French government that had decided to evacuate the Rhineland and that in spite of that, he had been arrested. While he was not asking anybody's help, he had been liberated at President Laval's request as president of the Chamber of Deputies for the anticipated session of the National Assembly, made necessary by the turn of events. He had returned to Paris with Pierre Laval and, at the town hall, had refrained from any action—such as a speech or an official reception—that could have a political implication. But despite all this discretion, the SS German troops had come to arrest him. The ambassador knew the rest of the story. He was ready to accept his fate, Herriot continued, but he asked only to be brought back to Maréville on French territory; he should not be forced to follow the now captive government into exile. Abetz looked very much embarrassed, as he had just received orders to the contrary and had so notified Herriot before the luncheon.

We were all very much moved, feeling that Herriot was entirely right. Not only was he being arrested again, not only was the entire government on the verge of arrest, but the Germans wanted to force Herriot to go with the government into exile. My parents were leaving under German duress, and we all felt the painfulness of the situation if Herriot was forced to undergo the same ordeal.

My father thought it imperative that the National Assembly be called in session so that the transfer of power should be accomplished legally. He had previously expressed himself on the subject: "Exceptional circumstances justified the July 10, 1940, meeting of the National Assembly, which granted regular powers to Marshal Pétain and to the government of the Republic. Changed circumstances should now put an end to those powers, and I felt it was indispensable that the National Assembly recover by normal means the powers that it had delegated. It was at all costs necessary to find a solution to provide continuity before the arrival of the Allied troops and avoid in France the possibility of the same kind of political adventurism that was in the making elsewhere." How right he was. But then the two pro-Nazi Frenchmen, Brinon and Déat, eager to take refuge in Germany and, at the same time, spite their opponents in France, had, before running away, influenced General Oberg, head of the SS in France and through him Himmler in Berlin. For us, it was heartbreaking to see how they had compromised, indeed, ruined my father's plan—a plan fully approved by Herriot and all the senators and deputies who had been calling on my father.

My mother then joined the discussion and said: "Mr. Ambassador, this departure, under these conditions, is an outrage. See for yourself the painful situation it would put us all in."

Herriot, raising his arms, said, "Please, listen to her, Mr. Ambassador. This is the voice of France." My mother pursued her plea. "These two men, of course, have not always been in agreement in the past. That was politics—France was happy then—but in the face of a great danger, now they come together. You cannot condone an action that would make it appear as if my husband had instigated unscrupulous tactics resulting in Monsieur Herriot's being forced to undergo the same fate as ours, under duress."

Abetz was dying of shame. He knew too much. He liked France and was honest enough to perceive how odious this situation was, entirely created, as it was, by his masters. He took it upon himself to say unequivocally that things would be done as we wished. It was very courageous of him, for one must not forget that from that very moment he lost the confidence of his chiefs and was dismissed the minute he got back to Germany.

Such a discussion could not have gone on much longer; our nerves were much too tense. So, by common accord, we fell back on anecdotes and reminiscences—The Duke of Windsor, Anthony Eden, the League of Nations, the Ethiopian crisis, etc.

We left around 4:30 in a communion of thought and feeling very close to one another. My husband promised to bring Herriot in his captivity at city hall some books and some cigars. He arrived there around 6:30 P.M. The SS were standing guard at the entrance. He suggested to Herriot, in agreement with the prefect, Bouffet, that he escape through the underground tunnels and hide at an apartment of an American friend of ours who had let us have it for any good purpose. Herriot hesitated for a while, then declined the offer, saying that he wanted to follow his fate. He then kissed my husband farewell.

If I recount this occasion, it is because, as I said earlier, it has remained engraved on my memory as one of those rare moments when all those present, knowing that they are in the face of tragedy, act out their roles not only with courage but with courtesy and elegance. It was in marked contrast to the spirit that prevailed in France in the months to come.

Since three o'clock on that same afternoon, the Gestapo had surrounded Matignon. President Herriot and his wife left with Abetz. They were driven in the company of an SS captain to the city hall. At 6:30, the Lavals were driven under heavy guard to Belfort and Sigmarigen, while Marshal Pétain was being arrested in Vichy by the Gestapo and deported to Germany.

EXHIBIT J

*Extract of Laval's Speech to a Delegation of Artisans**

Really, I don't need you, have no need of you in any capacity. For if you only knew—it's my one piece of vanity that I am confessing

*Published in *Métiers de France*, March 1944; reprinted in Baraduc.

here—the pride I feel within me, the contempt for whatever is the outward show of others' opinion! Perhaps you can imagine that at my age, after all I have done, I am satisfied only when at night, by myself, I can approve of myself. No matter what anybody may have said or done or thought that day, no matter what [condescending] smiles may have been exchanged in my presence, if I have the conviction that I have fought well in defense of my country and that the day just past has been added to the previous days toward the strengthening of my country, then I am happy. I say to myself, "As for everything else, never mind. We'll see later." My tombstone will have long been above me, and possibly nobody will have yet understood. But you, to whom I am speaking, look me straight in the eye: I am a man like you, a Frenchman; I love only my country, and I ask you to defend it side by side with me.

EXHIBIT K

Sketch of Mme. Laval by Pierre Laval, Written on Thursday, September 13, in the Chambers of the Examining Magistrate of Mme. Laval

We were born in the same little town of Châteldon, and we have always known each other. First her father, then her brother, was the mayor of our community for many years. My wife had five sisters and two brothers. One of them, an officer in an infantry regiment, was wounded during the battle of Verdun and died a few days later at the hospital. Her other brother, a doctor, became the socialist deputy for our district in 1911 and served until his death in 1925. One of her sisters married an officer, Colonel Gonnard, who was taken prisoner in World War I.

My wife's family was staunchly Republican, and it was her father who replaced Mr. Chassaigne-Goyon, a former prefect of the empire, as conseiller général of the Puy-de-Dôme department.

She was brought up in a political atmosphere. Her parents, who lived in Clermont-Ferrant before our marriage, had many friends who were members of Parliament, conseillers généraux, and mayors from Puy-de-Dôme. Her father had fought in the Franco-Prussian war of 1870. He was a strong Republican, a patriot, full of anti-Prussian feelings. His judgments were ironic and severe when he spoke of the Italians.

We were married in Châteldon in 1909, and our union was based on mutual affection. Neither of us had wealth.

After our marriage, I became a member of the Paris bar and quickly went into politics. Five years later, I was elected deputy from Aubervilliers, of which I remained mayor until the decree of revocation after my arrest by the Germans.

My wife has always been my trusted friend, my comfort, and my guide. She approved or disapproved, and I always attached great value to her advice. My greatest successes were often due to her inspiration. When I was faced with difficulties, she always gave me strength. Her affection helped me overcome all hardships.

There were times when I disagreed with her on important questions. She disagreed with me when I decided to campaign actively in Parliament in favor of the granting of powers to Marshal Pétain in July 1940. She understood the main reason that prompted me to do so, but she blamed me for not heeding the advice given to us by friends who felt that the marshal and I would not get along. She would have sympathized with my decision if it had been in favor of a man like Marshal Lyautey. Marshal Lyautey died a few years before the war. I did not heed her advice, and events proved her to be right.

A month before, in June, we were in Châteldon, and she did not want me to go to Bordeaux because she felt that I would be led to participate in the government. Yet she refused to let me go alone, because at the time I was in poor health. She greatly deplored my accepting ministerial office, since I had assumed no responsibility in the war, much less in our defeat. She could not understand why I was willing to accept such a responsiblity after our defeat. Besides, she did not approve of my working with Marshal Pétain and his new ministers, who were no friends of ours, and several of whom I did not even know.

I did not follow her advice, and the event of December 13 proved she had been right. In that event, she and our daughter, who had just returned from America, had to undergo the same house arrest as I did, and their ill feeling toward the marshal was, if anything, strengthened. On December 17, in agreement with her, I refused the cabinet post that the marshal asked me to take.

It was in 1942, when the marshal again asked me to enter the government, that her reaction was the strongest. The situation had greatly worsened. The Germans were increasing their pressure and demands, and she was aware of the conversation I had had with Goering a few days before, during which he had advised me not to accept a position in the government if it should be offered to me. She foresaw what the attitude of the Germans would be. She had no confidence in them. "They are double-crossers and cheats," she used to say. I elaborated the role I could play in acting as a screen to protect the French, emphasizing that it was my duty. With perspicacity and insight, she told me that my role would not be understood, that people would be ungrateful. My plight is even worse today, but I ask that my wife be treated according to her sentiments and her actions.

She never had anything to do with my government activities except occasionally, to bring to my attention cases of misfortune or injustice. She lived practically alone at Châteldon, where I would join her late every evening. We never had guests. She was very insistent on living a life of seclusion. It was her rule, and she always adhered to it, more strictly so during the entire occupation. She complained when occasionally a German diplomat would express the wish to call upon her. She found it obtrusive and ill-bred to ask to come to our home when they could see me and the marshal freely in Vichy.

I recall an incident that occurred at a diplomatic dinner given by Marshal Pétain. The conversation happened to turn to the French who were in the underground. "They are brave fellows!" she exclaimed in front of the German minister and other diplomats. While I smiled discreetly, I noticed the stiffness that followed.

The day of our arrest and deportation to Germany, April 17, 1944, at the Hôtel Matignon, in Paris and in the presence of President Herriot and Mme. Herriot, she denounced the German Ambassador Abetz in terms that were moving and severe. She stressed the bad faith of the Germans and the brutality of their methods. I remember that M. Herriot was moved by my wife's comments.

In Germany, at Vangen, while the Germans were trying to lead us in a direction opposite to the one we wanted to follow and we energetically refused, my wife told Herr Fischer, the consul general, what she thought of the way the German government and its representatives were treating us. "A bullet, sir, would be much cleaner," she said. Such was the tone of our relations during the last days of our deportation in Germany.

My wife followed me because she had not the slightest confidence in my surviving the fate that was awaiting me in view of her opinion of the Germans and the conditions under which I had been arrested. I was greatly pained to see her suffering when, on December 13, 1944, we were told that we were to be evacuated to Silesia. We succeeded in delaying the departure, and thanks to the subsequent military events, we were forced to move but no more than twenty kilometers from Sigmaringen.

EXHIBIT L

The Questioning of Mme. Laval by the Examining Magistrate, September 7, 1945

A week before the cross-examination of Pierre Laval by Judge Marchat, the same judge had Mme. Laval undergo her one and only interrogatory. She was still imprisoned at Fresnes, accused of having impaired the internal security of the state and of "intelligence with the enemy." The examination concerned only her relationship with her husband.

Question: What was the nature of your political activity, in concert with your husband, particularly during his official trips?

Answer: I never engaged in politics, Your Honor. During the thirty-five years that my husband has been in politics, my name has never been associated with his. My husband has made official visits to almost every European country, but I have never accompanied him. Indeed, I thought that considering the important interests he had to defend, the presence of a woman was, to say the least, inopportune. I feel that a woman disturbs. She wastes time, because, out of politeness, she has to be taken care of. Such was my attitude before the war. Why should I have changed during the occupation?

Question: Did you go to Vichy? Did you see or associate with any Germans, men or women?

Answer: It is well known that I never lived in Vichy. In 1940, I retired to my country home, cutting down on our standard of living to set an example. I was received once or twice at the marshal's table and readily realized that material life was easier in Vichy than at Châteldon. It took a certain willpower, because winters are often rough in our parts, but I preferred to stay in our home. I have never dealt with, invited, or received in our home any German, man or woman. In the evening, I did my correspondence. I took care of the families of the war prisoners, busying myself with the services I could render to the people of our village. All this was a family tradition.

Question: You are known, madame, for having a certain influence on your husband. Were you in agreement with his policy?

Answer: My husband explained to me the policy he wanted to follow; he convinced me that this policy was the only one likely to avoid the worst for his country; that if he did not succeed, it was not his fault.

Several times, he felt like giving up. But I can still see him clenching his jaw, bringing his fist down on the dinner table, and saying, "I have no right to leave." He believed that if he left, he would be replaced by adventurers and that the country would suffer more and more. He therefore sacrificed himself.

For years and years, my husband had only one policy: to avoid war. Had he been at the head of the government in 1939, war would not have broken out until he had exhausted every possibility of avoiding such a cataclysm.

You speak of my husband; we were the closest couple that could be. I know better than anyone else that what he strived to do above all else was to alleviate the pains and the sufferings of his country.

Question: Why did you go with him?

Answer: I had no confidence in the Germans, whose prisoner he was. I knew how he felt about them. I would have followed him to the devil's lair. It was to me a moral obligation. My daughter would never have forgiven me, otherwise. She herself would have set me that example of abandoning everything, her home and her husband, to follow her father.

EXHIBIT M

Telegram from the Files of the Office of Chief of Counsel for War Crimes

May 30, 1944

For Ambassador personally,

In the matter of carrying out retaliatory measures against the execution of "Tunis fighters," the Führer has agreed that as a retaliatory measure against the execution of another "Tunis fighter," the former French ministers Léon Blum, Georges Mandel, and Paul Reynaud should be ordered shot by the French government. The Führer moreover said care should be taken that the French government not set them at liberty after they have been arrested.

Signed: *Hilger*

To:

Secretary of State Keppler
Under Secretary of State Pol.
Ambassador Ritter
Ambassador Gaus
Director Division Personnel
Director Division Commerce and Transport
Director Legal Division
Director Cultural Division
Director Press Divison
Director Broadcasting Divison
Chief Pol.
Dirigent Pol.
Chief Inland I
Chief Inland II
Ambassador von Rintelen
Minister Benzler
Minister Frohwein
Minister von Grundherr
Senior Legation Counsellor Melchers
Dr. Megerle
Legation Counsellor von Grote

EXHIBIT N

The Last Words Written by Laval in His Prison Cell, in Answer to the Accusation That He Had "Humiliated" France

It remains for me to say what I think of the humiliation I am supposed to have brought upon France and to answer complaint of having, by my policy, caused moral and material harm, for which France today is paying the price. The real crime was not that of having been present when the humiliation of defeat was inflicted upon us. The real crime was to have launched France upon a war obviously lost in advance, since no preparation, either diplomatic or military, had been made to forestall defeat.

My crime, if it were one, would have been to accept, during the occupation, those burdens that in all justice should have been borne by those who were responsible for our disaster. My error was to have accepted the receivership in a bankruptcy that I myself had sought by every means to avoid.

The real crime was to have failed to see soon enough the formidable danger personified in Hitler and, even more terrible, not to have foreseen the danger and to have done nothing to prevent it.

These crimes, I did not commit. I denounced them indignantly over the years, particularly during the last months preceding the war. I shall read at my trial the official and secret records of the sittings of the Foreign Affairs Committee of the Senate and the report of the secret committee meeting of March 1940. The stand I took will then be clear to all the world.

In 1931, I wanted our country to live on neighborly terms with Germany. I advocated understanding and agreement with Germany, and even in 1935, a good-neighbor policy. But at the same time, knowing as I did Hitler's boundless ambition, the growing power of his armies, his design to build the greater Reich and ensure German hegemony over Europe, I also undertook by every means to encircle Germany politically.

It was with this object in view that I signed, with Mussolini, the Rome agreements. With this same end in view, I facilitated the reconciliation between Italy and Yugoslavia and persuaded Austria, in order to defend herself, to arrange for military help from Czechoslovakia, Yugoslavia, and Romania. Again, it was with this end in view that I negotiated and signed the Franco-Soviet Pact.

The real crime was to have broken the Italian agreements. There can be no explanation or excuse for this blunder. The consequences were immediate and disastrous: the remilitarization of the Rhineland was the first sign of Hitler's devastating enterprise. It was the immediate consequence of breaking the political and military agreements I had signed with Italy.

From the very moment that Mussolini, in exasperation, threw himself into the arms of Hitler, the drama was certain to develop rapidly. Austria was annexed; Italy was the first to pay dearly for her mistake. From then on, she was to have a common frontier with Germany.

The real crime was to go to Munich and explain to Hitler that he had nothing to fear from the Western powers, that he might quietly digest Austria; and, in addition, to offer him the Sudetenland. But the ogre's appetite was insatiable. Austria was not sufficient. He annexed Czechoslovakia.

After Munich, nothing was done to renew diplomatic relations with Rome. Still worse, I was prevented from renewing my contact with Mussolini. When he realized the danger to his country of this policy, he expressed through informal channels a desire to meet me. I shall read at my trial the report of a secret session of the Senate. In my interpellation of March 1939, I referred to the conversation I had had on this subject with M. Daladier, at that time prime minister.

The French government also failed to turn toward Russia. All the advantages and means of defense that could have been derived from the Franco-Soviet pact were neglected. Our government ignored and snubbed the Soviets. The possibility was not even envisaged that their armies could move into Poland to meet the Germans in the event of a German attack against Poland.

The real crime was to follow a policy toward Russia that inevitably led the Soviets to seek a direct agreement with Germany. Ideological differences were not enough then to prevent Stalin and Hitler from reaching an agreement. That is where our government made another blunder. It failed to realize that imperious and immediate realities must take precedence over ideological conflicts. Hitler had learned from Bismarck—and the defeat of 1918 confirmed the lesson—that the German army cannot with any prospect of victory fight a war simultaneously on the eastern and western fronts.

He wanted to attack Poland first, in order to recover the territory that the Versailles treaty had taken from Germany. He knew how to divide his adversaries. He was not worried about the west. All he needed was to come to terms in the east. He wished to avoid a fight with the Soviet army at all costs.

And Stalin at that time wanted peace. He knew of Hitler's plans to conquer the Ukraine and the Caucasus. He knew the military might of Germany. He could no longer rely on collective security. Munich, to which he was not invited, had destroyed Geneva, and he feared that the Western powers had abandoned the east of Europe to Hitler.

Thus, the two dictators did not hesitate to sign, in August 1939, the Moscow Agreement. The Munich Pact accounts for the Moscow Pact.

The sequel is known, all too well known. Poland was attacked and rapidly crushed, and war was declared by France alone, or practically alone, since Great Britain was not at all ready. It was because the French ministers were unable to conceive the necessity for security and the essential need for a realistic foreign policy that we were drawn into a dreadful adventure, which we and Europe as a whole might have escaped.

I stated in March 1940, at the secret session of the Senate, amid unanimous applause, that the government had plunged us into war with extraordinary levity.

How, under these circumstances, can the humiliation of France be attributed to me? When I gave up the office of prime minister in January 1936, France and Great Britain were rivals at Geneva for the first place in Europe. Our country was prosperous and happy, her budget had been successfully balanced, her currency was sound. We enjoyed every liberty. We possessed a powerful army, a fleet, an empire, the reserves of the Bank of France were overflowing with gold, and the left bank of the Rhine was demilitarized.

Who, then, brought down calamity upon us? Hitler without a doubt; but we might have neutralized and foiled his efforts. Why did irresponsible politicians succor and assist his schemes?

I was not of their number. I repeatedly denounced them. I voiced my indignation. I had foreseen and had repeatedly declared that the policy they were following would lead us to ruin and humiliation. Our country will now be obliged to struggle through long, hard years to reconquer the place she then held in the world. How can I be charged with the humiliation to which she was subjected through the fault of others?

On September 3, 1939, when the government asked us to vote a special appropriation for war purposes, I moved for a secret session so as to enlighten my colleagues. France was being plunged into war, though it was both whispered and thought that she might never really have to fight that war. I have never witnessed such incompetence and recklessness as was displayed at the start of what was soon to be called the "phony war."

No, I did not humiliate France, my country. I defended her interests passionately. It was my only reason for being at the head of the government. I deplored our misfortunes, but I never doubted our country's future. Germany had overrun the frontiers of Europe, but Russia remained intact, and England was not vanquished.

In order to understand my policy during the occupation, it is essential to distinguish the two periods. When I returned to the government in 1942, I no longer held the views that I advocated in 1940. The war had evolved. Russia and America were fighting Germany.

In 1940, the German government, at least until Gauleiter Burckel expelled the inhabitants of Lorraine, had proceeded with the correctness that might be expected from a victor who respects his adversary. In 1942, there would be no mistake as to the German attitude after my conversation with Goering: Germany intended to treat us with harshness and without any regard for the future relations between our two countries.

Why did I, then, return to power? As I have already said, it was to defend and protect our country.

True, if I committed a crime then, it was a crime against myself and my dearest ones. How can I be blamed for a sacrifice made for my country's sake? How can ingratitude go further?

I have nothing to fear from enlightened public opinion. I have worked too hard, struggled too long, suffered too much, not to want the truth to be made known.

Courageous men, honest public servants of all ranks, did not hesitate to serve during the unhappy period of the occupation. Ministers, secretaries, great prefects (I should like to name them all), had, like myself, no other thought than their country's welfare. They have been struck down or threatened. Why this ostracism? It can come only from ignorance of the facts and circumstances or from a desire to nurse in our land a spirit of hatred and division.

Why should those who served France be ranked with the handful of men who voluntarily put themselves at Germany's service? Does not France today need all her children, all those who are honest and courageous, to assist in her material and moral resurrection? When I examine my conscience, I find no echo of reproach. No reasoning, no threat, no judgment, can trouble my peace of mind. My soul is pure and unsullied by the enemy.

I am accused of humiliating France; why not rather acknowledge all that I have endured for her sake?

Was it not logical that France should have a government to limit the exigencies of the victor? I had no links with de Gaulle's committee, but it can well be imagined that we might have been in accord. He in London or Algiers, ready to participate in the liberation and anxious to hasten V-Day, and I in Vichy or Paris, protecting the country, maintaining our administration and the financial and economic structure of our nation.

During the years of German occupation, I went through many long hours when I was near to desperation. At times, I uttered certain words or did certain acts. My purpose was always to avoid the necessity for compliant action, often to obviate the necessity for any action at all.

I constantly tried to salve our wounds, to break our chains, and to counter the perpetual German menace. More and more I made promises that I was determined not to keep. Against men like Hitler, Oberg, or Sauckel, I had no resources to draw upon except patience and tenacity of purpose. I had no forces at my command except my gift for negotiation and my power to persuade.

I applied my whole intelligence to my country's service. I knew that my interlocutors had no faith except bad faith and that their methods were brutal and extreme. I mobilized all my wits, all my heart, and all my mind, matured by many years of political experience. I fought continually, day by day, and often night by night, to reach some difficult concession, to reduce seizure of property, to prevent heartless requisitions, to forestall the departure of workmen, to return prisoners to their homes, to save poor creatures condemned to death.

I devoted every waking minute to saving France, to preserving its framework and its life. There was untold suffering, wounds that never will be healed, but this I could not prevent. I say in modest humility that I preserved in the body of France that breath of life that permitted her to survive, to be liberated, and to begin her renascence.

I did my best. That is all I claim. But who could have done better than I did when confronted by an enemy as harsh, as unprincipled, and as pitiless as the Germans were? Another man would have saved his honor, you may say. Yes, perhaps, if he had looked at things in a different light. And in so doing, he would surely have helped to crucify France.

I have a different conception of honor. I subordinate my personal honor to the honor of my country. My ideal of honor was to make every sacrifice in order to spare our country the final indignity of being ruled by a Gauleiter or by a band of adventurers, to avoid a declaration of war on the Anglo-American powers, and to obviate an alliance with the German Reich. I achieved my goal.

For me, the road of honor consisted in lightening the burden of suffering and sorrow for the whole French people. Tens of thousands of men and women, Frenchmen and Frenchwomen, owe me their lives. Hundreds of thousands more can thank me for their freedom.

EXHIBIT O

The Sorrow and the Pity, *a Film*

The Sorrow and the Pity, a "documentary" directed by Marcel Ophuls, conveyed to many thousands of viewers a definite impression of Pierre Laval as a German "puppet" minister. In a book with the same title as the film and by the same Mr. Ophuls, we now read:°

There is a well-known phenomenon in the world of film: during the editing, nearly all directors from time to time take sides for or against some of their characters. One morning, one finds oneself enamored of Catherine Deneuve, so one adds some close-ups of her at the expense of Yves Montand. The next day, one identifies oneself with the character played by Montand, and the slightly cold beauty of his partner annoys you instead of moving you. Result: one cuts out the added close-ups. This is a kind of behavior that all film editors know well and that actors are leery of with good reason. The

° *Le Chagrin et La Pitié* (Pans, Editions Alain Moreau), 1980, p. 248.

documentary film being no more and no less subjective than any work of fiction, there is no reason at all to suppose that the same fits of temper, the same transfers of sympathy, the same prejudices and the same lapses, do not afflict the directors of documentary films. In my own case, I could observe that these changes of mood did not occur only with regard to the protagonists that I had come to know myself at the time of filming, but also—which is a more curious phenomenon—with regard to the great dead who asserted their being within the film I was making: Pétain, Laval, de Gaulle, Churchill, Hitler, and the rest. And so it is perfectly true that as I got into the subject further and further, as I lived with it, as I spoke with the main characters, as I tried to pierce their secrets and penetrate their inner lives, Pierre Laval seemed to me less and less hard to bear and Pétain more and more so. René de Chambrun, if he should read these lines, will no doubt be surprised: I have the impresison that Laval was a courageous man who knew how to take risks and who amply demonstrated this during the atrocities of the trial that he was subjected to during the liberation. . . .

INDEX

209